A Textbook Of Fire Assaying

Edward Everett Bugbee

Nabu Public Domain Reprints:

You are holding a reproduction of an original work published before 1923 that is in the public domain in the United States of America, and possibly other countries. You may freely copy and distribute this work as no entity (individual or corporate) has a copyright on the body of the work. This book may contain prior copyright references, and library stamps (as most of these works were scanned from library copies). These have been scanned and retained as part of the historical artifact.

This book may have occasional imperfections such as missing or blurred pages, poor pictures, errant marks, etc. that were either part of the original artifact, or were introduced by the scanning process. We believe this work is culturally important, and despite the imperfections, have elected to bring it back into print as part of our continuing commitment to the preservation of printed works worldwide. We appreciate your understanding of the imperfections in the preservation process, and hope you enjoy this valuable book.

A TEXTBOOK
OF
FIRE ASSAYING

BY

EDWARD E. BUGBEE

Assistant Professor of Mining Engineering and Metallurgy,
Massachusetts Institute of Technology

NEW YORK
JOHN WILEY & SONS, INC.
LONDON: CHAPMAN & HALL, LIMITED
1922

COPYRIGHT, 1922
BY
EDWARD E. BUGBEE

TECHNICAL COMPOSITION CO.
CAMBRIDGE, MASS., U. S. A.

PREFACE

This book is the outgrowth of a set of mimeograph notes prepared in 1911 and intended for use in the course in fire assaying at the Massachusetts Institute of Technology. The mimeograph notes were succeeded by a book of 150 pages published by the author in 1915. The present volume has been revised and enlarged and is offered as a small contribution toward the scientific explanation of the ancient art of fire assaying. It contains some hitherto unpublished results of research, as well as considerable new data derived from a careful search of all the available literature, none of which have previously appeared in book form.

Although intended primarily as a college textbook, it is not entirely elementary in character and it is hoped that it will be found sufficiently complete and fundamental to be of service to the more mature student of the science. Every effort has been made to avoid the old "cook-book" method of presentation so common in books of this kind and to give the underlying scientific reasons for the many phenomena which occur, as well as the rationale of each process and detail of manipulation.

The object of instruction in fire assaying should not be merely the training of students to obtain results of a certain degree of precision by blindly following some set procedure, as is unfortunately too often the case. On the contrary, their attention should be focussed on the physical and chemical principles which govern the various operations. If they truly understand the reasons for the use of each of the reagents and for the various details of technique, they will not have to hunt over the pages of a receipt book when confronted by an ore of unfamiliar constitution, but will be able to make up their own assay charges and outline their own details of manipulation.

The author believes that a course in fire assaying is the logical place to introduce the study of metallurgy. The study of general metallurgy, which is abstract and uninteresting by itself, is made concrete and intensely interesting if the various processes of fire assaying are used to illustrate its principles. Most of the principles of metallurgy are utilized in one stage or another of the fire assay and if taught in this connection, the student's interest is awakened, the principles are understood and the study of this branch of metallurgy becomes a pleasure and not a burden. With this end in view, emphasis has been laid on those metallurgical principles which are of importance in fire assaying, for example, the thermochemistry of the metals and of their oxide and sulphide compounds, the nature and physical constants of slags, the characteristics of refractories and fuels, the principles of ore sampling, the behavior of metallic alloys on cooling and the chemical reactions of oxidation and reduction.

In the short time allowed for instruction in fire assaying in the crowded curricula of our technical schools, the time factor is an important consideration. With large classes and a limited number of laboratory instructors, the author's experience leads him to the conclusion that it is inadvisable to rely too much on verbal instruction in the classroom and laboratory, particularly during the first few weeks when so much that is entirely new has to be mastered before any real progress can be made. Explicit directions are given, therefore, for the first analyses; thus saving the student's time and conserving his efforts by making it possible for him to attack the subject intelligently and without any unnecessary delay. As the work progresses, less stress is laid upon detailed procedure and the student is placed more upon his own resources and encouraged to work out his own assay charges from his knowledge of fundamental principles, aided by a study of typical examples.

The order of arrangement of laboratory work is the logical one beginning with cupellation, first in the qualitative and then in the quantitative way. The assay of lead bullion leads naturally to parting for the determination of the gold, after which either scorification or crucible assaying may be undertaken.

When available, the source of what may be termed "new information" has been acknowledged, but this has not always been possible and the author trusts he may be pardoned for any serious omissions in this particular. Although it is hoped that in the present book all of the errors which occurred in the author's edition have been eliminated, some new ones may have crept in and the author will esteem it a favor to have these called to his attention. He would also be pleased to receive any suggestions and criticisms which might be embodied in a subsequent edition, if such should be required.

To the many friends who have supplied material or helped in other ways the writer wishes to express his gratitude. The officials of the Anaconda Copper Mining Company and of the United States Smelting, Refining and Mining Company have been especially helpful in this way. The author is particularly indebted to Mr. Rufus C. Reed for many helpful suggestions and for reading the type script. He wishes also to express his appreciation of the courtesy of the Allis-Chalmers Mfg. Co., the Braun Corporation, the Denver Fire Clay Co., the Thompson Balance Co., and the United States Bureau of Mines for furnishing photographs and electrotypes.

CONTENTS

CHAPTER I

ASSAY REAGENTS AND FUSION PRODUCTS 1–15
    Definitions. Reagents. Chemical Reactions of Reagents. Fusion Products.

CHAPTER II

FURNACES AND FURNACE ROOM SUPPLIES 16–38
    Crucible Furnaces. Muffle Furnaces. Fuel. Coal Furnaces. Wood Furnaces. Coke Furnaces. Gasoline Furnaces. Gas Furnaces. Fuel Oil Furnaces. Furnace Repairs. Muffles. Crucibles. Scorifiers. Furnace Tools.

CHAPTER III

ORE SAMPLING 39–70
    Definitions. Methods. Commercial Considerations. Principles of Sampling. Sampling Practice. Hand Cutting. Machine Cutting. Grab Sampling. Moisture Sampling. Duplicate Sampling. Finishing the Sample. Size of Assay Pulp. Sampling Ore Containing Malleable Minerals.

CHAPTER IV

BALANCES AND WEIGHTS 71–88
    Flux Balance. Pulp Balance. Assay Balance. Theory of Balance. Directions for Use of Balance. Weighing by Equal Swings. Weighing by Method of Swings. Weighing by No Deflection. Weighing by Substitution. Check Weighing. Adjusting and Testing Assay Balance. Weights. Calibration of Weights.

CHAPTER V

CUPELLATION 89–117
    Bone Ash. Making Cupels. Description of Process. Practice in Cupellation. Assay of Lead Bullion. Loss of Silver in Cupeling. Loss of Gold in Cupeling. Effect of Silver on the Loss of Gold in Cupeling. Influence of Impurities on the Loss of Precious Metals during Cupellation. Rule Governing

Cupellation Losses. Indications of Metals Present. Indications of Rare Metals. Retention of Base Metals. Portland Cement and Magnesia Cupels. Color Scale of Temperature.

CHAPTER VI

PARTING.. 118–126

General Statement. Parting in Porcelain Capsules. Inquartation. Parting in Flasks. Influence of Base Metals on Parting. Indications of Presence of Rare Metals. Errors Resulting from Parting Operations. Testing Nitric Acid for Impurities. Testing Wash Water. Testing Silver Foil for Gold.

CHAPTER VII

THE SCORIFICATION ASSAY.................................... 127–142

General Statement. Solubility of Metallic Oxides in Litharge. Heat of Formation of Metallic Oxides. Ignition Temperature of Metallic Sulphides. Assay Procedure for Ores. Chemical Reactions. Indications of Metals Present. Assay of Granulated Lead. Scorification Assay of Copper Matte. Losses in Scorification. Scorification Charges for Different Materials.

CHAPTER VIII

THE CRUCIBLE ASSAY.. 143–195

Theory of the Crucible Assay. Classification of Ores. Crucible Slags. Classification of Silicates. Action of Borax in Slags. Fluidity of Slags. Acidic and Basic Slags. Mixed Silicates. The Lead Button. The Cover. Reduction and Oxidation. Reducing Reactions. Reducing Power of Minerals. Oxidizing Reactions. Testing Reagents. Slags for Class 1 Siliceous Ores. Slags for Class 1 Basic Ores. Assay Procedure for Class 1 Ores. Assay of Class 2 Ores. The Niter Assay. Slags for Pure Ores. Slags for Impure Ores. Conduct of the Fusion. Physical and Chemical Changes Taking Place in Niter Fusion. Preliminary Fusion. Estimating Reducing Power. Calculation of Assay Charge. Procedure for the Regular Fusion. The Soda-Iron Method. Chemical Reactions. The Slag. Procedure. The Roasting Method. Assay of Class 3 Ores.

CHAPTER IX

THE ASSAY OF COMPLEX ORES AND SPECIAL METHODS.......... 196–210

Assay of Ores Containing Nickel and Cobalt. Assay of Telluride Ores. Assay of Ores and Products High in Copper. Assay of Zinc-Box Precipitate. Assay of Antimonial Ores.

CONTENTS

Assay of Auriferous Tinstone. Corrected Assays. Assay of Slag. Assay of Cupels.

CHAPTER X

THE ASSAY OF BULLION.................................. 211–232

Definitions. Weights. Sampling Bullion. Lead Bullion. Copper Bullion. Doré Bullion. Gold Bullion. Assay of Lead Bullion. Assay of Copper Bullion. Scorification Method. Crucible Method. Nitric Acid Combination Method. Mercury-Sulphuric Acid Method. Assay of Doré Bullion. United States Mint Assay of Gold Bullion.

CHAPTER XI

THE ASSAY OF SOLUTIONS................................. 233–239

Evaporation in Lead Tray. Evaporation with Litharge. Precipitation by Zinc and Lead Acetate. Precipitation as Sulphide. Precipitation by Cement Copper. Precipitation by Silver Nitrate. Precipitation by a Copper Salt. Electrolytic Precipitation. Colorimetric Method.

CHAPTER XII

THE LEAD ASSAY.. 240–247

General Statement. Lead Ores. Accuracy and Limitations of Method. Quantity of Ore and Reagents Used. Manipulation of Assay. Influence of Other Metals. Procedure for Assay. Assay of Slags. Chemical Reactions.

INDEX.. 249–254

A TEXTBOOK OF FIRE ASSAYING

CHAPTER I.

ASSAY REAGENTS AND FUSION PRODUCTS.

Assaying is a branch of analytical chemistry, generally defined as the quantitative estimation of the metals in ores and furnace products. In the western part of the United States, the term is employed to include the determination of all the constituents, both metallic and non-metallic, of ores and metallurgical products.

Fire assaying is the quantitative determination of metals in ores and metallurgical products by means of heat and dry reagents. This involves separating the metal from the other constituents of the ore and weighing it in a state of purity.

An **ore** is a mineral-bearing substance from which a metal, alloy or metallic compound can be extracted at a profit. The term is loosely used to include almost any inorganic substance that may occur in nature. An ore generally consists of two parts, the metalliferous or valuable portion, and the "gangue" or valueless portion. Gangue minerals are divided, according to their chemical composition, into two classes, acid and basic. Silica is a type of the former; lime, magnesia, and the oxides of iron, manganese, sodium and potassium are examples of the latter.

An ore may be acid, basic or "self-fluxing" according to the preponderance of one or the other group of slag-forming gangue constituents. A self-fluxing ore is one which contains acid and basic material in the right proportion to form a slag.

The metallurgical products which come to the assayer include bullion, matte, speiss, drosses and crusts, litharge, flue-dust and fume, as well as solutions and precipitates resulting from hydrometallurgical operations.

The reagents used in fire assaying may be classified as fluxes, acid, basic or neutral, and as oxidizing, reducing, sulphurizing or desulphurizing agents. Some reagents have only one property, as for instance silica, an acid flux, others have several different properties, as litharge, a basic flux but also an oxidizing and desulphurizing agent.

A **flux** is something which converts compounds infusible at a certain temperature into others which melt at this temperature. For instance, quartz by itself is fusible only at a very high temperature, but if some sodium carbonate is added to the pulverized quartz it can be fused at a temperature easily obtained in the assay furnace.

The student should remember that to aid in the fusion of an acid substance, a basic flux such as litharge, sodium carbonate, limestone, or iron oxide should be added while for a basic substance an acid flux such as silica or borax should be used.

A **reducing agent** is something which is capable of causing the separation of a metal from the substances chemically combined with it or of effecting " the stepping down " of a compound from a higher to a lower degree of oxidation.

An **oxidizing** agent is one which gives up its oxygen readily.

A **desulphurizing agent** is something which has a strong affinity for sulphur and which is therefore capable of separating it from some of its compounds.

The principal reagents used in assaying follow:

Silica, SiO_2, is an acid reagent and the strongest one available. It combines with the metal oxides to form silicates which are the foundation of almost all slags. It is used as a flux when the ore is deficient in silica and serves to protect the crucibles and scorifiers from the corrosive action of litharge. Care must be taken to avoid an excess of silica, as too much of it will cause trouble and losses of precious metals by slagging or by the formation of matte. Silica melts at about 1625° C. to an extremely viscous liquid. It should be obtained in the pulverized form.

The fluxing effect of silica is shown in the accompanying freezing-point curve[*] of the lime-silica series. The series shows three eutectics and two compounds. The combination having the lowest melting-point is the eutectic with 37 per cent of CaO which melts at 1417° C. Another eutectic containing 54 per cent CaO melts at 1430° C. Lying between these is the compound calcium bi-silicate, corresponding to the formula $CaSiO_3$, which fuses at

[*] Day and Shepard Am. Jour. Sc. **22**, p. 255.

1512° C. A second compound, corresponding to the formula Ca_2SiO_4, the calcium singulo-silicate melts at 2080° C. A cursory glance at this curve will be sufficient to suggest the desirability of trying to make approximately a bi-silicate slag when assaying ores which contain considerable lime

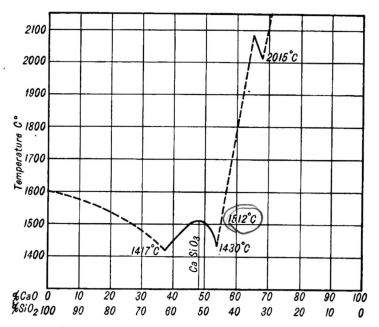

FIG. 1. — Freezing-point curve of lime-silica series.

Glass is used by some in place of silica. Ordinary window-glass, a silicate of lime and the alkalies with the silica in excess, is best. Its acid excess is always doubtful and so is not commonly used. If used, a blank assay should be run on each new lot to insure against introducing precious metals into the assay in this way. Its chief advantage is that 5 or 10 grams too much glass will ordinarily do no harm in a fusion whereas 5 or 10 grams of silica in excess might spoil the assay.

Borax. — $Na_2B_4O_7$, $10H_2O$, is an active, readily fusible, acid flux. It melts in its own water of crystallization, beginning at the lowest visible red heat, and becomes anhydrous at a full red heat. It intumesces in fusing and on account of this behavior may, if used in large amounts, tend to force part of the charge out of the crucible, especially if not thoroughly mixed with the charge.

In small amounts, however, it lowers the temperature of slag formation and promotes a quiet and orderly fusion.

Borax is often used as a cover for crucible fusions. When properly used it is believed to prevent the mechanical loss of fine ore which frequently results when a large volume of gas escapes rapidly at a temperature below that of incipient fusion. Borax, containing, as it does, 47 per cent of water, loses approximately half of its weight by fusion, and consequently when used as an acid flux, approximately twice as much borax as borax-glass is required.

Borax-Glass. — $Na_2B_4O_7$, is made by fusing borax to drive off its water of crystallization and then cooling and crushing the solidified glassy residue. It is usually purchased in the powdered form and should be kept in air-tight containers, as the fine material takes on moisture from the air and tends to cake. Under ordinary conditions it behaves like a true glass, having no definite freezing- or melting-point. If, however, it is subjected to rapid vibration when cooling it may be induced to solidify in the crystalline form at a definite temperature. This crystallized borax-glass melts at 742° C. If not subjected to vibration it remains a viscous fluid even below a visible red. Finely divided amorphous borax-glass begins to sinter at about 500° C. It is extremely viscous when melted, even when heated well above its melting temperature.

Its rational formula, $Na_2O, 2B_2O_3$, indicates an excess of acid, and experiment proves this to be present. At a red heat it becomes a strong acid and dissolves and fluxes practically all of the metallic oxides both acid and basic. It is one of the best fluxes for alumina.

Five borates of alkalies and alkaline earths are recognized, the chemical classification being as follows:

TABLE I.

CLASSIFICATION OF BORATES.

Name	Oxygen ratio Acid to base	Formula R = bivalent base
Ortho-borate	1 to 1	$3RO.B_2O_3$
Pyro-borate	1½ to 1	$2RO.B_2O_3$
Sesqui-borate	2 to 1	$3RO.2B_2O_3$
Meta-borate	3 to 1	$RO.B_2O_3$
Bi-borate	6 to 1	$RO.2B_2O_3$

According to the metallurgical classification, *i.e.*, the ratio of oxygen in acid to oxygen in base, the first of these would be neutral and the others acid. Ditte* studied the fused borates of the alkaline earths and classified them as acid, neutral and basic. He called the meta-borate neutral. The writer's experiments with alkaline borates show that the meta-borate is decidedly viscous when fused but that at the same time it shows a strong tendency to crystallize during cooling. The pyro-borate, when fused, was decidedly fluid, being comparable to the sub-silicate of soda. It would seem proper, therefore, to consider the sesqui-borate as the neutral one when considered from this standpoint.

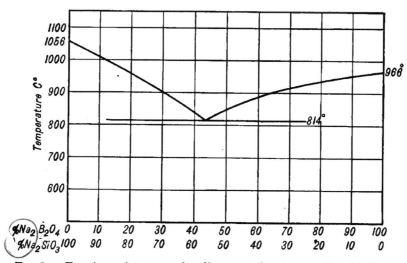

Fig. 2.—Freezing-point curve of sodium meta-borate — sodium bi-silicate series.

Fusing as it does at a low temperature, borax helps to facilitate the slagging of the ore, and in the hydrous or anhydrous condition is used in almost every crucible assay. In general, it may be said to lower very appreciably the fusing-point of all slags, and this, in addition to the fact that it is such an excellent solvent for the metallic oxides, accounts for its almost universal use in fire assaying. The borates of lead and the alkalies are more viscous than the corresponding silicates. This viscous effect persists far below the apparent solidification-point unless the slag is decidedly basic.

If too much borax is used in the assay of siliceous ores there

* Compt. rend. **77**, p. 785, p. 893 (1873).

results a very tough, glassy or stony slag which holds tenaciously to the lead button. This is probably due partly to the effect of borax in reducing the coefficient of expansion of the slag and partly to its action in preventing crystallization. When the attempt is made to separate the lead and slag, a film of lead will often adhere to the slag and give the assayer much trouble.

The remedy for this condition is, first, to reduce the quantity of borax used and then, if necessary, to increase the bases. No more than 5 or 10 grams of common borax or its equivalent in borax-glass should be used per assay-ton of siliceous ore.

The melting-point curve of the sodium meta-borate — sodium bi-silicate series, according to Van Klooster*, is shown in Fig. 2. The melting-point of sodium bi-silicate does not agree exactly with that given by Niggi but, none the less, the diagram serves to illustrate the effect which borax has in reducing the melting-point of assay slags.

The eutectic containing 56.5 per cent of Na_2SiO_3 freezes at 814° C.

Sodium bicarbonate, $NaHCO_3$, is still used by some assayers as an alkaline flux, mainly because of its cheapness and purity. It is, however, decomposed when heated to 276° C., forming the anhydrous normal carbonate with the liberation of water vapor and carbon dioxide. The large volume of water vapor and carbon dioxide released, passing up through the charge before it has softened, is bound to carry off more or less of the fine ore and thus contributes to the so-called " dusting " loss.

The bicarbonate contains but 63.1 per cent of Na_2CO_3 and therefore when it is used as a substitute for the normal carbonate 158 parts are required for each 100 parts of the normal carbonate. Because of the above serious disadvantages the use of the anhydrous normal carbonate is recommended in all cases. The only advantage which can now be claimed for the bicarbonate is that it does not deliquesce.

Sodium carbonate, Na_2CO_3,* is a powerful basic flux and by far the cheapest one available for assay purposes. Owing to the ease with which alkaline sulphides and sulphates are formed it also acts to some extent as a desulphurizing and oxidizing agent. Pure anhydrous sodium carbonate melts at 852° C. When molten it is very fluid and can hold in suspension a large proportion of

* Zeitschr. anorg. Chemie, **69**, p. 122 (1910).

finely ground, infusible and inactive material such as carbon or bone-ash.

The commercial normal carbonate of this country, made by the Solvay process from the bicarbonate, is easily obtained in a pure state. It tends to absorb water from the air and is, therefore, unsatisfactory for use in some climates. The variety known by the trade as 58 per cent dense soda-ash has been found particularly satisfactory for assay purposes, and is but little affected by atmospheric moisture.

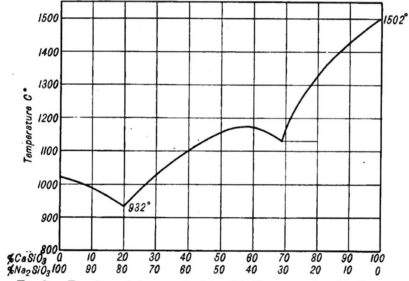

FIG. 3. — Freezing-point curve of calcium bi-silicate — sodium bi-silicate series.

When sodium carbonate is heated to about 950° C., it undergoes a slight dissociation with the consequent evolution of a small amount of carbon dioxide. Analysis of sodium carbonate which has been melted shows it to contain about 0.4 per cent of free alkali. When silica is added to the fused carbonate this free alkali first disappears and then a reaction takes place between the silica and sodium carbonate and a certain amount of carbon dioxide is evolved. The amount evolved is directly proportional to the amount of silica added and to the temperature. Niggi* showed that the system $Na_2CO_3 - SiO_2$, for a constant temperature and

* Jour. Am. Chem. Soc. **35**, pp. 1693–1727.

pressure of CO_2, reaches a state of equilibrium, which condition may be expressed by the equation:

$$Na_2CO_3 + Na_2SiO_3 \rightleftarrows Na_4SiO_4 + CO_2.$$

He found that in order to displace all the CO_2, at least one mol of SiO_2 for each mol of Na_2O must be added. Combinations less acid than the bi-silicate retain CO_2 indefinitely. The bi-silicate melts at about 1018° C.

The fluxing effect of sodium carbonate is shown in the accompanying freezing-point curve* of the calcium bi-silicate — sodium bi-silicate series.

Between the melting-point of sodium bi-silicate, 1018° C. and that of calcium bi-silicate, 1502° C., Wallace found indications of a eutectic containing 20 per cent $CaSiO_3$ which melted at 932° C. It may be concluded from this that if we are to flux limestone with soda and silica alone, we should add 4 mols of Na_2CO_3 for each mol of $CaCO_3$, or roughly 60 grams of Na_2CO_3 for $\frac{1}{2}$ A.T. of pure $CaCO_3$, together with sufficient silica for a bi-silicate. The addition of borax will materially reduce the melting-temperature of the mixture.

Potassium carbonate, K_2CO_3, is a basic flux, similar in its action to sodium carbonate. It melts at 894° C. It has the disadvantage of being more expensive, weight for weight, than sodium carbonate, and because of its greater molecular weight more of it is required than of sodium carbonate to produce a given result.

Niggi† showed that a small amount of silica displaces an almost equivalent amount of CO_2 from fused potassium carbonate, and that successive additions of silica displace a progressively smaller quantity of CO_2, until when the proportions are 2 mols of SiO_2 to 1 mol of K_2O, the silica displaces only half the equivalent amount of CO_2, at which condition the last of the CO_2 passes off. He gives the following equation as expressing the conditions of equilibrium:

$$K_2CO_3 + K_2Si_2O_5 \rightleftarrows 2K_2SiO_3 + CO_2.$$

Willorf‡ contends that diminution of the partial pressure of CO_2 causes considerable displacement of the equilibrium toward the right-hand side of the equation. With this, Niggi does not

---

* Zeitschr. anorg. Chemie, **63**, p. 1 (1909).
† loc. cit.
‡ Zeitschr. anorg. Chemie, **39**, 187 (1904).

agree and argues that the influence of the partial pressure of CO_2 is inconsiderable. He cites experimental data as well as theoretical grounds for this belief.

As is the case with a mixture of sodium and potassium carbonates, a mixture of sodium and potassium silicates melts at a lower temperature than either one alone, and for this reason the mixture is used whenever it is desired to maintain a low temperature during the assay. The lead assay is an example and in fact is now about the only case in which it is still customary to use potassium carbonate in fire assaying.

Litharge, PbO, is a readily fusible basic flux. It acts also as an oxidizing and desulphurizing agent and on being reduced it supplies the lead necessary for the collection of the gold and silver. It melts at 883° C., and contains 92.8 per cent of lead.

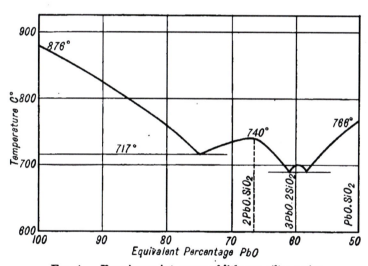

Fig. 4.—Freezing-point curve of litharge-silica series.

Mixtures of finely pulverized litharge and silica, ranging from $6PbO.SiO_2$ to $PbO.SiO_2$, begin to sinter at about 700° C. According to Mostowitch* the sub-silicate, $4PbO.SiO_2$, is completely liquefied at 726°; the singulo-silicate, $2PbO, SiO_2$, forms a viscous liquid at 724° but does not flow readily until heated to 940° C. The bi-silicate, $PbO.SiO_2$, melts at 770° and eutectic mixtures both lower and higher in silica fuse at lower temperatures.

* Trans. A.I.M.E. **55**, p. 744.

The freezing-point curve of part of the $PbO - SiO_2$ system, according to Hilpert-Nacken,* is shown in Fig. 4. The melting-points of compounds shown do not agree exactly with those of Mostowitch. Compared with sodium bi-silicate, which melts at 1018°, the corresponding lead silicate is decidedly more fusible. This explains why it is customary to provide for the presence of litharge in almost all assay slags.

Litharge has such a strong affinity for silica that if the crucible charge does not contain enough of the latter, the acid material of the crucible itself will be attacked. If left long enough, a hole may be eaten through it.

Litharge readily gives up its oxygen if heated with carbon, hydrogen, sulphur, metallic sulphides, iron, etc. It thus acts as an oxidizing and, in the presence of sulphur, as a desulphurizing agent. Examples of these reactions are shown below:

$$2PbO + C = CO_2 + 2Pb \text{ (oxidizing)},$$
$$3PbO + ZnS = ZnO + SO_2 + 3Pb \text{ (desulphurizing and oxidizing)}.$$

The liberated lead is then available for the collection of the gold and silver.

The reaction with carbon begins below 500° C., and is rapid at 600°. Reduction by CO starts below 200°.

Litharge begins to volatilize at 800° C. which is considerably below its melting-point.

Lead silicates do not readily give up their lead to carbonaceous and sulphurous reducing agents. The higher the proportion of silica, the less readily is the silicate broken up. In order that all the lead may be extracted it must first be set free by the use of a stronger basic flux. Hofman† says, "metallic iron decomposes all fusible lead silicates at a bright red heat, provided enough is added to form a singulo-silicate."

Ordinarily commercial litharge contains a small amount of silver, varying from 0.2 ounce to 1.0 ounce or over per ton. A practically silver-free variety is made from Missouri lead by giving a zinc treatment, as for the Parkes process, and then cupeling. It is never safe to assume, however, that litharge is silver-free until

* Métallurgie 8, p. 157 (1911).
† Metallurgy of Lead, p. 38 (1918).

it has been proven so by assay. Each new lot received should therefore be carefully mixed to make it uniform, and assayed.

Assay litharge should be free from bismuth, as this will be reduced during the fusion and, owing to its slow rate of oxidation, will concentrate in the lead during cupellation, finally giving irregular silver results.

Lead in the granulated form, test lead, is used in the scorification assay as a collector of the precious metals and as a flux. When oxidized by the air of the muffle it becomes a basic flux. Ordinary test lead may contain more or less silver and every new lot should be assayed before being used.

Test lead may be made by pouring molten lead, just above its freezing-point, into a wooden box and shaking it violently in a horizontal direction just as it becomes pasty and continuing until it becomes solid. The fine material is sifted out, the coarse is remelted.

Lead in the form of foil is used in the fire assay of gold, silver and lead bullion. Lead melts at 326° C. Like litharge it should be free from bismuth.

Argols is a reducing agent and basic flux. It is a crude bitartrate of potassium obtained from wine barrels, and is one of the best reducing agents.

Cream of tartar, $KHC_4H_4O_6$, is refined bitartrate of potassium. Being free from sulphur it is used as a reducing agent in the copper assay. Both argols and cream of tartar break up on heating as follows:

$$2KHC_4H_4O_6 + \text{heat} = K_2O + 5H_2O + 6CO + 2C.$$

The K_2O thus liberated is available as a flux.

Charcoal, sugar, flour etc. are also reducing agents because of the carbon that they contain. Flour is very commonly used in flux mixtures and is satisfactory in every respect.

Iron is a desulphurizing and reducing agent. When it is heated with the sulphides of lead, silver, mercury, bismuth and antimony the sulphides are decomposed, yielding a more or less pure metal and iron sulphide. Copper, nickel and cobalt sulphides are partly reduced by iron, as would be expected from a study of the heats of formation of the same.

Iron also reduces most of these metals and some others from their oxide combinations, as for example:

$$PbO + Fe = Pb + FeO,$$

the iron oxide formed acts as a basic flux. Iron decomposes all fusible lead silicates by replacing the lead, thus:

$$x\text{PbO.SiO}_2 + x\text{Fe} = x\text{FeO.SiO}_2 + x\text{Pb}.$$

It should therefore always be used in the lead assay.

It is used in the form of spikes or nails, and sometimes, especially in Europe, an iron crucible is employed.

Potassium nitrate, KNO_3, commonly known as niter, is a powerful oxidizing agent. It melts at 339° C. and fuses at a low temperature without alteration, but at a higher temperature it breaks up, giving off oxygen, which oxidizes sulphur and many of the metals, notably lead and copper.

It is used in the fire assay especially to oxidize sulphides, arsenides, antimonides, etc.

If fused alone it is stable until a temperature of 530° C. is reached, when it begins to decompose, giving off oxygen. When it is fused with charcoal, the two begin to react at about 440° C. The reaction between niter and carbon, according to Roscoe and Schoerleman, is as follows:

$$4KNO_3 + 5C = 2K_2CO_3 + 3CO_2 + 2N_2$$

According to the same authority, sulphur and niter react as follows:

$$2KNO_3 + 2S = K_2SO_4 + SO_2 + N_2.$$

Niter begins to react with silica at about 450° C.,* probably according to the following reaction:

$$4KNO_3 + 2SiO_2 = 2K_2SiO_3 + 5O_2 + 2N_2.$$

In a charge containing a large excess of soda and litharge the reaction with pyrite is as follows:

$$6KNO_3 + 2FeS_2 + Na_2CO_3 =$$
$$Fe_2O_3 + 3K_2SO_4 + Na_2SO_4 + CO_2 + 3N_2.$$

Many assayers object to the use of niter because of its oxidizing effect on silver. Large amounts of niter cause boiling of the crucible charge and necessitate careful heating to prevent loss. It is found to give less trouble when the crucible is uniformly heated, as in the muffle, than when the charge begins to melt first at the bottom, as in the pot-furnace.

* Fulton, A Manual of Fire Assaying, p. 59

Potassium cyanide, KCN, is a powerful reducing and desulphurizing agent. It combines with oxygen, forming potassium cyanate, thus:

$$PbO + KCN = Pb + KCNO \text{ (reducing action)},$$

and also with sulphur, forming sulphocyanide, as follows:

$$PbS + KCN = Pb + KSCN.$$

It is sometimes used in the lead assay and usually in the tin and bismuth assays. It is extremely poisonous, and should be handled with great care. It fuses at 526° C.

Salt, NaCl, is used as a cover to exclude the air, and to wash the sides of the crucible and prevent small particles of lead from adhering thereto. It melts at 819° C.

It does not enter the slag, but floats on top of it. It is often colored by the different metallic oxides of the charge and sometimes helps to distinguish assays which have become mixed in pouring.

TABLE II.

Assay Reagents.

Name	Formula	Properties in order of their importance
Silica	SiO_2	Acid flux
Glass	$xNa_2O.yCaO.zSiO_2$	Acid flux
Borax	$Na_2B_4O_7.10H_2O$	Acid flux
Borax-glass	$Na_2B_4O_7$	Acid flux
Sodium bicarbonate	$NaHCO_3$	Basic flux, desulphurizing
Sodium carbonate	Na_2CO_3	Basic flux, desulphurizing
Potassium carbonate	K_2CO_3	Basic flux, desulphurizing
Litharge	PbO	Basic flux, desulphurizing, oxidizing
Potassium nitrate	KNO_3	Oxidizing, desulphurizing
Argols	$KHC_4H_4O_6 + C$	Reducing agent, basic flux
Cream of tartar	$KHC_4H_4O_6$	Reducing agent, basic flux
Flour		Reducing agent
Charcoal	C	Reducing agent
Lead	Pb	Collecting agent
Iron	Fe	Desulphurizing and reducing agent
Potassium cyanide	KCN	Reducing and desulphurizing agent
Salt	NaCl	Cover and wash
Fluorspar	CaF_2	Neutral flux
Cryolite	$AlNa_3F_6$	Neutral flux

Fluorspar, CaF_2, is occasionally used as a flux in fire assaying. Its melting-point is 1378° C. and it would, therefore, seem to be of doubtful value in fire assay fusions which seldom exceed 1200° C.

When melted it is very fluid and assists in liquefying the charge, although it is inert and does not ordinarily enter into chemical combination with the other constituents of the charge. Karandéeff* shows a melting-point curve of $CaF_2 - CaSiO_3$ series with a eutectic, containing 54 molecular per cent of $CaSiO_3$, which fuses at 1128° C.

Cryolite, $AlNa_3F_6$, is a powerful flux, commonly used in the manufacture of enamels and occasionally in the melting of bullion. It may sometimes be useful in fire assaying. Cryolite melts at about 1000° C. and has the property of dissolving alumina. It increases the coefficient of expansion of the slag.

Fusion Products. — Every gold, silver or lead assay fusion, if the charge is properly proportioned and manipulated, should show two products, a lead button and, above it, a slag. Two undesirable products, matte and speiss are occasionally also obtained. When a cover of salt is used, or if niter is used in the assay, a third product will be found on top of the solidified slag. In the first case this is almost entirely sodium chloride, in the latter case it is a mixture of the sulphates of sodium and potassium.

THE LEAD BUTTON should be bright, soft and malleable and should separate easily from the slag. It should contain practically all of the gold and silver which were in the ore taken for the assay.

SLAG is a fusible compound of earthy or metallic oxides and silica or other acid constituents. The slags made in fire assaying are usually silicates or borates of the metallic oxides contained in the ore and fluxes used.

Slags should be homogeneous and free from particles of undecomposed ore. A good slag is usually more or less glassy and brittle. When poured, the slag should be thin and fluid and free from shots of lead. If too acid, it will be quite viscous and stringy, and the last drops will form a thread in pouring. If too basic, it will be lumpy and break off short in pouring. When cold, the neutral or acid slag is glassy and brittle, the basic one is dull and stony-looking.

Slags in the molten state are usually solutions, but in rare cases they may be chemical compounds. In the solid state they are usually either solid solutions or eutectic mixtures; occasionally they may be chemical compounds.

* Zeitschr. anorg. Chemie, **68**, p. 188 (1910).

MATTE is an artificial sulphide of one or more of the metals, formed in the dry way. In assaying it is most often encountered in the niter fusion of sulphide ores when the charge is too acid. It is found lying just above the lead button. It is usually blue-gray in color, approaching galena in composition and very brittle. It may form a layer of considerable thickness, or may appear simply as a granular coating on the upper surface of the lead button. This matte always carries some of the gold and silver and, as it is brittle, it is usually broken off and lost in the slag in the cleaning of the lead button. The student should examine the lead button as soon as it is broken from the slag and if any matte is found, he may be certain that his charge or furnace manipulations are wrong.

SPEISS is an artificial, metallic arsenide or antimonide formed in smelting operations. As obtained in the fire assay, it is usually an arsenide of iron approaching the composition of Fe_5As. Occasionally the iron may be replaced by nickel or cobalt. The antimony speiss is very rare. In assaying, speiss is obtained when the iron method is used on ores containing arsenic. It is a hard, fairly tough, tin-white substance found directly on top of the lead and usually adhering tenaciously to it.

If only a small amount of arsenic is present in the ore, the speiss will appear as a little button lying on top of the lead; if much arsenic is present, the speiss will form a layer entirely covering the lead. It carries some gold and silver. If only a gram or so in weight, it may be put into the cupel with the lead and will be oxidized there, giving up its precious metal values to the lead bath. A large amount of speiss is very hard to deal with as it is difficult to scorify. The best way is to assay again, by some other method.

CHAPTER II.

FURNACES AND FURNACE ROOM SUPPLIES.

Furnaces for assaying may be divided into the two following classes:

1. Crucible or Pot-Furnaces. — These are furnaces used solely for melting purposes, in which the crucible is in direct contact with the fuel or flame and the contents, therefore, more or less subject to the action of the products of combustion.

2. Muffle Furnaces. — These are furnaces in which the charge to be heated is in a space, the muffle, apart from the fuel or products of combustion. The muffle is a semi-cylindrical receptacle of fire-clay or other refractory material, set horizontally and so arranged that the fuel or products of combustion pass around and under it. Thus, the material to be heated is entirely separated from the products of combustion.

As muffle furnaces may be used for melting purposes as well as for scorification and cupellation, many assayers in America use this type of furnace exclusively, especially in connection with soft coal fuel. The advantages of muffle furnaces for melting are the greater ease and saving of time in charging and pouring, the better control of temperature and the better distribution of heat for melting purposes. Crucibles also seem to stand more heats in a muffle furnace than they will in pot-furnaces, probably on account of the slower and more uniform heating.

Pot-furnaces have the advantage of size, so that in dealing with low-grade ores, for instance, a larger charge and crucible may be used than in muffle furnaces of the ordinary size. A higher temperature may be obtained in pot-furnaces than in muffles and this, occasionally, is an advantage of the pot-furnace.

The furnaces themselves are made of fire-brick or fire-clay tile and may be set in an iron jacket or surrounded by common red brick. Fire-brick is best laid in a mortar made from a mixture of 2 parts ground fire-brick and 1 part fire-clay. Sometimes a small amount of Portland cement is added. In any event the brick and tiles should be thoroughly wet before the mortar is applied. Finally, as little mortar as possible should be used, since the bricks are much harder than the solidified mortar.

Assay furnaces are made to burn practically all kinds of gaseous, liquid and solid fuels. Those most commonly used are natural and artificial gas, gasoline, kerosene, fuel-oil, wood, charcoal, coke, bituminous and anthracite coal.

Gas is the cleanest, most easily controlled, most efficient in combustion and, except in the case of a natural supply, the most expensive fuel. When gas is used for firing, a blower is usually required to supply air under a low pressure.

Oil is nearly as clean and as convenient to use as gas, the efficiency of combustion is high and in localities near the oil-fields it may be very cheaply obtained. The calorific power of the hydrocarbon fuel-oils is high, about 50 per cent more than the best coals, which makes them particularly suited for use in isolated localities where freight charges are high. Gasoline is forced under pressure through a heated burner where it is vaporized, and the gas injected into the furnace carries with it a sufficient supply of air for combustion. Fuel-oil requires steam or air under pressure to aid in atomizing the oil, preliminary to proper combustion. Gasoline and kerosene both have a heating value of about 21,000 B.t.u. per pound, crude petroleum about 18,500.

Solid fuels are usually the cheapest and are therefore more extensively used than any of the others. In isolated districts where coal or coke is not available, wood is occasionally used as fuel in assay furnaces. For this purpose the wood should be felled in winter and thoroughly air-dried for at least six months or longer, according to the climate. The air-dried wood will still retain from 20 to 25 per cent of water and in this condition has a heating value of about 6000 B.t.u. per pound. Charcoal is seldom used in this country for assay purposes on account of the abundance of other fuels.

Bituminous coal is the most satisfactory solid fuel for muffle-furnace firing and coke for pot-furnaces. Good soft coal has a calorific power of about 14,500 B.t.u. per pound. It should be low in sulphur and the ash must not be too readily fusible. Coke should be hard, strong and low in sulphur, and the ash should be infusible at the temperature of the furnace. That is to say, it should be high in silica and alumina and low in iron, calcium, magnesium and the alkalies, to prevent clinkering of the walls of the furnace.

Gas and Oil vs. Solid Fuel. — Gaseous and liquid fuels have many advantages over solid fuels for assay purposes. Some of these advantages are as follows:

1. The fire is kindled in an instant and the furnace may be quickly heated to the desired temperature for work.

2. The temperature is readily controlled and may be quickly varied to suit the requirements of the work.

3. A high efficiency of combustion is possible in properly designed furnaces, and as soon as the work is completed the fuel supply may be shut off and fuel consumption stopped.

4. The avoidance of labor in firing gives the assayer more time for other duties.

5. The cleanliness in operation, due to absence of solid fuel and ash, is obviously a great advantage in any analytical laboratory.

On account of the expense, however, coal is much more generally used than either oil or gas. It is easy to make a comparison of the costs of any of the fuels by considering the heat units. For instance, with soft coal at \$10 per ton and gasoline at 25 cents per gallon, 1 cent invested in soft coal may be said to buy $2 \times 14,500 = 29,000$ B.t.u. and the same amount invested in gasoline to buy approximately $\frac{1}{25} \times 6.0 \times 21,000 = 5040$ B.t.u. That is to say, the gasoline is over six times as expensive as the coal on the basis of heat units, and for steady running this may be taken to be approximately correct. However, for a small amount of work, a gasoline furnace may be cheaper to run even with the cost of fuel as above assumed, for the small furnace is quickly heated and as soon as the work is completed the oil supply may be shut off and the expense stopped, while a coal furnace takes much longer to heat and then must be allowed to burn out after the work is completed.

Coal Furnaces. — This type of furnace is used in many of the large custom and smelter assay offices in this country.

The furnace may be built either with a tile or fire-brick lining. The tile lining is more easily set up, but whether or not it is as durable as a properly constructed fire-brick lining is open to question. The outside of the furnace is usually laid up with common hard-burned red brick. If the furnace is to be lined with fire-brick several rows of "headers" should be left to hold the lining securely in place. The furnace is held together with angle-irons, stays and tie-rods.

Fig. 5.—Twin double-muffle soft coal furnace.

A great improvement in the construction of these furnaces may be made by introducing a single course of insulating brick between the fire-brick and the red brick. The use of these brick permits a quicker heating of the furnace, affords a considerable economy in fuel and provides a much more comfortable working place, because of a large reduction in the heat losses due to radiation.

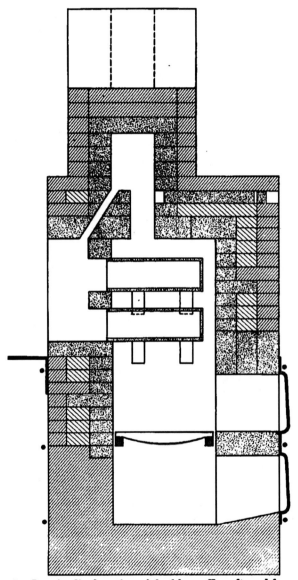

Fig. 6.—Longitudinal section of double-muffle soft coal furnace.

In Figs. 5, 6 and 7 are shown front elevation, longitudinal and transverse sections of twin double-muffle soft coal furnaces using NN muffles. In Fig. 5 is also shown an iron-topped pouring table with slagging-anvils made of sections of steel rails. The

Fig. 7.—Transverse section of double-muffle soft coal furnace.

operator stands between the table and the furnace when working at the furnace, and on the other side of the table when hammering out his lead buttons. Insulating brick is used in the construction of these furnaces, and the system of bonding the wall with "headers" is shown in the sections.

In the furnace, as ordinarily constructed, the muffles are supported by "jamb" bricks projecting from the sides. When these are used, it is well to leave a hole or loose brick on the outside of the furnace, to facilitate the removal of the stubs when these bricks become broken off and the ends slagged in. Fulton recommends using long tiles which meet in the center, thus giving better support for the muffle. He claims a prolonged life for the muffle with this arrangement. The writer has found the Scotch Gartcraig brick to outlast 3 or 4 best American fire-brick for muffle supports. Another method of supporting muffles in furnaces of this type is by the use of iron pipes or castings which extend directly across the furnace and through which cooling water is circulated.

These furnaces occupy a floor space of approximately $3\frac{1}{2}$ by 4 feet. They are built in a variety of sizes; those taking NN, QQ and UU muffles are the sizes most commonly used. The NN muffle is $10\frac{1}{2}$ by 19 by $6\frac{1}{2}$ inches outside, the QQ is $12\frac{1}{2}$ by 19 by $7\frac{3}{4}$ and the UU is 14 by 19 by $7\frac{1}{4}$ inches outside.

Each NN muffle will hold twelve 20-gram, or eight 30-gram crucibles, allowing in each case for a row of empty crucibles in front to act as warmers, while the QQ muffle will hold fifteen 20-gram, or twelve 30-gram crucibles, also allowing for a row of empty crucibles in front.

The furnaces are best arranged to be fired from the rear, although they may be arranged to be fired from the front or sides. The flue makes off from near the front of the furnace, thus tending to heat the muffle uniformly throughout its entire length. It should be from one-sixth to one-eighth the grate area.

The stack for one of the furnaces will need to be at least 20 feet high and possibly higher, depending largely on the character of the coal. It should not be built directly on the furnace but may be placed directly over the furnace if supported by arches and cast-iron columns, or it may be put to one side of the furnace and in this case will extend down to the ground. When the stack is supported independently of the furnace it allows the furnace to expand and contract with less danger of cracking and also permits of tearing down and rebuilding the furnace without interfering with the stack.

With long-flame coal these furnaces are best fired with a rather thin bed of fuel, say 6 inches. The sequence of firing will consist, first, of running the slice bar along the entire length of the grate in one or two places and lifting up the fire to break up any large cakes and thus allow free passage of air through the fire, second, of pushing the well coked coal forward with the hoe and, third, of adding 1 or 2 shovels of fresh coal near the firing door. As this coal is heated it begins to coke and the gas given off passes over the white-hot coal of the fire and is there mixed with heated air. This results in a free draft and good volume of hot flame. If instead of being added near the firing door the fresh coal is spread all over the fire it will quickly cake and tend to smother the fire by shutting off the draft.

It is not necessary to use the slice bar every time, but only when the fire is tightly caked or after a long run when the grate is covered with clinkers.

The temperature of the muffle may be regulated at will by manipulating the draft- and firing-doors. For instance, after a batch of cupels have started, the draft may be closed and the firing-door opened, to admit cold air above the fire and quickly cool the muffles to any required degree.

Soft coal furnaces have the advantage of simplicity and low initial cost. They burn from 40 to 50 pounds of good bituminous coal an hour.

Wood Furnaces. — Wood-burning furnaces are made with single and double muffles and are much like the soft coal furnaces except that a larger firebox and grate are used. Wood is usually sawed in 2-foot lengths and with dry wood the muffle may be easily heated sufficiently for assaying. Hard wood is much to be preferred as it does not burn out as rapidly, but almost any kind of dry wood may be used.

The large firebox and the grate, which is set about 8 inches below the bottom of the fire-door are the principal distinguishing characteristics of a wood-burning assay furnace.

Coke Furnaces. — Coke is still used to a considerable extent in pot-furnaces, but for muffle-furnace fuel it is fast falling into disuse, at least in this country.

Compared with the soft-coal muffle furnace, the coke furnace has the advantage that it can be more quickly heated to a cupeling temperature and that it requires less frequent stoking. On the other hand it is harder to regulate the temperature, especially to cool it off quickly when cupeling; the stoking is harder work and in most localities the fuel cost per assay is higher.

The great advantage of the coke pot-furnace is the very high temperature which may be obtained and the fact that, even though the crucibles boil over or eat through, no harm is done to the furnace. Coke furnaces should be supplied with an especially good quality of fuel. If the ash tends to melt, the walls quickly become covered with clinkers and are bound to be more or less damaged when these are removed.

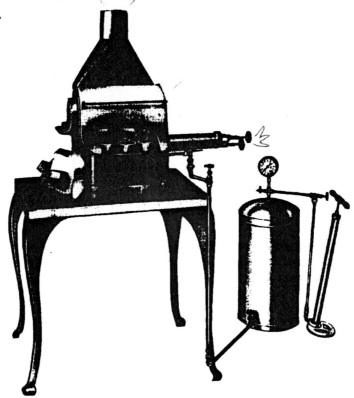

FIG. 8.—Gasoline furnace outfit.

Gasoline Furnaces. — A gasoline furnace outfit consists of a furnace, which may be either a muffle, crucible or combination of the two, a burner with piping, etc., and a gasoline tank with pump. The tank for a small assay office, is an ordinary tinned-steel pressure tank equipped with a hand pump, pressure-gage and the necessary piping connections. These range from 2 to 15 gallons capacity.

A complete gasoline furnace outfit is shown in Fig. 8. This is a combination crucible and muffle furnace made in several sizes ranging in capacity from 6F or 4G crucibles to 10F or 6G crucibles. In the illustration the crucible compartment is shown open although, of course, when actually in use, it is closed with special fire-clay covers. The muffle is situated directly above the crucible chamber. The advantage of this type of furnace is that fusions may be started within fifteen minutes after the heat is turned on, and while the fusions are in progress the muffle is heating. At the end of two rounds of fusions, the muffle is hot enough for cupellation.

The burners are usually constructed of special bronze alloys capable of withstanding oxidation at high temperatures. They consist of a filtering chamber for purifying the gasoline, a generating chamber where the gasoline is vaporized, a generating pan and valve for the initial heating of the burner, a spraying nozzle and valve through which the gasoline vapor is injected into the furnace and a mixing chamber where the proper amount of air for combustion is mixed with the gas. From the filter the gasoline passes around the interior of the burner face, the generating chamber, where it is heated by the heat radiated from the furnace and vaporized, so that once the furnace is under way the generating burner may be shut off. Gasoline is supplied to the burner under a pressure of from 20 to 50 pounds per square inch.

The great object to be sought and one of the hardest to attain in any gasoline furnace is an even distribution of heat. Another objectionable feature in many gas and gasoline furnaces is the poor draft through the muffle. Owing to the fact that the pressure inside the furnace is slightly greater than that of the atmosphere there is a great tendency for the products of combustion to work back through the hole in the rear of the muffle, thus to a large extent excluding the air and unduly prolonging cupellation or scorification.

In operating a gasoline burner care should be taken to see that combustion takes place only in the furnace. All burners have more or less tendency to back-fire, that is for the flame to jump back and remain in the mixing chamber. If this is allowed to continue, the burner gets so hot that the metal oxidizes and then it is only a matter of a short time before it is entirely destroyed. Every furnace should be provided with a shut-off valve between the burner and the gasoline tank. When it is desired to shut off the furnace, close this valve, letting the burner continue as long as any pressure is left and never entirely close the burner valves. The valve stem or needle is of steel and the seat is of bronze, and owing to the different rates of expansion of these metals, the valve is injured if these are left in close contact when the burner is cooling. This precaution is especially to be observed when the burner is provided with the ordinary needle valve, as when this opening is once enlarged the efficiency of the burner is destroyed.

Gas Furnaces. — Gas furnaces are used in some assay offices, especially where a natural gas supply is available. Where artificial gas has to be used this type of furnace proves decidedly expensive, if used for any considerable amount of work. As the gas is not usually under sufficient pressure to carry in its own supply of air for combustion, these furnaces are customarily supplied with air from a blower, which adds to the expense and difficulty of the furnace operation.

Fuel-Oil Furnaces. — When a cheap oil supply is available, oil is an ideal fuel for assay furnaces. Fuel-oil and kerosene cannot be vaporized in the burner as they deposit carbon when heated and thus clog the passages. Consequently, to ensure complete combustion, the oil must be thrown into the furnace in as fine a state of mechanical subdivision as possible. This is accomplished by atomizing the oil with a jet of air or steam.

The air for atomizing the oil may be supplied, (1), by a high-speed motor-driven fan giving a large volume of air at a pressure of from 6 to 14 ounces; (2), by a positive pressure blower giving a pressure of from 1 to 5 pounds; or (3), directly from a compressor. In the last case, the air is reduced to any desired pressure by a suitable regulating valve.

The burner used must be designed to operate properly with air at the available pressure. Therefore, there are low-, medium- and high-pressure burners. The high-pressure systems are noisy and therefore objectionable from this standpoint, as well as because of the large amount of power required. The low-pressure burner, operating usually at 6 or 8 ounces air pressure makes very little noise and requires a comparatively small amount of power. It is said, moreover, to use less oil and to cause less damage to the furnace, and is therefore most commonly used. A section of a low-pressure oil burner is shown in Fig. 9. This burner is adjustable for oil and air so that a wide range of temperature variation is available. The oil is introduced through the central channel and the quantity admitted is regulated by a needle valve. The oil channel terminates in an enlarged orifice through which the oil is discharged in a thin, circular film. It is caught by a rotating air blast and discharged from the nozzle

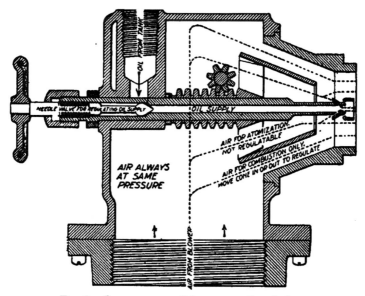

Fig. 9.—Low pressure oil burner, sectional view.

as a fine mist. Air for atomizing passes through the cone and is given a whirling motion by fins which project from it. Extra air for combustion passes in around the outside of the cone, which is operated from the side by means of a rack and pinion, and may be completely shut off by moving the cone out as far as it will go.

Any fuel-oil lighter than 18° Baumé at 60° F. may be used in these burners with gravity feed and only a few feet of head. A heavier oil may be used if heated, although in this case a pressure feed may be desirable. The oil consumption for assay furnaces runs from $1\frac{1}{2}$ to $2\frac{1}{2}$ gallons per hour, dependent on the size of furnace and grade of oil.

The muffle type of furnace is commonly used both for fusions and cupellations. The furnace proper may be considered to consist of three parts; a combustion chamber where the oil is ignited, a muffle chamber which contains the muffle and where combustion is completed, and the damper block which contains the dampers for controlling the atmosphere in the muffle and the flow of gases through the furnace. The combustion chamber serves to protect the muffle from the intense direct heat of the flame and is lined with removable tiles. Between it and the muffle is a heavy fire-clay plate which serves as a support for the muffle and protects it from the flame. By adjusting the dampers, either an oxidizing or reducing atmosphere may be obtained in the muffle.

Care of Muffles. — Muffles are expensive, and care should be taken to make them last as long as possible. They are subject to injury by corrosion due to basic reagents, principally litharge, and by cracking, due to sudden changes of temperature. Care should be taken, particularly in the case of oil furnaces, to bring the heat up slowly so that all parts of the furnace may become heated gradually. To prevent injury by corrosion try to avoid accidental spilling, and so proportion the size of crucibles to the charges that boiling over is impossible. Cupels should weigh 20 per cent more than the button to be cupeled in order to prevent litharge from running through and on to the muffle floor. Cracking due to changes of temperature is much more rapid when the inside of the muffle is glazed. This is due to the different rates of expansion of the glazed and unglazed parts.

When any lead or slag is spilled in the muffle, or a fusion is found to have eaten through its container, the muffle must be quickly scraped out and the spot well covered with bone-ash. The bone-ash absorbs the litharge and forms a thick paste with the slag so that it can be easily cleaned out with a scraper. It is well to keep a thin layer of bone-ash in the muffle at all times.

When not in use the drafts and muffle doors should be kept closed, and at the end of the day the furnace should be allowed to cool down slowly.

Furnace Repairs. — Fire-clay usually forms the basis of mortars used in furnace construction and repairs, as lime mortar and hydraulic cement are not suitable for use with masonry exposed to high temperatures. Fire-clay is a clay containing only very small amounts of iron, lime, magnesia and the alkali oxides. It forms a more or less plastic and sticky mortar; on heating it loses its moisture and plasticity and the mortar hardens.

All clays shrink more or less on drying and burning, and to prevent this as far as possible, as well as to make the mortar strong, a certain amount of crushed fire-brick or sand should be added. Crushed fire-brick is better than sand owing to its porous and irregular shaped grains, as these give a better mixture with the clay and a stronger cement.

A good mortar for general use around assay furnaces is made with a mixture of 2 parts fire-brick ground through 12-mesh and 1 part fire-clay. A small amount of Portland cement or molding clay, say not over $\frac{1}{4}$ part, will cause the mixture to adhere better and make the mortar harder when set. For work at very high temperatures the Portland cement must be omitted as it acts as a flux for the other materials and causes the whole to melt.

All mortars should be made up dry and thoroughly mixed before the required amount of water is added. The water should be thoroughly mixed in and the mortar should be sticky and of the right consistency. It is well to mix the mortar several hours before using. When bricks are being laid or repairs made about a furnace, the bricks and brickwork should be thoroughly wet before the mortar is applied, as otherwise the bricks absorb so much water that the mortar does not form a good bond with them.

In laying fire-bricks, as little mortar as possible should be used as the bricks are always harder than even the best of mortar. The mortar should be made to fill every crevice. The best way to attain this is to put an extra amount of fairly thin mortar on the wet brick and then drive or force it firmly into place, allowing the excess mortar to squeeze out.

The ash from many coals is quite readily fusible and results in the formation of clinkers and accretions on the sides of the furnace, especially just above the grate. When the furnace is cold these adhere very tenaciously to the walls of the furnace and when they are broken off, pieces of the brick are removed with them. To remove these accretions with the least possible damage to the furnace cut them off with a chisel bar just after a hot fire has been drawn.

In putting in a new muffle, first remove the old one with the mortar that held it, also any clinkers which would interfere with the working of the furnace. Patch the lining of the furnace if necessary and see that the bricks or other supports for the muffle are in place and in good condition. After trying the muffle to see that it rests properly on the supports, remove it, sponge over the brickwork where the mortar is to come in contact with it, place some rather thick mortar on each of the supports and replace the muffle. See that it rests evenly on the different supports and on the front wall of the furnace. The muffle should be level or slope slightly toward the front end. Fill up the space between the muffle and the front wall of the furnace with some rather thick mortar, working from both inside and outside of the furnace. This outside joint should be finished up neatly with the aid of a trowel. It is best to allow the furnace to dry for a day or two if possible, but if necessary it may be used as soon as finished by heating up slowly.

For patching the linings of furnaces use the mixture recommended for general use or try the following which is recommended by Lodge. Fire-brick through 12-mesh 7 parts; Portland cement 2 parts, fire-clay 1 part. Put this on as dry as possible and it will make a patch almost as hard as the original brick.

Cracked and broken muffles may be made to last much longer if patched with one of the above-mentioned mixtures.

Metallurgical Clay Goods.

Under the caption, "Metallurgical Clay Goods," are included muffles, crucibles, scorifiers, roasting-dishes, annealing cups etc. These embrace many of the most important utensils of the assayer and upon their good properties much of his success depends. Fire-clay is the only material which answers the double purpose of satisfactory service and inexpensive construction. Refractory clay or fire-clay, as it is commonly called, is a clay which will stand exposure to a high temperature without melting or becoming, in a sensible degree, soft or plastic.

All clays contract both upon drying and upon burning and this leads to more or less warping and cracking of the finished product. To prevent this shrinkage as far as possible and also to add strength to the finished article it is customary to add a certain amount of sand or well-burned clay to the mixture. Burned clay is usually preferred to sand for this purpose, not only because its rough porous grains give a better bond with the fire-clay and make a stronger cement, but also because it makes an article which is less readily corroded by assay slags and fusion products. The intermixture of coarse grains of burned clay also helps in that it makes a product better able to withstand sudden changes in temperature.

The exact proportions of raw and burned clay used by any manufacturer are carefully guarded trade secrets and depend, of course, very much on the clay used as well as on the article to be manufactured. The larger the article the more care must be taken to prevent warping and cracking. Usually however, the proportion of raw to burned clay will lie between the limits of 1 to 1 and 1 to 2.

Muffles. — Muffles may be made of a variety of materials, but for assay purposes fire-clay muffles are used exclusively. They are made in a great variety of sizes and shapes. However, when crucible fusions are to be made in the muffle, a nearly rectangular cross-section is preferred, as this gives a muffle of almost uniform height without any appreciable waste space.

Muffles, as well as other fire-clay ware, should be stored in a warm, dry place and should be heated and cooled slowly and uniformly. The life of a muffle is also much influenced by the way it is supported.

Crucibles. — Assay crucibles are made either of a mixture of raw and burned clay or of a mixture of sand and clay, the first being known as clay or fluxing crucibles and the second as sand crucibles. The raw clay is finely ground, mixed with the right proportion of coarser particles of sand or burned clay and water, and the whole well kneaded and compressed in molds of the proper shape.

Good crucibles should have the following properties:
1. Ability to withstand a high temperature without softening.
2. Strength to stand handling and shipping without breaking.
3. Ability to stand sudden changes of temperature without cracking.
4. Ability to withstand the chemical action of the substances fused in them.
5. Impermeability to the substances fused in them and to the products of combustion.

Of course it is impossible to get any one crucible which will possess all of the above good properties to a high degree. For instance if a crucible is to be made as nearly impermeable as possible, it will be made of very fine-grained material and tightly compressed. Such a crucible, however, will not stand handling or sudden changes of temperature as well as one made with a skeleton of coarser material. Furthermore the manner and temperature of burning has much to do with the ability of crucibles to stand handling and shipping. A fairly hard-burned crucible will be stronger and less likely to be broken in handling, but on the other hand it will not stand sudden changes of temperature as well as a soft-burned crucible. Crucibles made of clay containing little uncombined silica and of burned clay of the same nature will stand a high temperature and chemical corrosion much better than those made of sand and clay or of clay containing much free silica.

Crucibles are tested for resistance to chemical corrosion by actual service and also by fusing litharge in them and noting the time it takes to eat through. To make a test of this sort which is of any value, care must be taken to see that the temperature, the quantity of litharge and all other conditions are the same for the crucibles being tested. A crucible may be tested for its permeability to liquids by filling it with water and noting the time it takes before it becomes moist on the outside.

Crucibles come in a great variety of shapes and sizes. Those most commonly used for assaying may be classified into two groups as follows:

Pot-Furnace Crucibles. — These are comparatively slim, heavy walled crucibles with practically no limit as to height. The base is small, so that they may be forced down into the fuel and for this reason they are easily tipped over and are not suitable for muffle work. The sizes most used are the E, F, G, H, J and K. Crucibles of the same designation but made by different manufacturers vary considerably in capacity. The approximate capacity of some of the pot-furnace crucibles is shown in the following table:

TABLE III.

CAPACITIES OF POT-FURNACE CRUCIBLES.

Crucible designation	E	F	G	H	I	J	K
[1] Battersea	180 c.c.	210 c.c.	300 c.c.	420 c.c.	....	600 c.c.	750 c.c.
[2] Denver	180 c.c.	240 c.c.	400 c.c.	....	530 c.c.	685 c.c.	950 c.c.

[1] Made by the Morgan Crucible Co., London, England.
[2] Made by the Denver Fire Clay Co., Denver, Colorado.

Muffle Crucibles. — These are made with a broader base so that they may stand securely on the floor of the muffle, and are usually not more than 4 inches high. Muffle crucibles are designated by gram capacity, the 10-, 15-, 20- and 30-gram sizes being most frequently used. The numbers are intended to indicate the grams of ore-charge which the crucibles will take. They are usually generously proportioned, so that often an assay-ton of ore (29.166 grams) may be treated in a 20-gram crucible. The approximate capacity of the more important muffle crucibles is shown in the following table:

TABLE IV.

CAPACITY OF MUFFLE FURNACE CRUCIBLES.

Crucible designation	5 gm.	10 gm.	12 gm.	15 gm.	20 gm.	30 gm.
Denver	70 c.c.	100 c.c.	140 c.c.	160 c.c.	190 c.c.	260 c.c.
Battersea	70 c.c.	100 c.c.	.....	135 c.c.	190 c.c.	260 c.c.

Scorifiers. — These are shallow fire-clay dishes used in the scorification assay of gold and silver ores. They should be smooth on the inside, dense and impermeable to lead and slag and should be composed so as to withstand, as much as possible, the corrosive action of litharge. Scorifiers are designated by their outside diameters. Of the large number of sizes made, the following are the most commonly used: $2\frac{1}{4}$ inches, $2\frac{1}{2}$ inches, $2\frac{3}{4}$ inches, 3 inches, $3\frac{1}{2}$ inches. The Bartlett scorifier is shallower than the regular one and was designed for the treatment of heavy sulphide ores containing considerable metallic impurities. Scorifiers should be made of clay containing a minimum of uncombined silica, as the scorifier slags are usually very basic. Particularly when they contain copper, they attack the silica of a scorifier with avidity, and one with a siliceous skeleton may become perforated and allow its contents to escape to the floor of the muffle, thus spoiling the assay and injuring the muffle.

FURNACE TOOLS.

The more important furnace tools consist of crucible, scorifier, cupel and annealing cup, tongs, cupel rakes and shovels, muffle scrapers and spatulas and the various pouring molds, cupel and annealing cup trays, hammers, slagging forceps, anvils etc.

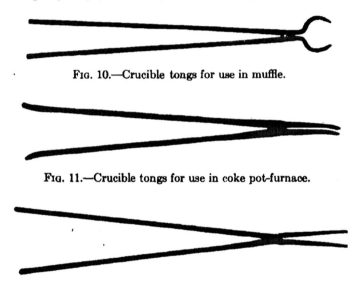

FIG. 10.—Crucible tongs for use in muffle.

FIG. 11.—Crucible tongs for use in coke pot-furnace.

FIG. 12.—Crucible tongs for use in gasoline melting-furnace.

Crucible Tongs. — Two types of crucible tongs are in common use, those which grasp the body of the crucible and those which grip the top edge of the crucible inside and out. In Fig. 10 is shown a pair of crucible tongs of the first type, suited for use in a laboratory where the fusions are made in the muffle. Thirty inches is a convenient length for these tongs. Figure 11 illustrates a good strong pair of the second type of tongs, especially suited for coke pot-furnace work. These may be made somewhat shorter, say 26 inches long. Figure 12 shows a lighter construction of the second type for use in gasoline melting-furnaces and in muffle work. These should be about 30 inches long. A combination of these two types of tongs is listed by most supply houses, but is of little practical use as it cannot be used in a muffle full of crucibles to grasp the body of the crucible, owing to its shape, and neither is it as satisfactory as the one illustrated in Fig. 12 for use in gasoline melting-furnaces. Another convenient tool for crucible furnace work is shown in Fig. 13. This is known as a charging fork. It consists of a fork-shaped piece of steel, which fits the crucible about midway, mounted on the end of a long rod. This is used principally for charging and occasionally for pouring; 46 to 48 inches is a convenient length.

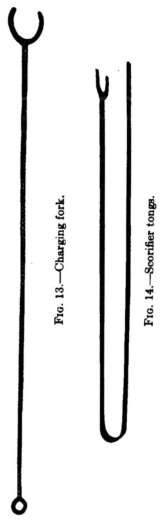

Fig. 13.—Charging fork.

Fig. 14.—Scorifier tongs.

Scorifier Tongs. — Several different designs of scorifier tongs are employed, the first and oldest being shown in Fig. 14. The curved fork fits the bottom of the scorifier while the long arm extends across the top. These are preferably made of $\frac{3}{4}$ by $\frac{1}{8}$ inch steel and should be about 30 inches long. They may be flattened enough at the bend to give the right degree of spring. Several different sizes should be supplied to handle the different sizes of scorifiers, although a pair made with a space of $1\frac{5}{8}$ inches between the two members of the fork will handle $2\frac{1}{2}$, $2\frac{3}{4}$ and 3 inch scorifiers perfectly. The form of crucible tongs illustrated in Fig. 12 is also occasionally used for handling scorifiers. With these, scorifiers may be lifted from the rear of the muffle without disturbing those in front. They are convenient in that one pair of tongs will fit any size of scorifier.

Cupel Tongs. — A good form of cupel tongs is illustrated in Fig. 15. It may be made of half-inch half-round stock and should be about 30 inches long. It is best to curve the points of these tongs to conform to the cupel, so that if the operator happens to grasp a cupel below its center of gravity it cannot turn over and spill the contents. For handling a large number of cupels at one time, a cupel shovel of light weight iron is often used. This may be made of any convenient width and from 24 to 30 inches long. The cupels are moved on or off the shovel with a rake or rabble of the same width.

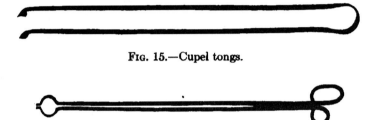

FIG. 15.—Cupel tongs.

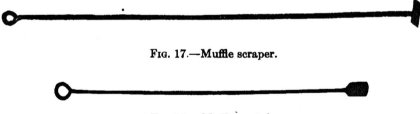

FIG. 16.—Annealing cup tongs.

Annealing and Parting Cup Tongs. — A pair of tongs arranged to handle annealing cups is shown in Fig. 16. They should be made so that when closed they fit the cup somewhat above its center. When a large number of annealings are to be done at one time the cups may be placed in some form of clay dish and all put in the muffle together.

FIG. 17.—Muffle scraper.

FIG. 18.—Muffle spatula.

Muffle Scrapers and Spatulas. — The muffle scraper, as its name implies, is a tool intended for the prompt removal of anything spilled upon the floor of the muffle. A muffle spatula is a long rod of say $\frac{1}{4}$ inch iron, flattened at the end. It is useful in spreading bone-ash over a slagged spot in the muffle, as well as in adding reagents, etc., to crucibles and scorifiers already in the muffle. In Figs. 17 and 18 are shown a muffle scraper and spatula.

Molds. — Various forms of molds to receive the molten charge are in use. They are usually made of cast iron and should be

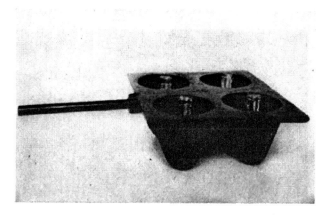

Fig. 19. — Four-hole crucible mold.

machined on the inner surface. For crucible fusions, the writer prefers one having a fairly sharp (50°) conical cavity holding about 60 cubic centimeters and with a slightly rounded bottom. In Fig.

Fig. 20. — Cupel tray holding 16 cupels.

19 is shown a four-hole mold of this description. This leaves the lead button in good shape for pounding and permits a good separation of lead and slag. Some assayers prefer a solid block mold

with a conical cavity, claiming that the fusions cool more rapidly. A mold of this type, however, is heavier to handle and more expensive. If a muffle full of crucibles is poured at one time, it will be found that those first poured are ready for slagging almost immediately, even if the lighter molds are used.

Fig. 21. — Clay dish holding 24 annealing cups.

For scorification fusions, molds with smaller cavities are used. They are made with spherical or with flatly-coned cavities and both types are satisfactory. A convenient form of mold is one in which the number of cavities equals the number of scorifiers which the muffle will hold.

Cupel Trays, etc. — A convenient cupel tray is illustrated in Fig. 20. A clay dish for annealing is shown in Fig. 21. Any form of hammer will serve for slagging the buttons, but one with a round section is preferable. Ten-inch forceps are satisfactory both for holding buttons while slagging and for removing the nails from iron-nail fusions.

CHAPTER III.

ORE SAMPLING.

A sample is a small amount which contains all the components in the proportions in which they occur in the original lot.

Object. — The object of sampling an ore is to obtain, for chemical or mechanical tests, a small amount which shall contain all the minerals in the same proportion as the original lot. In the subsequent discussion the word " sample " will be taken to mean that fraction which is taken to represent the whole, whether or not it does so. The compound words correct-sample, representative-sample, true-sample, will be used to represent the ideal conditions.

In the intelligent operation of a mine or metallurgical plant, it is necessary to sample and assay continually. In most mines, the different faces of ore are sampled every day. In concentrating plants, it is customary to sample the products of every machine at frequent and regular intervals, to ascertain whether the machine is doing the work expected of it. In smelters, it is necessary to sample and assay every lot of ore, as well as fluxes and fuels, in order to calculate a charge which will run properly in the furnace. The slag, flue dust and metallic products must also be sampled and assayed, with a view to maintaining control of the operations. In lixiviation plants, the ore and tailings, as well as the solutions, must be sampled in order that the daily work of the plant may be controlled and checked. In fact, careful sampling and assaying cannot be disregarded, and are becoming more and more important every day as the grade of ore decreases and the margin of profit becomes less.

The assayer will usually have the major part of the sampling done for him, but he is expected to know how to do it when called upon. He usually has to prepare only the final sample, but will occasionally receive lots of 10 to 100 or more pounds to assay, in which case he will have to do his own sampling. The following discussion will deal principally with the assay laboratory problems of sampling; the question of mine sampling is entirely omitted, but methods used in sampling mills are briefly reviewed for the sake of completeness.

Methods. — The question of ore sampling is probably the most complicated of all sampling problems, because of the great variety of constituents and the lack of uniformity in their distribution throughout the whole mass. It is obvious that, however we may proceed, the problem is to select a method, such that every particle of our non-homogeneous mixture, the ore, shall have nearly the same chance of being included in the sample. Several methods may be followed to secure this result and, assuming the ore to have had a preliminary crushing, the available methods are:

1. Random selection
2. Selection by rule
3. Mixing and cutting

The first two are rough, preliminary methods generally known as " grab-sampling." The last is capable of mathematical precision and may be repeated through all stages of the sampling process. It is the only method which should be used when an exact sample of the precious metal ores is desired. Iron ores are so uniform that " grab-sampling " is likely to yield satisfactory results.

When it is considered that the final sample for chemical analysis usually weighs only half a gram and for fire assay somewhat less than 15 grams, and that each must truly represent from 1 to 5 carloads of ore weighing from 50 to 250 tons, the enormous practical difficulties of the problem may be appreciated.

Precise sampling may usually be considered to consist of three distinct operations, repeated as many times as necessary. These operations are crushing, mixing and cutting. The cutting gives a sample and a reject. By a repetition of the three operations the sample may be further reduced until it has reached the desired weight.

The whole science of ore sampling depends primarily on a correct knowledge of the proper relation between the maximum size of the ore particles and the weight of the sample taken. The problem to be solved in each case is somewhat as follows: when a particular ore has been crushed to a certain size, how small a sample is it safe to take from this and still keep within the limit of allowable error? It is necessary to know the ore, the limit of allowable error, and the mathematical principles involved.

Sampling is classed as hand sampling when the mixing and cutting down is done by men with shovels, and as machine sampling when it is done by some form of automatic machine.

Commercial Considerations. — The most certain method of obtaining a representative sample of a lot of ore would be to crush the whole to 100-, 120-mesh or finer, mix it thoroughly and then cut down to the desired weight. This method can be followed for small amounts of a pound or so, but in the case of large lots it would entail too much labor and would usually unfit the ore for future treatment. The method generally adopted is a compromise and consists in crushing the whole lot to a certain predetermined maximum size and then taking out a certain fraction as a sample. This sample is again crushed to a smaller size and cut down as before, and this process repeated until finally the assay sample is obtained.

The care which is required in sampling, as well as the size to which a lot of ore or other material must be crushed before a sample is taken, depends upon the value and uniformity of composition of the material. The more uniform it is, the smaller may be the sample taken after crushing to any particular size. For instance, in the case of a solid piece of galena containing silver uniformly distributed as an isomorphous silver sulphide, a piece may be broken off anywhere, and after being crushed, will give a lot of ore which is truly a sample of the piece. If, however, the specimen is not solid galena, but is made up of galena and limestone, the silver still being contained in the galena, it will be necessary to crush the whole lot to a uniformly fine size before taking out a fractional part for a sample. Furthermore, it will readily be seen that the greater the difference in the grade of the different minerals in the ore, the finer the ore must be crushed before a sample of a given size should be taken from it.

Since ores are never perfectly uniform in composition, a certain amount of crushing is evidently necessary in every case. To determine the amount of crushing it is important to consider the commercial side of the question, that is, to determine how far it will pay to go with the process. Evidently a mistake of 1 per cent in the iron contents of a carload of iron ore worth $3 a ton is less serious than the same percentage error in the copper contents of a car of copper ore worth $50 a ton. Therefore it may be seen, that it will pay the seller or buyer of the copper ore to go to more pains and expense in the sampling of the ore, than if he were dealing with the less valuable iron ore.

The commercial conditions are met when the ultimate sample obtained comes within an allowable limit of error, usually 1 per cent, of the ideal or true figure, provided also that it has been obtained without undue delay and at a reasonable cost.

PRINCIPLES OF SAMPLING.

Varying Relation of Size of Sample to Maximum Particle. — Every ore-sampling operation is in effect a laboratory experiment in probability, and the variation of any portion or sample of a lot from the average composition of the whole may be considered to be due to the excess or deficit of one or more particles of the ore.

The effect upon the results will be greatest when the piece or pieces which are in excess or deficit are of the largest size, greatest specific gravity and greatest variation in quality from the average.

Disregarding for the moment the last two of these factors and supposing the ore particles to be approximately uniform in size, it is evident that the sample must contain so many particles that one additional particle of the richest mineral would cause practically no variation in the value. This means that the sample of the ordinary ore must contain a very large number of particles 500,000 in some cases, 5,000,000 in others.

Having determined how many particles of the ore it is necessary to include in the sample, and assuming the different minerals to be entirely detached from one another, it would be fair to take such a weight of ore after each reduction as would contain this established number of particles. Or, as the weight of a lump is proportional to the cube of its diameter, the weight of ore taken for the sample should be proportional to the cube of the diameter of the largest particle of the ore.

In the ordinary ore, however, the different minerals are not entirely detached from one another, but approach this condition more and more closely as the size of the ore is reduced. Hence a fixed number of the particles of the fine ore is less likely to be a true average of the whole than the same number of pieces of the lump ore before it was broken. Therefore as the size of the ore is reduced a larger and larger number of particles should be taken for the sample. To conform to this condition the following rule was proposed by Professor R. H. Richards: "For any given ore the weight taken for a sample should be proportional to the square of the diameter of the largest particle."

The accompanying table, based on figures taken from the practice of several careful managers, to a certain extent conforms to this rule. The table was arranged and is now published with the permission of Professor Richards.

TABLE V.

WEIGHTS TO BE TAKEN IN SAMPLING ORE.

Weights of sample pounds	1	2	3	4	5	6
	Diameter of largest particles — millimeters					
	Very low grade or very uniform ores	Low grade or uniform ores	Medium ores		Rich or spotted ores	Very rich and spotted ores
20,000.000	207.00	114.00	76.20	50.80	31.60	5.40
10,000.000	147.00	80.30	53.90	35.90	22.40	3.80
5,000.000	107.00	56.80	38.10	25.40	15.80	2.70
2,000.000	65.60	35.90	24.10	16.10	10.00	1.70
1,000.000	46.40	25.40	17.00	11.40	7.10	1.20
500.000	32.80	18.00	12.00	8.00	5.00	.85
200.000	20.70	11.40	7.60	5.10	3.20	.54
100.000	14.70	8.00	5.40	3.60	2.20	.38
50.000	10.70	5.70	3.80	2.50	1.60	.27
20.000	6.60	3.60	2.40	1.60	1.00	.17
10.000	4.60	2.50	1.70	1.10	.71	.12
5.000	3.30	1.80	1.20	.80	.50	
2.000	2.10	1.10	.76	.51	.32	
1.000	1.50	.80	.54	.36	.22	
.500	1.00	.57	.38	.25	.16	
.200	.66	.36	.24	.16	.10	
.100	.46	.25	.17	.11		
.050	.33	.18	.12			
.020	.21	.11				
.010	.15					
.005	.10					

The first column shows the safe weight in pounds for a sample of ore of any of the six grades shown and for sizes as indicated in the respective columns. Column 1 applies to iron ores, column 2 to low-grade lead, zinc and copper ores and even to low-grade pyritic gold ores, without native gold, where the pyrite is evenly distributed through the ore. Columns 3 and 4 apply to ores in which the valuable minerals are less uniformly distributed. Columns 5 and 6 apply to ore containing fine particles of native gold or silver, also to telluride and other " spotty ores. "

It should be remembered that the above-mentioned rules for sampling will not hold for ore containing large pieces of malleable minerals such as native gold, silver, silver sulphide, chloride etc. These roll out and do not crush and must be treated by special methods. See " Sampling Ores Containing Malleable Minerals."

In using the table, it is not necessary to crush successively to all of the sizes shown in any of the columns. The ore may be crushed to any fineness convenient and then a sample of the weight shown in the table may be taken. In sampling-mill practice it is customary to reduce the diameter of the coarsest particles one-half at each stage or crushing, thus reducing the volume to one-eighth or 12.5 per cent. It is also customary in practice to take a 20 per cent sample at each stage; consequently the ratio between the weight of sample and size of maximum particle is constantly increasing throughout the sampling process, thereby meeting theoretical conditions previously discussed.

Relation of Size of Sample to Grade of Ore and Effect of Specific Gravity of Richest Mineral. — Although it had long been appreciated that the size of the sample would have to be greater as the ratio of the grade of the richest mineral to the average grade increased, it remained for Brunton* to develop a formula by which the proper ratio between these could be scientifically controlled. According to him, each of the following factors must be included in any formula to be used for the control of sampling operations.

W = weight of sample in pounds.
k = grade of richest mineral in ounces per ton.
c = average grade of ore in ounces per ton.
s = specific gravity of richest mineral.
n = number of maximum-sized particles of richest mineral in excess or deficit in sample.
f = a factor expressing the ratio of the actual weight of the

* Trans. A.I.M.E. **25**, p. 826 (1895).

largest particle of richest mineral which will [pass a screen]
of a given size to the weight of the largest [particle of the]
same mineral which will pass the screen.

p = allowable percentage error in sample.
D = diameter in inches of the holes in the scr[een, or the]
normal diameter to which the ore is crushe[d.]

From these Brunton finds

$$D = .65 \sqrt[3]{\frac{Wcp}{fsn(k-c)}}.$$

Making p, the allowable percentage error, $= 1$, the formula becomes

$$D = .65 \sqrt[3]{\frac{Wc}{fsn(k-c)}}.$$

To determine a value to use for n, he made a number of assays on two different lots of high-grade ore crushed to pass a certain limiting screen. The average deviation from the mean $= p$ was substituted in the formula, and results of 2.64 and 3.14 respectively were found for n. Assuming that 3 is a safe value for n and cubing each side we find

$$D^3 = \frac{Wc}{10.8fs(k-c)},$$

or

$$W = \frac{10.8fsD^3(k-c)}{c},$$

from which may be found the safe weight in pounds for a sample of any ore whose largest particle is D inches. Taking four examples, using as the richest minerals pyrite, galena, native silver and native gold and assuming different values for D, k, c and f the following table was made after the style of the table first shown in Hofman's "Metallurgy of Lead." The values for f used for the fine sizes were those determined by Brunton's experiments, i.e., 4 for pyrite and galena and 6 for native silver and native gold. This value of f is reduced gradually, until for 1 inch diameter, it is made equal to 1, this variation therefore tending to compensate for the greater uniformity of value of the particles as they become larger.

A TEXTBOOK OF FIRE ASSAYING

The following table is probably the best and certainly the most conservative of all. A good deal of intelligent discrimination may often be used, however, and mere formulas can never be made to cover all possible contingencies. For instance, in sampling an ore in which the valuable mineral is finely and uniformly disseminated

TABLE VI.

WEIGHTS TO BE TAKEN IN SAMPLING ORE.

Specific gravity Richest mineral	Size of particles		Safe weight in pounds when largest particles are of size given in second column					
	Mesh	Diam. Inch	Grade of richest mineral divided by average grade					
			10	50	200	600	1,500	2,500
5.0	120	.0043			.003	.010	.025	.043
	100	.0055	.0003	.0018	.007	.021	.053	.089
	50	.0100	.0017	.0095	.039	.116	.291	.485
	14	.0364	.0585	.319	1.29	3.90	9.76	16.3
	4	.145	2.96	16.1	65.5	195.	494.	823.
	2	.338	30.0	163.	664.	2,000.	5,000.	8,340.
		.5	75.9	413.	1,680.	5,050	12,600	21,100.
		1.0	486	2,650.	10,700.	32,300.	80,900.	140,000.
7.5	120	.0043			.005	.015	038	.064
	100	.0055	.0005	.0027	.011	.032	.080	.134
	50	.0100	.0026	.0143	.058	.174	.437	.727
	14	.0364	.0878	.479	1.94	5.85	14.6	24.5
	4	.145	4.44	24.2	98.3	293.	740.	1,230.
	2	.338	45.0	245.	996.	3,000.	7,500.	12,500.
		.5	114.	620.	2,520.	7,580.	19,000.	31,600.
		1.0	729.	3,970.	16,100.	48,500.	121,000.	211,000.
10.5	120	.0043	.0005	.0027	.011	.032	.081	.135
	100	.0055	.0010	.0055	.022	.068	.170	.283
	50	.0100	.0041	.0222	.090	.272	.679	1.13
	14	.0364	.148	.804	3.26	9.83	24.6	41.0
	4	.145	7.78	42.4	172.	518.	1,300.	2,160.
	2	.338	78.8	429.	1,740.	5,250.	13,100.	21,900.
		.5	230	1,250.	5,080.	15,300	38,200.	63,800.
			1,500	3,000	6,000	15,000	30,000	60,000
17.6	150	.0036	.0798	.159	.319	.798	1.59	3.19
	120	.0043	.136	.272	.544	1.36	2.72	5.40
	100	.0055	.284	.569	1.14	2.84	5.69	11.4
	50	.0100	1.14	2.28	4.56	11.4	22.8	45.6
	14	.0364	41.2	82.5	165.	412.	825.	1,650.
	4	.145	2,170.	4,350.	8,690.	21,700.	43,500.	86,900.
	2	.338	22,000.	44,000	88,100.	220,000.	440,000.	881,000.

throughout the gangue, a much smaller sample than that given in the table may be taken for the coarse sizes, although for the fine sizes the full quantities shown in the table should be taken. Another ore, with perhaps the same ratio of value of the richest mineral to average grade, having the rich mineral in larger crystals or masses, will have to be sampled as carefully as indicated by the table throughout the entire operation.

It should be noted also, that except in the case of native metals, the richest minerals are usually more finely divided by crushing than the gangue; therefore the extreme case provided for by the formula is seldom met in practice.

One of the most difficult things an assayer may be called upon to do is to sample such mill products as vanner concentrates. In these the particles of gangue minerals are two or three times the diameter of the average rich mineral and good mixing is impossible. The material stratifies whenever handled and the greatest care must be taken if the sampling is to be successful.

SAMPLING PRACTICE.

Recording. — Every lot of ore coming into an assay office, laboratory, custom mill or smelter should be given a lot number which should never be repeated. The lot should be immediately labeled with this number. A record book, kept for this purpose, should show the number of the sample, date of receipt, name of mine, company or individual from whom received, the gross and net weight, as well as notes on the general mineral character, etc.

Weighing. — Large lots of ore are first weighed, and a moisture sample is sometimes taken at this point. Small lots may be first dried and then weighed.

Crushing. — All of the ore, unless already fine enough, is broken or crushed to pass a screen of some limiting size. This size depends upon the value of the ore and other factors to be considered later. The finer the pulp is crushed, the more uniform in size are the particles and more thorough mixing and better sampling is possible. If the ore is to be smelted, most of it should be left in the coarse state, as fine ore is undesirable. If it is to be roasted or leached, on the other hand, fine ore is not objectionable, and the first crushing may be carried further. As a rule, however, the aim is to minimize the crushing, thus saving in cost and keeping down the dust.

Machines for crushing should be rapid in action and easy to clean. Jaw breakers and rolls fulfill these requirements; ball mills and pebble mills do not.

Mixing. — This step in the process of sampling is often omitted or allowed to take care of itself. It is a necessary forerunner of quartering and channeling, but is usually omitted before the other methods of cutting. Especially in the handling of small lots of ore in the laboratory, it is best to be over-careful in this particular rather than the reverse, and, as it adds but little labor, to give each lot of crushed ore a thorough mixing before cutting. The mixing of small lots will be discussed under the head of finishing the sample.

The final step in the sequence of sampling operations consists in taking out a fraction of the whole, say a quarter or a half, in some systematic, impartial manner. The part taken out is called the sample, and the operation of taking it is the cutting.

Hand Cutting. — The following methods of hand cutting are occasionally used, but whenever possible are being replaced by machine cutting.

FRACTIONAL SHOVELING. — This is a rough starting method, suited only to large lots of low-grade or fairly uniform ore. When the ore is being taken away from the crusher or shoveled out of cars, as the case may be, every second, third, fifth, or tenth shovelful, depending on the value and uniformity of the ore, is taken and placed in a separate pile, which is afterwards cut down by some of the methods described later. When the ore is being shoveled, care must be taken that each shovelful is taken from the floor. Lumps which are too large for the shovel should be broken and put back on the pile. The method is open to the serious objection that it is a very simple matter for a prejudiced person to make the sample either higher or lower in grade than the average, by selection of his shovel samples.

QUARTERING. — This is the method of cutting which accompanies coning. It presupposes a thorough mixing by coning, as the two always go together.

CONING. — The sample is shoveled into a conical pile, each shovelful being thrown upon the apex of the cone so that it will run down evenly all around. When a large lot of ore is to be mixed by coning, it is first dumped in a circle and then coned by one or more men who walk slowly around between the cone and the circle of ore. The best results are obtained by coning around a rod, as by this means the center of the cone is kept in a vertical line. Coning does not thoroughly mix an ore, but rather sorts it into fine material which lies near the center and coarser material which rolls down the sides of the cone. If the ore is practically uniform in size and specific gravity, the mixing may be more thorough. A slight dampening of the ore is said to allow of better mixing by coning. The floor, for this and other hand sampling operations, should be smooth, and free from cracks which would make good cleaning difficult or impossible. A floor made of sheet-iron or steel plates is preferable.

Fig. 22. — Cone of crushed ore.

Figure 22,* a cone of crushed ore, shows clearly the inherent defect of this method of sampling, the segregation of coarse and fine ore, caused by dropping shovelful after shovelful on top of a cone.

When the cone is completed, it is worked down into the form of a flat truncated cone by men who walk around and around, drawing their shovels from center to periphery, or starting at the apex and working the shovel up and down in the path of a spiral. The point to be observed here is not to disturb the radial distribution of the coarse and fine ore. After flattening, the cone is divided into four 90-degree sectors or quarters by means of a sharp-edged board, or better, by a steel-bladed quarterer. These

* From U. S. Bureau of Mines Technical Paper No. 86: Ore Sampling Conditions in the West.

quarters should, of course, radiate from the position of the center of the original cone. Two opposite quarters are taken out and rejected and the two others are then taken for the sample. Care must be taken at this point to sweep up all dust belonging to the

Fig. 23. — Partly flattened cone

Fig. 24. — Truncated cone from which reject quarters have been removed.

rejected portions before proceeding, so that this dust shall neither be lost nor mixed with the sample. This sample may be again mixed by coning and quartered, or crushed, coned and quartered as the case may require.

Figure 23* shows a partly flattened cone and Fig. 24* a cake from which the reject quarters have been removed.

When properly carried out, this method may be made to yield fairly accurate results, but at best it is a slow and tedious process, and requires the most conscientious work on the part of the laborers to ensure correct results. It is open to the objection that it affords opportunity for manipulation of the sample by dishonest operators.

Coning and quartering is the old Cornish method of ore sampling and was almost universally used thirty years ago. It is still used to some extent as a finishing method at sampling works and by engineers in the field where no machinery is available.

BENCH SYSTEM OF CONING. — The tendency to segregate, which is the principal objection to coning, can be largely overcome by what is known as the bench system of coning. Under this system all of the ore is not piled in a single cone; a part of it is coned first and this small cone is worked out into a layer of considerable diameter and but little thickness. Another part of the ore is then coned on top of this and the cone truncated. This is repeated until all of the ore is used. This method is said to give working results which are much more satisfactory than those obtained by the regular system.

RIFFLE CUTTING. — Riffle cutting or splitting is the most accurate laboratory method available. The riffle, splitter or split-shovel consists of a number of parallel troughs with open spaces between them, the spaces usually being of the same width as the troughs. These troughs are rigidly fastened together and either provided with a handle, making a split-shovel, or set up at an angle of about 45° making an inclined riffle. Figure 25 shows a split-shovel with pan and shovel. These may be made in different sizes but are useful only for small-scale work.

The ore is taken up on a flat shovel or special pan and spread over the troughs, care being taken not to heap the ore above the troughs. Either the ore which falls in the troughs or that which falls between them may be taken as the sample. The cutting may be repeated as many times as is deemed desirable. For the best results in cutting any sample of ore by this method, care should be taken to have only a thin stream of ore falling from the

* From U. S. Bureau of Mines Technical Paper No. 86: Ore Sampling Conditions in the West.

Fig. 25. — Split shovel and pans.

Fig. 26. — Brunton splitter.

pouring pan and to move this pouring pan back and forth over the split shovel, in a horizontal direction perpendicular to the riffles, so that every part of the stream of ore is being directed alternately and rapidly first into the sample and then into the reject. The more irregular in size, specific gravity and value are the minerals, the greater the care which should be taken in this particular. The sample should be mixed before recutting.

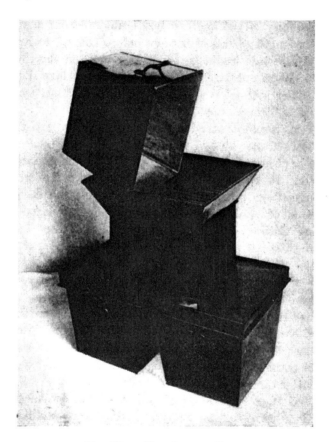

FIG. 27. — Closed type splitter.

A modification of the riffle or split-shovel known as the Jones sampler, or simply as a "splitter," is in general the most convenient form of sampler for finishing work. It is a riffle sampler in which the bottoms of the riffles are steeply inclined, first in one direction and then in the other. The ore is spread over the riffles in the Jones sampler exactly as over the split-shovel, and is caught in two pans placed underneath.

The Jones splitter and those similar to it have one decided advantage over the flat type shown in Fig. 25, in that the riffles cannot be overloaded, a very common fault of the shovel type. In Fig. 26 is shown a very substantial form known as the Brunton riffle, the operation of which is self-evident.

One objection to the Jones sampler and other similar models, is the possibility of the loss of considerable fine ore dust, due to the greater length of fall of the ore before coming to rest. One way to obviate this would be to slightly moisten the thoroughly mixed ore before cutting. A better way is to close the bottom of the sampler and set it directly on the pans. An example of this type of splitter is shown in Fig. 27.

In selecting a split-shovel or riffle cutter for any particular sampling operation, care should be taken that the distance between the riffles be at least four times the diameter of the maximum particle of ore. It is found that a slight bridging action may occur if this precaution is not observed. Riffle cutting is the most rapid method of hand sampling and is also the most accurate.

Machine Cutting. — A large number of machines have been devised to take the place of the slow, laborious methods of hand sampling. All these machines depend on taking the sample from a stream of falling ore. They may be classified as continuous and intermittent samplers. The continuous samplers take part of the stream all the time, by placing a partition in the falling stream of ore to separate sample from reject. The intermittent samplers, as the name implies, deflect the entire stream at intervals to make the sample. This is accomplished by passing a sample cutter directly across the stream.

The continuous method of sampling is open to the objection that it is impossible to get a stream of falling ore containing coarse and fine particles which is uniform across its entire section. This is because the ore on its way from the preceding crusher, bin or elevator practically always passes through a sloping chute in which the large lumps roll away from the small ones and the heavy minerals become more or less separated from the lighter ones. Therefore, any continuously taken sample will be either richer or poorer than the average. Because of these conditions this type of sampler will not give reliable results, and is now but little used.

The intermittent method of sampling gives better results. The machine should be so designed that it takes equal portions all across the stream at frequent and regular intervals. In one mill the first time-sampler cuts 24 and the last one 76 sections per minute.

While it is not possible to produce a stream of ore which is uniform in value throughout its entire length, and no single cut would be likely to give an exact representation of the lot, yet if a large number of small samples be taken entirely across the

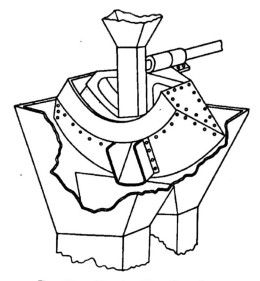

Fig. 28. — Brunton Time Sampler.

stream, the composite thus obtained will, according to the theory of probability, approach very close to the composition of the entire lot. It is essential that the percentage of sample taken from all parts of the delivery pipe be the same; in other words, that the vertical sample section, taken in a direction parallel to the motion of the intake-spout, should be a rhomboid.

Three machines of this type have come into general use; these are the Brunton, the Vezin and the Snyder.

Figure 28 is a line drawing of the Brunton Time Sampler. It consists of an oscillating divider swinging back and forth, in a vertical plane, beneath the end of the feed spout. It is suspended on a horizontal shaft and swings through an arc of 120°. It receives its motion through a train of gears, a disc crank and rocker arm, and by a change of gears any proportion of the stream, from 5 to 20 per cent, may be taken.

The sample cutter, which has horizontal edges not shown in the figure, deflects the sample forward into a hopper. The rest

Fig. 29. — Vezin sampler.

of the ore is deflected in the opposite direction into a chute leading to the reject bin. It is essential that the sample cutter move entirely out of the stream in each direction and that its velocity be uniform while any part of it is underneath the falling stream.

Otherwise, it would take too much from one part of the stream and not enough from other parts.

This type of sampler requires less head-room than any of the others and thus, by reducing the necessary height of building, saves in the cost of mill construction. Its rocking motion helps to dislodge any rags or strings which may have fallen on the cutting edges and its short cutting edges render accidental distortion impossible. A further advantage claimed for the Brunton ma-

Fig. 30. — Snyder sampler.

chine is that centrifugal force assists in the discharge of ore from the sampler and the machine can, therefore, be run at a much higher rate of speed than any of the sector machines.

The Vezin sampler, shown in Fig. 29, is probably the best-known automatic sampler. Various modifications in shape are possible, but generally speaking, it consists of one or two sample cutters which rotate about a vertical shaft and pass through a falling stream of ore, taking out a part of it and conveying this part through a central spout to a sample hopper. The theory of sampler design requires that the horizontal cutting edges be radii of the axis of revolution. This is necessary in order to ensure taking the same amount of ore from every part of the stream. The entire mechanism is supported in a frame, the bottom of which forms a hopper to collect the reject.

Particularly in the case of coarse ore, this sampler requires more head-room than the Brunton and its long cutting edges are liable to be distorted. It is designed to take a definite proportion, usually one-fifth of the stream, and this proportion cannot be altered after the machine is made.

The Snyder sampler, shown in Fig. 30, is the simplest of all. It consists of a circular casting much the shape of miner's gold-pan, mounted on the end of a horizontal shaft. One or more holes are made in its sloping flange and the edges of these project both on the front and back sides of the flange. The sampler revolves from ten to thirty times a minute and the material to be sampled comes to it by way of a sloping chute, not shown in the cut. The ore stream falls on the inside of the sloping flange and either passes through the opening into a suitable sample hopper or slides off the flange into a hopper leading to the reject chute.

The sides of the sample spout should lie in planes passing through the axis of revolution. Such a sampler, 60 inches in diameter, will take material $3\frac{1}{2}$ inches in diameter.

Figure 31 is a section through a sampling mill and shows how a number of crushers and samplers are combined in an automatic plant. To simplify the drawing, the roll feeders have been omitted. Such a plant will treat a 50-ton carload in less than an hour. It is cleaned by brushing with the aid of compressed air.

Hand and Machine Sampling Compared. — In comparing hand and machine sampling it may be said that machine sampling is generally cheaper, and, with a properly designed machine, is more accurate than coning or fractional shoveling. Perhaps the most important advantage of all is that, being strictly mechanical in operation, it affords less opportunity for manipulation of the sample.

Precaution to be Observed. — Besides the danger of "salting" from crushing machines, elevators, sampling machines etc., special attention must be paid to the disposition of the fine ore dust. As a rule the rich minerals in the ore are more brittle than the gangue, with the result that the ore dust is far higher in grade than the average of the ore. Whence is seen the necessity of

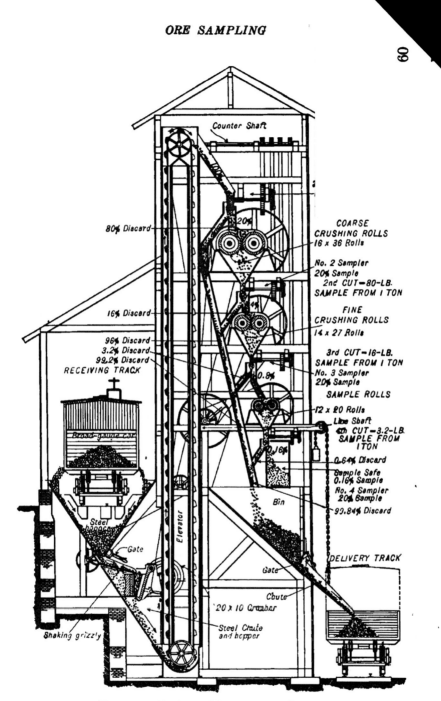

Fig. 31. — Taylor and Brunton sampling system.

preserving all of the ore dust and of taking pains to see that the sample contains its proper proportion of the same.

Grab-Sampling. — This is a rapid method used for sampling large quantities of low-grade and uniform material, such as iron or coal. It may also be used to obtain rough samples of the less homogeneous ores containing copper, lead, zinc, gold and silver. The methods of sampling iron ore and coal are fairly well standardized and consist in taking small shovelsful from definite points in the car or vessel as the material is being unloaded. These are combined and worked down by some of the standard finishing methods.

The method is obviously both rapid and inexpensive, but is so unscientific that no one considers it suitable for obtaining a sample from which the amount of gold, silver, copper or lead contained in an ore is to be determined. Unfortunately, however, some smelters still continue to use the grab-sample to determine the amount of moisture in custom ores.

Moisture Sample. — Assays and chemical determinations are always made on dry samples and the value of a lot of ore is always figured on the moisture-free basis. Except in cases when the entire lot may be dried, it is necessary to take a sample from which to determine the moisture. This sample must be taken as quickly as possible after the ore is weighed. If, as is still too often the case, a grab-sample is used as the basis for a moisture determination, much of the careful work of obtaining the sample for the determination of the other constituents may be nullified. Inasmuch as fines will ordinarily contain very much more moisture than lump ore, and as the grab-sample is small in amount, it is clear that any sample of mine-run ore thus taken will tend to carry more than its due share of moisture. Such a result leads to an undervaluation of the ore, due to the fact that the net weight reported is too small. In this connection it should not be forgotten that this so-called sample is taken by an interested party, an employee of the smelting company, who may be entirely honest but who certainly will not purposely lean over backwards in his efforts to be fair to the shipper. At any event, it is safe to say that samples for the determination of moisture should be taken with the same amount of care as samples for the determination of metallic contents, and that apparently the simplest and only scientific way of obtaining them from shipments of mine-run ore is to take them from the sample safe or reject from the last mechanical sampler.

Since the ore is weighed on the cars before it is sampled, and since in dry climates there is obviously some loss of moisture by evaporation from the ore in its passage through the crushing, elevating and sampling machinery, it is customary to make a correction to the moisture-figure, as determined by this latter method, to compensate for this loss. This correction usually consists of the addition of an arbitrary percentage. Brunton* finds 10 per cent in summer and 7 per cent in winter a fair average figure. For instance, if the sample showed 5 per cent moisture for a lot of ore shipped during the summer months a fair figure for the actual moisture content would be 5.5 per cent.

This addition of a more or less arbitrary correction is not entirely satisfactory and the reason for it is not always understood by the shippers, but in spite of this practice the latter method of arriving at the moisture content of an ore is far superior to that which depends on the grab-sample, and with its use there are fewer disputes and less ill-feeling between seller and buyer.

Moisture determinations are made in duplicate on samples weighing from 2 to 5 pounds. These are weighed out into porcelain or enameled-iron dishes and dried at 105° C., the loss of weight being called moisture.

The moisture-figure, either because of the method of taking the sample, or the amount of the compensating correction applied, still continues to be a frequent source of dissatisfaction on the part of sellers of ore. The practice of taking one or more grab-samples from each car of ore is the most unscientific part of the whole ore-purchasing business. This practice is unfortunately still in common use even when the ore is of such a nature that it must be passed through a mechanical sampling plant to obtain the sample used for determining the metallic contents. In this latter case, grab-sampling has nothing to recommend it, unless it be the opportunity for manipulation or error, and it should be abandoned. In case the ore is of such a nature that a satisfactory sample for the determination of metallic contents can be obtained without mechanical sampling, the same method may ordinarily be applied to obtain a moisture sample.

* Trans. A.I.M.E. **40**, p. 567 (1909).

Duplicate Sampling. — To check the accuracy of the sampling operations, we may resort to the process of duplicate sampling or to resampling. Duplicate sampling in the laboratory should consist in first cutting the entire lot into two portions and then sampling each one separately. As a general rule, the results should check within 1 per cent. If they do not, it indicates either poor mixing and cutting or a too rapid reduction of sample.

Some sampling mills are arranged to allow for taking duplicate samples, so that they have constant checks on the accuracy of their sampling operations. The following results of assays made on original and resampled lots are taken from D. K. Brunton's paper on "Modern Practice of Ore-Sampling" in the Transactions of the American Institute of Mining Engineers[*] and shows how closely such work is made to check.

TABLE VII.

RESULTS OF RESAMPLING.

Lot No.	Sample Ounces gold per ton	Resample Ounces gold per ton
3192	3.62	3.64
3198	5.04	5.015
3219	2.70	2.67
3235	3.18	3.16
3310	1.17	1.17
3324	6.52	6.51
3340	0.71	0.78
3388	1.70	1.84
3424	9.24	9.20
3471	30.64	30.52

FINISHING THE SAMPLE.

The 12- or 14-mesh ore cut by the last sampler is further reduced in size by the use of sample grinders, and its weight is reduced by coning and quartering or by riffle cutting. The principles of sampling laid down in the first part of the chapter should be followed throughout, even to the final portion which is weighed out for assay determination.

As the sample grows smaller more and more care has to be taken to prevent contamination or "salting." A few particles of rich ore, which if introduced into the original lot would have had no

[*] Trans. A.I.M.E. **40**, p. 567 (1909).

material effect on the average, might seriously alter the result if allowed to enter the final sample.

Before the final pulverizing is begun, the sample should be thoroughly dried by heating to 100° or 110° C. No greater degree of heat than this should be used, as there is danger of roasting the sulphides or otherwise altering the composition of the ore.

Mixing. — In addition to coning, the following methods of mixing are frequently used in some stage of the finishing treatment of ore.

1. ROLLING. For lots of 100 pounds or less the method of mixing, whereby the ore is rolled on canvas, rubber sheeting or paper, is often used. When the ore particles are fairly uniform in size and specific gravity, this method is satisfactory, but for ordinary ores in the coarse state, it should be avoided. For ore crushed so fine that it has little or no tendency to stratify, as for example the assay pulp ground to 100- or 120-mesh, the method is found satisfactory when the operation is properly performed. This method is almost universally used by assayers for mixing the final lot of pulverized ore, just before taking out the assay portion.

2. POURING. For small samples the method of pouring from one pan into another is sometimes employed, especially as a preliminary to riffle cutting. Like the one above, it is imperfect when performed on an ordinary mixture of coarse and fine ore.

3. SIFTING. For mixing small lots of ore or fluxes, the method of sifting is particularly good. The apertures in the sieve should be two or three times as large as the largest particles. The ore should be placed on the sieve a little at a time and allowed to fall undisturbed into a flat receiving pan, until all the ore has passed the sieve. Two or three siftings are equivalent to 100 rollings. Sifting has the further advantage over the other methods that all lumps are broken up and the ore composing them distributed. It should be noted that sifting with a screen, the apertures of which are smaller than the coarsest particles of ore, will tend to separate hard and tough minerals which resist grinding, from soft and brittle ones which tend to become very finely pulverized.

Grinding. — Two kinds of grinders are used for finishing work, the cone-grinders and the disc-pulverizers. They should be so constructed that they may be easily and thoroughly cleaned. Many excellent pulverizers are unsuited for sampling work on

Fig. 32. — Disc pulverizer closed

Fig. 33. — Disc pulverizer open for cleaning.

account of the labor and difficulty involved in cleaning them effectively.

Figure 32 shows a thoroughly reliable and efficient disc-pulverizer which takes ¼-inch ore and reduces it in one operation to 100-mesh or finer. It is as nearly dust-tight as possible, and the grinding plates are renewable. It is shown open for cleaning in Fig. 33.

The bucking-board is now but little used for grinding ores except in the case of very small samples weighing less than 100 grams where, because of ease of cleaning and small dust loss, it may still be used. It is also used to regrind the last oversize resulting from screening.

One of the best methods of cleaning the bucking-board or sample-grinder is to brush it out, then grind a quantity of some barren material, such as sand or crushed fire-brick, and follow this by a second brushing.

Screening. — It is customary in careful work to screen all final samples of assay pulps. Although a good pulverizer, properly adjusted, will grind practically everything fine enough to pass 100- or 120-mesh in one pass, the exact adjustment is difficult to get and to maintain on account of wear and expansion due to heating. Besides, there is always a small amount of ore remaining in the feed chute, which has not been ground and which in itself necessitates screening of the pulp. The screens should be at least 9 inches in diameter to give satisfactory capacity, and the screen wire should be of uniform grade. The screen itself consists of a suitable frame in which the screen wire is stretched, fitting into a pan which holds the sifted ore. They should both be free from crevices which might provide lodging places for ore, which would be given up later to enrich a subsequent sample.

The operation of screening consists of a combination of shaking in a horizontal plane and tapping of the screen against the table-top or work-bench to keep the meshes clean. In most cases it is neither necessary nor desirable to use washers or a brush to assist in screening. They both tend to force oversize particles through the screen. Screens should be carefully brushed out after sifting each sample, and after a high-grade ore has been screened some of the barren material put through to clean the grinder should be sifted and then thrown away.

The sifted ore should be thoroughly mixed before sampling,

as screening under these conditions favors a certain amount of segregation.

Size of Assay Pulp. — For assay purposes, all ore should be reduced to at least 100-mesh and rich spotty ores should be pulverized to 120- or 140-mesh or finer to ensure a fair sample being obtained for the final crucible or scorification assay. For a crucible assay using 1 assay-ton, an ore may be left coarser than for a scorification assay where only 0.1 assay-ton charge is used. If the assayer has difficulty in obtaining results checking within one-half of one per cent he may well look for the difficulty in the size of the assay pulp. Very often a regrinding to a finer size will overcome the difficulty.

When any portion of ore has been selected as a sample and is to be passed through a sieve, it is essential that the whole sample be made to pass. The harder portions which resist crushing the longest are almost invariably of a different composition from the remainder and if rejected render the whole sample worthless.

ORES CONTAINING MALLEABLE MINERALS.

In the crushing of ores containing native gold, silver and copper also chloride, bromide, iodide, or sulphide of silver, as well as other malleable minerals, more or less of these will be left on the sieve as flat scales, cylinders or spheres. When an ore which might be expected to contain such minerals, is being sampled great care should be observed, first, in watching for the metallics and seeing that they are saved, as the inexperienced operator is likely not to appreciate their value and to throw them away, and second, to so conduct the grinding that they may be removed at every opportunity. The coarser these particles are the more difficult it becomes to obtain an accurate sample, both from the standpoint of sampling theory and from the fact that a larger amount of highly intelligent and painstaking labor is necessary throughout each stage of the sampling and assaying process.

Two mistakes are common. The first is to throw away a small amount of residue resting on the screen without carefully examining it to ensure the absence of any valuable constituent. The second arises from the practice, occasionally noticed, of putting the metallics back on the bucking-board or into the grinding machine with a small amount of the pulverized ore and continuing the grinding until everything passes the sieve. This latter practice is fully as objectionable as the first, both on account of the impossibility of obtaining an even distribution of the metallic particles in the final sample of assay pulp weighed into the crucible and because of the loss resulting from the smearing of the metallics on the working surfaces of the grinding machines. A secondary disadvantage of this latter practice is the danger of salting the next sample from the metal remaining on the grinding surfaces, particularly if the sample is low-grade. Lodge* gives an example of this kind to illustrate the necessity of a thorough cleaning of machines and bucking-boards after rich ore has been ground. In this case sand carrying 0.04 ounce per ton in gold, after grinding in a " salted " machine, was found to assay 0.78 ounce per ton.

When an ore containing metallics is being sampled the original sample must be carefully weighed, the particles found on each sieve must be separately preserved and weighed, and the pulp resulting from each sampling and sifting must also be weighed. This not only gives the data from which to calculate the true or "metallic" assay of the sample submitted but also acts as a check on any carelessness in the whole sampling operation. If the pellets are gold or silver they are wrapped in lead foil, cupeled, weighed and parted. If of copper, as in the case of an ore containing native copper, the weight of the metallic contents is otherwise established, perhaps by cleaning in hydrochloric acid and direct weighing, or by making a fusion as in the Lake Superior fire-assay. Other cases may arise; for instance, in the sampling of molybdenum ores flat scales of molybdenite left on the screen will require special attention. Various metallurgical products, as for instance, slag, matte, furnace or cupel bottom, dross, litharge, precipitate, etc., very often contain metallics and must be handled in this way.

Calculation of Results. — Various writers give rules and formulas both for assaying and calculating results of this sort. No simple formula can cover all cases and no rule nor formula can take the place of the experience and common sense of the practical assayer, so that each example should be made an individual problem with its proper assumptions based on actual knowledge of conditions and occurrences during the sampling. The following example obtained in the assay of an ore from Cobalt, Ontario,

* Notes on Assaying, p. 32.

will illustrate some of the problems which have to be taken into consideration.

DATA. — Dry weight of sample received 129.6 grams. Size 16-mesh. This was crushed to pass a 120-mesh screen and yielded metallics on the screen 5.60 grams and pulp through the screen 121.6 grams. The pellets were scorified and cupeled, giving 3.823 grams of silver. The pulp assayed 1992 ounces per ton silver.

SOLUTION. — It is at once seen that the sum of the weight of the pellets and pulp do not equal the weight of the original sample, the difference or loss being 2.4 grams. The assayer must decide what to with this loss before proceeding to calculate the assay. However, it should first be pointed out that some loss is inevitable, the dust in any grinding room being sufficient evidence of this. The assayer does not know how much metal value this lost ore actually carries, but he knows that it does carry some and for that reason he cannot neglect it. It is obvious, however, that he should observe every precaution to keep the loss at a minimum to reduce this uncertain factor. In the present case it was believed that all of the loss was in dust, which was assumed to assay the same as the fine ore pulp. The amount of silver in $129.6 - 5.6 = 124.0$ grams of pulp, assaying 1992 ounces per ton, is then calculated and added to the silver from the pellets. This then gives the total silver contained in the original sample of 129.6 grams.

Silver in metallics	3.823 grams
Silver in 124.0 grams of pulp $\dfrac{124.0 \times 1.992}{29.166} =$	8.469 "
Total silver in sample	12.292 "

The average amount of silver in one assay-ton of the original sample would then be found from the following proportion:

$$129.6 : 12.29 = 29.166 : x$$

When this is solved x is found to be 2.765 grams. Whence the "metallic" assay of the ore is 2765 ounces silver per ton.

In order to show the method clearly, the above calculation has been worked out with more precision than is ordinarily necessary. Whether the sample of 129.6 grams of 16-mesh ore is a reliable one is open to question, but it is obviously the duty of the assayer to analyze the material submitted to him to the best of his ability, regardless of the above consideration.

ORE SAMPLING

There may be a shorter method of calculating the "metallic" assay in the simple case shown above, but in the more complicated cases, where metallics are found on several screens in the reduction of a sample of considerable size, it is best to follow the general method illustrated as being less likely to lead to confusion and error. One additional assumption has to be made when a lot of ore reduced by stages yields metallics on different screens: in any sampling the reject contains the same proportionate weight and value in pellets as the sample. It need hardly be mentioned that if the proper ratio between size of sample and maximum grain has been maintained, the above assumption will be borne out in practice.

The following example illustrates the more complicated case:

CALCULATION OF ASSAY WHEN ORE CONTAINS COARSE PARTICLES OF NATIVE GOLD.

Data

A sample of 23.75 kilograms or 23,750 grams was crushed to pass a 40-mesh sieve.	On sieve 25 grams. This yielded 6.2750 grams of gold. Through sieve 23,600 grams (Loss 125 grams). A sample from this of 5825 grams was crushed to pass a 120-mesh sieve.	On sieve 3 grams. This yielded 1.6720 grams of gold. Through sieve 5802 grams (Loss 20 grams). The fine ore assays 1.21 ounces gold per ton.

CALCULATIONS.   Weight Gold

Total pellets from 23,750 grams of ore on 40-mesh   6.275 grams

Total 40-mesh ore assuming loss to be same as the rest, *i.e.*, sample now 23,725 grams.

Total pellets from 23,725 grams on 120-mesh
$= \dfrac{23,725}{5825} \times 1.6720 =$ 6.810 "

Assuming all of ore to be crushed through 120-mesh and no loss, there would be $23,725 - \dfrac{23,725}{5825} \times 3 = 23,713$ grams fine ore (assaying 1.21 ounces)

Total gold in this $= \dfrac{23,713 \times .00121}{29.166} =$ 0.981 "

                          Total gold in original lot   14.066 "

$29.166 : x = 23,750 : 14.066$

$x = .01727 =$ gold from 1 assay-ton

Ore assays 17.27 ounces per ton.

If the metallics are mainly iron or other barren material the metallic assay may be lower rather than higher than the assay of the fine pulp.

CHAPTER IV.

BALANCES AND WEIGHTS.

The reliability of every assay or other quantitative determination is directly dependent upon the accuracy of the weighing, both of the ore charge and more especially of the resultant product, for example, the silver bead or the parted gold. Any error made in the weighing will, of course, invalidate all the rest of the work, regardless of the care which may have been given it. The operator should, therefore, familiarize himself with the construction, sensitiveness and operation of his balance before he attempts to do any accurate assaying.

A good assay balance, used carefully and intelligently is capable of weighing to 0.01 milligram or 0.00001 gram. For the most delicate assay balances an accuracy of 0.000002 gram is claimed. The necessity of weighing to this degree of accuracy may be understood when it is considered that if the usual charge of ore, 1 assayton, is represented by a sample of 29.166 grams or about an ounce, and the resultant gold is weighed to the nearest 0.01 milligram, the value of the ore is only determined to within 20 cents per ton. This is usually sufficiently close, but any less degree of accuracy would not be so considered.

At least three grades of balances are necessary for the fire-assay laboratory. These are known as flux, pulp, and button or assay balances. In large assay laboratories, there are also usually found bullion and chemical balances as well as separate assay balances for gold and for silver.

Flux Balance. — The flux balance, for the weighing of fluxes, reagents, etc., should be an even balance scale, provided with a removable scoop-shaped pan, capable of weighing 2 kilograms and sensitive to 0.1 gram. Figure 34 shows a most satisfactory flux balance made with agate bearings and side-beam graduated from 0.1 to 5.0 grams. With this balance no weight smaller than 5 grams is required.

Fig. 34. — Flux balance

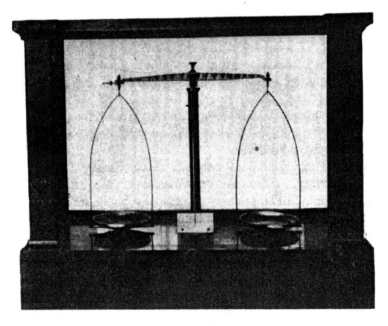

Fig. 35. — Pulp balance.

Pulp Balance. — The pulp balance for weighing the ore or pulp for assay and the buttons from lead assays, etc., should be an even balance scale. The pans should be made removable and should each have a capacity of at least 2 ounces of sand. The pulp balance should be enclosed in a glass case and should be sensitive to half a milligram. Such balances are sometimes listed in the manufacturers' catalogue as prescription balances. If more than one pulp balance is to be obtained, it is well to get one or more having a pan capacity of 4 or 5 ounces of sand. For one-half and 1 assay-ton charges the 2 ounce pan is to be preferred, as it is easier to transfer ore from it to the crucible than from a larger pan. Figure 35 shows a good type of pulp balance made with steel edges and agate bearings.

Assay Balance. — The button or assay balance is the most sensitive balance made. It should be capable of weighing to at least 0.01 milligram, should be rapid in action, making a complete oscillation in from 10 to 15 seconds, and should have stability of poise, that is to say that it should be so made that its adjustments will not change sensibly from day to day owing to slight changes of temperature and atmospheric conditions. The capacity of the assay balance need not be large, 0.5 gram maximum being sufficient, but the beam should be rigid at this load.

Such a delicate piece of apparatus must be handled with great care if good service is expected of it. It should be as far as possible from any laboratory or part of the plant where corrosive fumes are being evolved, and should be covered when not in use, to keep out the dust.

The balance beam should be as light as it can be made without sacrificing the necessary rigidity. For this reason the truss frame construction is usually adopted, giving the maximum strength with the minimum weight. The construction should be such that the two balance arms are of equal weight and length, and the three knife-edges should all lie in the same plane. The material of the beam should be non-magnetic for obvious reasons, and should have a small coefficient of expansion. The knife-edges and bearings should be of agate, ground, polished and mounted so as to have equal angles on each side. The knife-edges should be so sharp that a strong pocket-lens will show no flatness on the bearing edge and the agate bearings should appear perfectly smooth. All of the metal work of the balance should be protected from attack by chemical fumes, by some such means as gold-plating or lacquering. Lacquering seems to resist chemical fumes rather better than the ordinary gold-plating. The construction of the balance should be such that the rider may be placed on the zero graduation and used from the zero point to the end of the beam.

Fig. 36. — Gold assay balance.

The balance must be mounted in such a way that it will be free from vibration. Such a support may be obtained by placing the shelf, on which the balance rests, on one or more posts which are set in the ground and which come up through the floor without touching it.

There are a number of good assay balances, many of them provided with reading glasses and other special attachments. Figure 36 shows one of the inverted type, the principal advantage of which is that when the pointer is inverted, the ivory scale is on a level with the eye. This construction necessitates the offsetting of the zero graduation on the beam. By omitting the graduations, the beam may be made lighter and is not subject to strain and distortion due to graduating and numbering. The balance shown in the illustration has a very light trussed-beam which is not graduated. The beam is practically invisible in the cut but its reflection in the glass base-plate is quite clear. A white scale on the rider bar carries the graduations, and a pointer attached to the rider arm indicates on the scale the exact position of the rider on the beam.

Theory of the Balance. — The balance is essentially a light trussed beam, supported at its center by a knife-edge. At each end of the beam is hung a scale-pan. The two pans should be of equal weight.

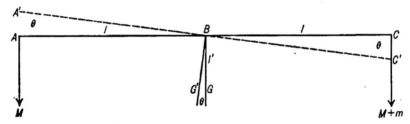

Fig. 37. — Line drawing of balance.

Let the three knife-edges A, B, and C, be in the same straight line. Let $AB = BC = l$. Let G be the center of gravity of the beam, whose weight is W. Let the distance of the center of gravity below the point of support, $BG = l'$.

With a load of M in each pan there will be equilibrium. Now if a small weight (m) be added to the right-hand pan, the balance will swing through a small angle θ and the beam will again come to equilibrium in a new position $A'BC'$. The condition for equilibrium will be obtained by taking the moments of the three forces, M, $M + m$ and W about the axis B. This gives the relation

$$Ml \cos \theta + l' \sin \theta \; W = (M + m) l \cos \theta$$

or $\dfrac{\sin \theta}{\cos \theta} = \tan \theta = \dfrac{lm}{Wl'}.$

The sensitiveness of a balance is usually denoted by the angle through which the beam will swing when a small weight, usually

1 milligram, (for assay balance 0.1 milligram) is added to one pan. For small angles the tangent and its angle may be taken as equal and therefore the expression deduced for tangent θ above may be taken as a measure of the sensitiveness of the balance.

The equation for tangent shows that the sensitiveness of a balance varies:

(a) Directly as the length of the balance arms.
(b) Inversely as the weight of the beam.
(c) Inversely as the distance of the center of gravity below the point of support. (Distance BG.)

The sensitiveness is seen to be independent of the load if the three knife-edges are in the same straight line, and most balance makers attempt to approach this condition in making assay balances. When B is above AC the sensitiveness is decreased with the load; when B is below AC it is increased up to a certain limit, beyond which the equilibrium becomes unstable.

The condition of uncreased sensitiveness with long beam and small weight (a) and (b) conflict, as the longer the beam is made the heavier it must be The length of the arm is also limited by the time of swing of the balance, which may be considered to be a compound pendulum. A period of about twelve or fifteen seconds is required for a complete oscillation. Formerly the long arm balances were common, but at present the makers are restricting the length of the beam to 5 inches.

By bringing the center of gravity nearer to the center of support the sensitivity is increased. As the center of gravity nears the center of support, the stability of poise decreases. If the two should coincide there would be no point of rest and the balance would be unstable or "cranky." The most difficult thing to obtain is a balance with great stability and extreme sensitivity. It is obtained by making the beam as light as possible and then keeping the center of gravity sufficiently below the center knife-edge to give the necessary stability. Most high-grade balances are provided with a screw-ball or sliding-weight so that the center of gravity may be adjusted. If the balance lacks stability, i. e., is cranky and over-sensitive, both of those conditions may be remedied by lowering this weight and thus lowering the center of gravity of the system.

In the above discussion the assumption has been that the arms of the balance were equal. Modern high-grade balances usually approach very closely to this condition. The process of "double weighing" serves to eliminate, however, any error in weighing that may be due to inequality of the arms. Call the observed weight of the body as weighed in pan A, W', and that in pan C, W''. Then W, the true weight, is found as follows:

$$W = \sqrt{W'W''}$$

when W' and W'' are nearly equal $W = \dfrac{W' + W''}{2}$.

General Directions for Weighing. — Brush off the pans and if necessary clean the front plate of the balance. See that the weighing rider is on the zero graduation or on the carrier, as the balance may require. Adjust, if necessary, to make the point of rest coincide with the center graduation on the ivory scale and try the adjustment every time you have any weighing to do, as it is never safe to assume that the balance will stay in equilibrium. Note the maximum load the balance will carry and do not exceed this.

Put the balance into action by gently lowering the beam onto the knife-edges. It may then start swinging slightly of its own accord. If it does not, set it swinging by gently fanning one pan with a motion of the hand, or by lifting the rider for an instant and then putting it back on the beam. The balance may be started swinging by blowing gently on one pan with a device such as a medicine dropper. If the balance is started swinging by fanning with the hand, it should be allowed to make one or two complete oscillations before a reading is taken, to prevent air currents from interfering with the normal swing. Have the amplitude of swing not more than 1 or 2 divisions each side of the center.

In reading the position of the pointer on the ivory scale, arrange always to have the reading eye in the same position relative to the ivory scale, that is, in a plane perpendicular to the scale and passing through the center graduation. A mark may be made on the glass door by which to line up the eye before each reading. The final reading must be made with the door closed.

Arrest the swinging of the balance when the pointer is at the center of the scale. This prevents any undue jarring of the beam, which is very likely to get the balance out of adjustment. Always turn the balance out of action before adding weights to the pan or taking them from it. When the balance is not in use, raise the beam from the knife-edges and leave the rider on the beam.

Do not allow the direct rays of the sun to strike the balance and never attempt to do close weighing unless the temperature of the room and balance can be maintained virtually constant.

Each silver bead should be placed on its side on a small anvil, hammered and then brushed before it is weighed.

To transfer the gold from the parting cup to the scale-pan, take the scale-pan with the forceps and place on the front part of the glass mounting base. Gradually invert the parting cup over it, tapping it gently. The gold should all slide into the pan. Any particles adhering to the cup may be detached by touching gently with the point of the forceps or by means of a small feather trimmed to a point.

Before weighing the gold, examine it carefully to see if it is clean and remove any foreign matter if present.

To remove gold from the scale-pan after weighing, pick up pan and all in the forceps and invert pan over the parting cup, brushing off lightly at the same time.

Weights should be placed only in the box or on the scale-pan and should be handled only with ivory-tipped forceps. Record the weight of the substance first, by noting the weights which are absent from the box, second, by checking off each weight as it is put back in the box. Record all weights in the notebook and not on scraps of paper.

For ordinarily accurate commercial work the weighing of the gold and silver is done by the "method of equal swings," using the rider for the final weighing. For extreme accuracy, as for instance in the calibration of weights, the weighing is done by "deflection," also called the "method of swings."

Weighing by "Equal Swings." — First of all, the balance is adjusted by the star wheel or preferably by the adjusting rider, if one is provided, until the needle swings exactly the same distance on each side of the center, reading always in the same order, say from left to right. For accurate gold weighing it will be necessary to estimate tenths of divisions on the ivory scale.

Put the substance to be weighed on the left-hand pan and add weights to the right-hand pan until their weight is within a fraction of a milligram of the weight of the substance. Apply the weights in a systematic manner, starting with one which is estimated to be too large. If too large, remove it and try the next smaller weight always working from larger to smaller weights until within 1 milligram of the true weight.

In trying any weight have the beam off the knife-edges, put the weight in the pan and gently turn the balance key until the pointer inclines slightly to one side or the other. This swing of only one or two divisions should indicate immediately whether the weight on the pan is too much or too little. Again turn the balance out of action before making any change of weight.

When within a fraction of a milligram of the correct weight, shift the right-hand, or weighing, rider about, until, when the balance is put into action the needle does not move very decidedly in one or the other direction. Then set the beam swinging 1 or 2 divisions each side of the center. If it does not swing evenly arrest the swing, change the position of the rider and try again. Repeat until the needle swings exactly as when adjusted. After one has become familiar with the balance only two or three trials of the rider will be necessary.

The weight of the substance is found from the sum of the weights on the pan plus the fractional part of a milligram indicated by the position of the rider on the beam.

Weighing by "Method of Swings." — First, determine the point of rest under zero load by noting the position of the pointer at the extreme swing on each side, taking 3, 5 or a greater odd number of consecutive readings. Call the center division zero and count divisions and estimate tenths to each side, calling those to the left of the center $-$, and to the right $+$.

Average the readings for each extreme, add the two and divide the sum by 2; the result is the point of rest. The method is illustrated in the following example.

```
          Left                    Right
         -3.9                      3.6
         -3.7                      3.4
         -3.5                   2 |7.0
       3 |-11.1                    3.5
         -3.7
         +3.5
       2 |-.2
         -.1 = point of rest.
```

Or the point of rest would be 0.1 division to the left of the center.

Call the point of rest under zero load r. Place the object to be weighed on the left-hand pan and weights on the right-hand pan until equilibrium is nearly established. With the rider determine the weight to the next smaller 0.1 milligram. Set the beam swinging as before and find the position of rest for the pointer. Call it r'. Shift the rider to the right, one whole division (= 0.1 mg.) so as to bring the point of rest on the opposite side of r, find the position of rest again, and call it r''. The fraction of a milligram to be added to the weights and rider reading when r' was found is then

$$\frac{r' - r}{r' - r''} \times 0.10 .$$

For instance let the weights and rider reading be 27.4 mg. and let $r' = -1.4$ and $r'' = +1.6$

then $\dfrac{r' - r}{r' - r''} = \dfrac{-1.4 + 0.1}{-1.4 - 1.6} = \dfrac{-1.3}{-3.0} = +0.43$

and the true weight would be $27.4 + (0.43 \times 0.1) = 27.44$ mg.

Another method of weighing by "deflection," requiring a knowledge of the sensitivity of the balance, is as follows: Suppose that a weight of 0.10 milligram will cause a deflection of the point of rest of 2.0 divisions on the ivory scale. Adjust the balance so that the point of rest with no load corresponds to the zero of the ivory scale. Place the substance to be weighed in the left-hand pan and again determine the point of rest. Suppose the deflection to be 1.2 divisions. Then the weight of the substance is 0.06 milligram. With a good balance this is a rapid and accurate method for small amounts of gold, but it is not very commonly used.

Weighing by "No Deflection." — A third method of weighing, called weighing by "no deflection," is sometimes employed for rough work. It consists in applying the necessary weights and then shifting the rider until the needle shows no deflection when the balance is lowered gently onto the knife-edges. This method disregards friction and inertia and is not as accurate as the two previously described methods.

Weighing by Substitution. — This method of weighing is the one usually adopted for the standardization or adjustment of weights, as it avoids any possibility of error due to inequality of arms. It consists simply in placing the substance to be weighed on one pan, counterbalancing it with weights placed on the other pan, and then removing the substance and adding standard weights until the balance is again in equilibrium. The weight of the substance is obtained from the substituted weights.

Check Weighing. — Students are advised to check all gold weighings in the following manner: Weigh and record weight of each lot of parted gold resulting from duplicate or triplicate assays, then place all on one scale-pan and obtain the total weight. Compare this with the sum of the weights obtained in the separate weighings. The figures should check within 0.01 or at most 0.02 milligram. If they do not, some of the weighings are at fault, some of the weights are in error, or the zero point has changed. By weighing the combined gold from 2 or 3 assays and reducing to milligrams per assay-ton, the accuracy of the assay is correspondingly increased. This practice is followed by all good assayers.

Accumulative Weighing. — A modification of the above method of check weighing is to weigh the gold accumulatively. For instance, suppose an assayer has fifty lots of gold to weigh, each one of them perhaps less than 1 milligram. He can save time by weighing one after the other, without bothering to remove the previous lot, until all fifty are on the scale-pan at one time. He records, of course, after the first weighing, the difference of weight caused by each increment of gold. Besides saving time, this method of weighing reduces to a negligible amount any constant error, such as change of adjustment, as instead of occurring in each one of the fifty weighings, the full amount of this error occurs only once in all, and but one-fiftieth of it applies to any one weighing.

ADJUSTING AND TESTING AN ASSAY BALANCE.

Leveling. — Level the balance by adjusting the footscrews and by observing the plumb-bob or level. Be sure that it rests firmly on the table or other support so that it will not be moved during the test. See that the beam, scale-pans and hangers are in their proper places and have not been forced out of normal position by previous careless usage.

Equilibrium. — Lower the beam carefully until the agate knife-edges rest on the agate supports. This motion and the reverse one must be gentle to prevent injury to the knife-edges and also to prevent a shock or jar, which would tend to change the adjustments. Adjust the balance so that the pointer swings equally on each side of the center. A star wheel, a small projecting piece of metal or " flag," revolving on a vertical axis at the middle of the beam, or preferably an extra rider, constitutes the attachment for this adjustment. If this adjustment cannot be made and the balance on starting to one side or the other continues to swing in that direction with increasing velocity, it is in unstable equilibrium, and the center of gravity must be lowered until the proper equilibrium is obtained.

Time of Oscillation. — Set the balance in motion and note the time of one complete oscillation, *i.e.*, swing from one extreme to the other and back again. For the modern 5-inch-beam assay balance this should be from twelve to fifteen seconds. If much faster than this the balance will probably not be very sensitive. If much slower than this the balance may lack stability and each weighing will take a correspondingly longer time.

Lowering the center of gravity of the beam results in decreasing the time of oscillation.

Stability. — By " stability " of a balance is meant its property of remaining in adjustment during use and in spite of moderate changes of room temperature. It is a common error of assayers to neglect testing for stability when selecting a fine balance, and yet stability is fully as important as a high degree of sensitiveness.

After each of the tests the beam should be lowered and the adjustment of the balance noted. If it no longer swings equally on each side of the center, due care having been taken to avoid disturbing any of the settings, it lacks stability. This may be due to excessive sensitiveness, which can be overcome by lowering the center of gravity of the system by means of the screw-ball, or it may be due to a defect in construction, arms of unequal length, etc., in which case it cannot be remedied.

Resistance. — If the knife-edges are dull or the supporting surfaces rough the frictional resistance to swinging will be considerable and the diminution in the amplitude of swing will be rapid. Note the position of the pointer on the scale at the extremes of several successive swings. The difference between successive readings on the same side will show the diminution in amplitude due to friction and to resistance of the air. In a good assay balance this should not exceed 0.1 of a division when the amplitude of swing is 1 division. The horizontal section of the beam and the area of the pans and other projecting parts should be as small as possible, to reduce the air resistance.

Let the balance swing until it comes to rest and read the position of the pointer, lift the beam from the knife-edges and repeat several times. The positions should not differ by more than 0.05 of a division. A greater difference than this indicates flatness of the knife-edges or roughness of the supporting surfaces. If the beam is exceedingly slow in coming to rest this test is unnecessary.

Sensitivity. — The sensitiveness of a balance is defined by physicists as the angle through which the beam moves when 1 milligram excess weight is added to one pan. If the scale graduations are laid out on the arc of a circle whose radius is the distance from the center knife-edge to the scale, the number of scale divisions passed over are proportional to the angle of deflection and in any given balance, may be taken as a measure of the sensitiveness. Unfortunately, however, there is as yet no standard distance between scale graduations and no uniformity of length of pointer, so that the number of scale divisions passed over cannot be used directly as a means of comparing the sensitiveness of balances of different makes.

From a practical point of view, the sensitiveness is the smallest difference in weight which the balance will indicate. Thus, when we say that a balance is sensitive to 0.01 milligram we mean that 0.01 milligram added to one pan will cause a noticeable difference in the swing or in the position of the point of rest.

Comparative Sensitivity. — With a distance between scale graduations of 0.05 inches it is easily possible to estimate the position of the pointer at each extreme of a swing to the nearest 0.2 division or to within 0.01 inch. Pointers on a number of the better American assay balances range from 5.5 to 6.75 inches in length and average about 6 inches. With the usual length of pointer, the position of the point of rest should be shifted at least 0.01 inch when an unbalanced weight of 0.01 milligram is placed in one pan, if the balance is to be termed sensitive to 0.01 milligram. With this as a basis anyone may work out his own method of comparing the sensitiveness of different balances, by taking into account the distance between graduations and the length of the pointer.

To Test Equality of Arms. — Adjust balance to swing evenly with no load and then place equal weights on each pan, equivalent to the full load of the balance. If the pointer does not now swing evenly the arms are of unequal length.

To Determine if Knife-Edges are all in Same Horizontal Plane. — Adjust balance and determine sensitivity with no load. Then place full load on each pan and again determine sensitivity. When the three knife-edges are in the same plane there should be no change of sensitivity with any weight up to the full load of the balance. When the full load of the balance is not known the sensitivity should be determined for gradually increasing loads and a curve of sensitivity drawn. If the three knife-edges are in the same plane this curve should be a straight line up to the point where the beam begins to be deflected by an overload.

WEIGHTS.

For the three balances above described we require four sets of weights, as follows:

For the flux balance we should have a block containing weights from 1 kilogram to 1 gram. These weights need not be extremely accurate.

For the pulp balance two sets are necessary, gram and assay-ton weights: gram weights, from 20 grams to 10 milligrams for weighing flour and ore for lead, copper and tin assays, as well as the buttons from the same: assay-ton weights, 2 A. T. to $\frac{1}{20}$ A. T. for weighing ore, matte, speiss and lead bullion for the gold and silver assay.

For the button balance is required a set of milligram weights of the utmost accuracy, from 1 milligram up to 500 or 1000 milligrams. These are preferably made of platinum, as an absolutely non-corrosive weight is imperative. Riders are used for determining fractions of a milligram. Riders are made of fine aluminum wire and are usually made to weigh 0.50 or 1.00 milligram. The balance beam is usually divided into 100 spaces on each side of the center and when a 1-milligram rider is used each space represents 0.01 milligram.

For many balances, a rider with a diamond-shaped loop, known as the Thompson rider, is to be preferred. Its principal advantage is due to its property of always hanging in a vertical position when on the rider arm. Even if it falls over to one side when on the beam it will slip back to the vertical position when lifted by the rider arm. The diamond-shaped loop prevents it from swinging or twisting around on the rider carrier and permits the rider to be placed squarely on the beam.

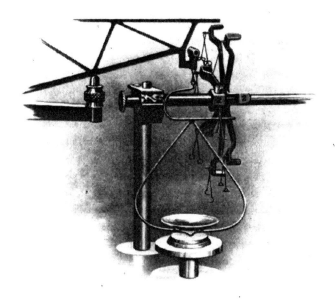

Fig. 38. — Thompson multiple rider attachment.

Multiple Rider Attachment. — Some of the balance makers are now supplying, on demand, what is called a multiple rider attachment, designed to do away with the use of the smaller weights. It consists of a carrier supplied with a number of riders of different weights, for instance, 1, 2, 3, 5, 10, 20, 30 milligrams, so arranged that any or all may be placed on a support provided for the purpose. This is equivalent to placing flat weights of the same value in the pan.

In Fig. 38 is shown a multiple rider attachment, the horizontal arm of which extends through the glass side of the balance and terminates in a milled head. The different riders are distinguished from each other by differently formed ends. An advantage claimed for this device is a saving in the wear and tear of weights, as the small flat weights, frequently handled by forceps, become broken and inaccurate, whereas the riders, on which there is practically no wear, will maintain their original weight almost indefinitely. A second advantage claimed is a saving in time, as with this attachment the riders can be manipulated much more quickly than the flat weights, which must be handled with forceps. It is not necessary to open the door of the balance in weighing any bead under 40 or 50 milligrams, and this alone is a saving of some time and also allows all air currents to subside before the final reading is made.

Assay-Ton Weights. — The assay-ton system of weights was devised to facilitate the calculation of the results of gold and silver assays. In the United States and Canada the results of such assays are reported in troy ounces of gold and silver per 2000 pound avoirdupois ton of ore. With the ordinary system of weights a tedious calculation would have to be made for each assay with the possibility of mathematical errors.

The basis of the assay-ton system is the number of troy ounces (29,166.+) in one ton of 2000 pounds avoirdupois. The assay-ton is made to weigh 29.166 grams. Then

1 ton avoirdupois : 1 ounce troy : : 1 assay-ton : 1 milligram.

Therefore, with one assay-ton of ore, the weight of the silver or gold in milligrams gives immediately the assay in ounces per ton.

In England and Australia the long ton of 2240 pounds is used, and the assay-ton weighs 32.666 grams.

In Mexico ores are bought and sold in metric tons of 1000 kilograms and assays are reported in grams of gold and grams or kilograms of silver per metric ton. In this case it is convenient to weigh out ore in grams.

Calibration of Weights. — The weights supplied by the makers cannot always be relied upon and even originally perfect ones are subject to changes of weight due to wear or accumulation of dirt. Therefore it behooves the assayer to check his weights occasionally and to determine the correction to be applied to the marked value. This requires the use of a standardized weight which should be carefully preserved and used for this purpose only.

The method of swings should be used and the weighing done by

BALANCES AND WEIGHTS

deflection after the sensitivity of the balance has been determined. First determine the position of rest and the sensitivity with no load, with 100, 250 and 500 milligram loads respectively. The sensitivity should not vary much throughout this range. The method to be followed can be understood from the following example.

CALIBRATION OF A SET OF ASSAY WEIGHTS.

Designate each weight by its marked value in the parenthesis and when there are several of the same value note some peculiarity by which each may be designated. The weights in the set, marked in milligrams are:

$(500) = a, (200) = b, (100) = c, (100') = d, (50) = e, (20) = f,$
$(10) = g, (10') = h, (10'') = (5) + (2) + (2') + (1) = i.$

The weight (100) is compared with the standard 100-milligram weight and the weights are then compared among themselves by the method of swings. The letters represent the true values.

In calibrating the weights from 100 milligrams to 10 milligrams, observations should be made on the following combinations:

Left-hand Pan	Right-hand Pan
(100)	100 mg. standard
(100)	(50) + (20) + (10) + (10') + (5) + (2) + (2') + (1)
(50)	(20) + (10) + (10') + (5) + (2) + (2') + (1)
(20)	(10) + (10')

The recorded observations are as follows:

$$100 \text{ mg.} = c \qquad -0.020 \text{ mg.}$$
$$c = e + f + g + h + i + 0.190$$
$$e = f + g + h + i + 0.020$$
$$f = g + h + 0.040$$
$$g = h + 0.015$$
$$h = i + 0.040$$

Solving these equations,

$$i = i$$
$$h = i + 0.040$$
$$g = i + 0.055$$
$$f = 2i + 0.135$$
$$e = 5i + 0.250$$
$$c = 10i + 0.670$$
$$c = 100.020 \text{ mg.}$$

From the last two values of

$$10i = 99.350 \text{ mg.}$$
$$i = 9.935 \text{ mg.}$$

Substituting this value for i in the above equations, we find the following values for the other weights of the set:

Designation	Actual Weight	Correction* to Marked Value
c	100.020	+ .020 mg.
e	49.925	− .075 "
f	20.005	+ .005 "
g	9.990	− .010 "
h	9.975	− .025 "
i	9.935	− .065 "

The smaller weights in i, may be calibrated in a similar manner. The large weights (100), (200) and (500) may be standardized by a simple modification of the above.

The process is made much simpler by having a complete set of standard weights which are very carefully handled and kept solely for standardizing purposes, and these the larger assay offices usually have.

Testing Riders. — Every new rider should be tested before use, as riders often vary 0.01 or 0.02 milligrams from their supposed value. If a rider is too heavy, a little bit at a time may be cut off with a pair of scissors until it comes down to the standard.

* A + correction means that the weight is heavier than the normal value.

CHAPTER V.

CUPELLATION.

In every assay of an ore for gold and silver, we endeavor to use such fluxes and to have such conditions as will give us as a resultant two products:

1st. An alloy of lead, with practically all of the gold and silver of the ore and as small amounts of other elements as possible.

2nd. A readily fusible slag containing the balance of the ore and fluxes.

The lead button is separated from the slag and then treated by a process called cupellation to separate the gold and silver from the lead. This consists of an oxidizing fusion in a porous vessel called a cupel. If the proper temperature is maintained the lead oxidizes rapidly to PbO which is partly (98.5 [*] per cent) absorbed by the cupel and partly (1.5 per cent) volatilized. When this process has been carried to completion the gold and silver is left in the cupel in the form of a bead.

The cupel is a shallow, porous dish made of bone-ash, Portland cement, magnesia or other refractory and non-corrosive material. The early assayers used cupels of wood ashes from which the soluble constituents had been leached. Agricola, writing about the year 1550, mentions the use of ashes from burned bones. Ashes from deers' horns he pronounces best of all; but the use of these was becoming obsolete in his time, and he states that assayers of his day generally made the cupels from the ashes of beech wood.

To-day it is thought that the bones of sheep are the best for cupels. The bones should be cleaned before burning and as little silica as possible introduced with them. It is important not to burn the bones at too high a temperature as this makes the ash harder and less absorbent. It is also advisable to boil the bones in water before burning them as this dissolves a great part of the organic matter, which if burned with the bones yields sulphates and carbonates of the alkalies.

[*] Liddell, Eng. and Min. Jour. **89**, p. 1264. (June, 1910.)

Properly burned sheep bones will yield an ash containing about 90 per cent calcium phosphate, 5.65 per cent calcium oxide, 1.0 per cent magnesium oxide, and 3.1 per cent calcium fluoride. Ordinary commercial bone-ash also contains more or less silica and unoxidized carbon. If more than a fraction of a per cent of silica is found in bone-ash, it is evidence that sufficient care has not been taken in cleaning the bones, and cupels made from such bone-ash are more likely than others to crack during cupellation, often resulting in the loss of small beads. If the bone-ash shows black specks it is an indication of insufficient oxidation and the assayer should allow the cupels to stand for some time in the hot muffle, with the door open, before using. Carbon is an undesirable constituent of cupels as it reacts with the lead oxide formed giving off CO and CO_2 which may cause a loss of the molten alloy due to spitting.

Bone-ash for cupels should be finely ground to pass at least a 40-mesh screen and the pulverized material should consist of such a natural mixture of sizes as will give a solid cupel with enough fine material to fill interstices between coarser particles. Opinions differ as to the best size of crushing for bone-ash and this will depend no doubt upon the character of the material. The bone-ash represented by the following screen analysis has, however, yielded particularly good cupels.

TABLE VIII.

SIZE OF BONE-ASH.

Size mesh	Size mm.	Per cent weight
On 40	0.380	9
Through 40 " 60	0.244	14
" 60 " 100	0.145	17
" 100 " 150	0.098	10
" 150		50

With cupels made from this bone-ash it was possible to reduce losses to 1.60 per cent, using 100 mg. of silver and 25 grams of lead, while with some other lots of bone-ash containing smaller proportions of −150-mesh material it was found impossible to keep the losses below 2.0 per cent.

Making Cupels. — Cupels are made by moistening the bone-ash with from 8 to 20 per cent of water and compressing in a mold. The bone-ash and water should be thoroughly mixed by kneading, and the mixture should finally be sifted through a 10- or 12-mesh sieve to break up the lumps. Some authorities recommend adding a little potassium carbonate, molasses or flour to the mixture, but with good bone-ash nothing but pure water need be added. The mixture should be sufficiently moist to cohere when strongly squeezed in the hands, but not so wet as to adhere to the fingers or to the cupel mold. Twelve per cent of water by weight is about right; but the amount used will depend

Fig. 39. — Cupel machine.

somewhat on the bone-ash and on the pressure used in forming the cupels. The greater the pressure the smaller the amount of water which is required. It is better to err on the side of making the mixture a little too dry than too wet.

The cupels may be molded either by hand or by machine. The hand outfit consists of a ring and a die. The ring is placed on the anvil and filled with the moist bone-ash, the die is inserted and pressed down firmly. It is then struck one or more blows with a heavy hammer or mallet, and turned after each blow; finally the cupel is ejected. The cupels are placed on a board and dried slowly in a warm place. The amount of compression is a matter of experience and no exact rule for it can be given;

but it may be approximated by making the cupels so hard that when removed from the mold they are scratched only with difficulty by the finger nail. One man can make about 100 cupels an hour, using the hand mold and die.

Several types of cupel machines are on the market and one of the best is shown in Fig. 39. This machine, has a compound lever arrangement which gives a pressure on the cupel equal to twenty times that applied to the hand lever. By adjusting, different degrees of compression may be obtained. These machines have interchangeable dies and rings so that different sizes of cupels may be made. The rated capacity of this machine is two hundred cupels an hour. Another machine made by the same company has an automatic charging arrangement. This machine is claimed to have a capacity of six hundred cupels an hour. Cupels should be uniform in hardness, and it would seem that with a properly designed machine a more uniform pressure could be obtained than by the use of hammer and die. Some assayers, however, still prefer hand-made cupels.

Cupels should be air-dried for several days, at least, before use. Most assayers make them up several months in advance so as to insure complete drying. They should not be kept where fumes from parting can be absorbed by them as, if this occurs, the CaO present will be converted into $Ca(NO_3)_2$. This compound is decomposed at the temperature of cupellation and may cause spitting of the lead button.

Cupels should not crack when heated in the muffle and should be so strong that they will not break when handled with the tongs. Good cupels give a slight metallic ring when struck together after air-drying. It is best to heat cupels slowly in the muffle as this lessens the chance of their cracking.

A good cupel should be perfectly smooth on the inside, and of the right porosity. If it is too dense, the time of cupellation is prolonged and the temperature of cupellation has to be higher, thus increasing the loss of silver. If the cupel is too porous it is said that there is danger of a greater loss, due to the ease with which small particles of alloy can pass into the cupel. The bowl of the cupel should be made to hold a weight of lead equal to the weight of the cupel.

The shape of the cupel seems to influence the loss of precious metals. A flat, shallow one exposes a greater surface to oxidation and allows of faster cupellation; it also gives a greater surface of contact between alloy and cupel, and as far as losses are due to direct absorption of alloy, it will of course increase these. The writer, using the same bone-ash and cupel machine, and changing only the shape of the cupel, has found shallow cupels to give a much higher loss of silver. In doing this work it was found harder to obtain crystals of litharge with the shallow cupel without freezing, and it was very evident that a higher cupellation temperature was required for the shallow cupel. The reason for this is that in the case of the shallow cupel the molten alloy is more directly exposed to the current of air passing through the muffle, and consequently a higher muffle temperature has to be maintained to prevent freezing. T. K. Rose[*] also prefers deep cupels on account of smaller losses. French found shallow cupels less satisfactory on account of sprouting.

A satisfactory size of cupel for general assay work is $1\frac{3}{4}$ inches in diameter and 1 inch high with a maximum depth of bowl of $\frac{11}{32}$ inch. A bone-ash cupel of these dimensions weighs slightly more than 40 grams and will hold the litharge from a 30-gram button with but little leakage. If necessary a 40-gram button may be cupeled in it, but if it is so used the bottom of the muffle should be well covered with bone-ash. A bone-ash cupel will absorb about its own weight of litharge.

Cupellation. — The muffle is heated to a light red, and the cupels, weighing about one-third more than the buttons which are to go into them, are carefully introduced and allowed to remain for at least ten minutes, in order to expel all moisture and organic matter. During this preliminary heating the door to the muffle is ordinarily kept closed, but if the cupels contain organic matter it is left open at first and then closed for five minutes or so before the buttons are introduced.

When all is ready the buttons are placed carefully in the cupels and the muffle door again closed. If the cupels are thoroughly heated, the lead will melt at once and become covered with a dark scum. If the temperature of the muffle is correct this will disappear in the course of a minute or two when the molten lead will become bright. The assays are then said to have opened up or "uncovered." This signifies that the lead has begun to oxidize rapidly, raising the temperature

[*] Eng. and Min. Jour. **80**, p. 934.

of the molten alloy considerably above that of its surroundings, whence it appears bright. It assumes a convex surface, and molten patches of litharge passing down over this surface give it a lustrous appearance. It is then said to "drive."

When the assays have uncovered, the door of the muffle is opened to admit a plentiful supply of air to promote oxidation of the lead, while at the same time the temperature of the muffle should be reduced. According to Fulton*, if the buttons are practically pure lead the temperature of uncovering is about 850° C. However, if antimony, cobalt, nickel etc., are present, the temperature of uncovering and also that required for cupellation will be higher.

The greater part of the lead oxide formed remains liquid and flows down over the convex surface of the molten alloy. If the temperature of the cupel is high enough this molten litharge is absorbed. A small part of the lead oxide is vaporized and appears as fume rising from the cupel.

After cupeling has proceeded for a few minutes, a ring, caused by the absorbed litharge, may be seen around the cupel just above the surface of the metal. If the temperature is right for cupeling this will be very dull red, almost black. If it is bright red, the temperature is too high. The color of the alloy itself will be much brighter than that of the absorbed litharge, as it is in fact much hotter than the cupel or surrounding air, on account of the heat generated by the rapid oxidation of the lead. Next to the formation of abundant litharge crystals, the appearance of the absorbed litharge is the best indication of proper cupellation temperature.

If the temperature is exactly right feather-like crystals of litharge form on the sides of the cupel above the lead. This is due to sublimation of some of the volatilized lead oxide. In cupeling for silver the temperature should be such that these crystals are obtained on at least the front-half of the cupel, and as the button grows smaller they should follow it down the side of the cupel, leaving, however, a slight clear space around it. If the temperature becomes too low for the cupel to absorb the litharge, the crystals begin to form all around and close to the lead in the cupel, and soon a pool of molten litharge is seen forming all around the annular space between the lead and the cupel.

* Western Chemist and Metallurgist, 4, p. 31. (Feb. 1908.)

If the temperature of the cupel is not quickly raised, this pool increases in size and soon entirely covers the lead and then solidifies. When this occurs the button is said to have "frozen," although the lead itself may be liquid underneath. Frozen assays should be rejected as the results obtained from them, by again bringing to a driving temperature, are usually low. If the freezing is noticed at the start, it may be arrested by quickly raising the temperature of the cupel in some way, i. e., by taking away the coolers, closing the door to the muffle, opening the draft, putting a hot piece of coke in front of the cupel, etc.

Beginners have difficulty in noting the first symptoms of freezing, but all should be able to see the pool of litharge starting. This gives the appearance and effect of oil; if the cupel is moved the button slides around as if it were greased.

Toward the end of the cupellation process the temperature must be raised again, because the alloy becomes more difficultly fusible as the proportion of silver in it increases, and in order to drive off the last of the lead a temperature of about 900° C. should be reached. The temperature should not be raised so high as to melt the crystals of litharge, for if this is done too great a loss of silver results.

As the alloy becomes richer in silver it becomes more and more rounded in shape and shining drops of litharge appear and move about on its surface. As the last of the lead goes off, these drops disappear, the fused litharge covering becomes very thin and, being of variable thickness, gives an effect of interference of light, so that the bead appears to revolve and presents a succession of rainbow colors. This phenomenon is termed the "play of colors." The colors disappear shortly, the bead becomes dull and after a few seconds appears bright and silvery. This last change is called the "brightening."

After brightening, the cupels should be left in the furnace for a few minutes to ensure removal of the last of the lead, and then moved gradually to the front of the muffle before they are taken out, so that cooling may be slow.

As the bead solidifies it will "flash" or "blick," i. e., suddenly emit a flash of light due to the release of the latent heat of fusion, which raises the temperature very much for a short time.

Cupels containing large silver beads should be drawn to the front of the muffle until they chill. Just as the bead is about to solidify a very hot cupel is placed over them and allowed to stand for several minutes, after which they are slowly withdrawn from the muffle. The hot cupel melts the outside crust of solid silver and causes solidification to go on from below. If this precaution is not taken, the beads may "sprout" or "spit." This action is caused by the sudden escape of oxygen which is dissolved in the molten silver and expelled when the bead solidifies. If the bead is allowed to solidify rapidly, a crust of solid silver forms on the outside, and as the central part solidifies this crust is violently ruptured by the expelled oxygen, giving a cauliflower-like growth on the bead and causing particles of silver to be thrown off. As a consequence the results obtained from sprouted beads are unreliable. Beads containing one-third or more of gold will not sprout even if rapidly withdrawn from the muffle. Sprouting is said to be an evidence of the purity of the silver.

The silver bead should appear smooth and brilliant on the upper surface, and should be silver-white in color and spherical or hemispherical in shape, according to its size. It should adhere slightly to the cupel and appear frosted on the under surface. If the bead is smooth on the bottom and does not adhere to the cupel, it is an indication of too low a finishing temperature. Such a bead will always contain lead. If it has rootlets which extend into cracks of the cupel the results are also to be taken as unreliable, as some of the silver may be lost in the cupel.

Lead buttons very rich in gold and silver have a peculiar mottled appearance after cupeling begins. Oily drops of litharge appear and move about on the surface of the alloy and finally run down the side of the convex surface and are absorbed by the cupel. This appearance is characteristic and once seen is easily recognized again. It may be seen toward the end of cupellation with any alloy containing much precious metal and is an indication of the approach of the end and a reminder that the temperature should be raised to ensure driving off the last of the lead.

The minimum temperature at which cupellation will proceed has been a more or less disputed point, owing largely to a difference in conception of the process and involved conditions. At least three methods of measuring the temperature have been proposed. One experimenter held his pyrometer junction one-quarter inch above the alloy in the cupel, another placed the junction inside the cupel, while a third measured the temperature of the alloy itself. According to Fulton* the alloy itself must be between 800 and 850° C. Litharge melts at 884° (Mostowitch), 906° (Bradford), but passes through a pasty stage before becoming liquid. It would seem that the cupel itself must be maintained above the melting point of litharge in order to allow of absorption. At any event the cupel is much hotter than the space around it partly because of the heat generated by the oxidation of the lead and partly because the cupel rests on the floor of the muffle and its interior portion becomes heated by conduction through the muffle floor on which it stands. Bradford† found 906° C. to be the minimum cupel temperature which would permit of absorption of litharge. Lodge‡ found that for silver cupellation with a moderate draft, the muffle temperature (taken one-quarter inch above the cupels) should be between 650° and 700° C.

FIRST EXERCISE. PRACTICE IN CUPELLATION.

Procedure. — Take from 0.10 to 0.20 grams of silver, but do not waste time in weighing. Wrap in 25 to 30 grams of sheet lead. Prepare two or three of these portions and cupel one at a time in order to become familiar with the operation, and with the correct temperature. To study the end phenomena " play of colors," " brightening," " blick " etc., the same or a larger amount of silver may be used with a smaller amount of lead, say 10 grams.

Have the muffle at a bright red; be sure that the cupels are dry and then heat gradually until they are red. Allow at least ten minutes for this. Be sure that the cupels weigh more than the lead, and that the bowl is sufficiently large to contain the melted alloy. Have a row of extra cupels in front of those which are to be used and keep them there throughout the process. Keep the door to the muffle closed and when the cupel is red throughout and heated to about 850° C. place the packet of lead and silver carefully in the cupel and close the door to the muffle so that the lead will fuse as quickly as possible. As soon as the assay begins to " drive," note the time, open the door of the muffle and lower the temperature of the cupel by checking the fire and by placing cold scorifiers, etc., around it. Continue to reduce the temperature until feather crystals of litharge are

---

* Western Chemist and Metallurgist, **4**, p. 31 (1908).
† Jour. Ind. and Eng. Chem. **1**, p. 181.
‡ Notes on Assaying, p. 62.

seen forming at least on the front half of the cupel. Then continue the cupellation at this temperature. Finally finish the assay at a somewhat higher heat, increasing the temperature by starting up the fire, removing the coolers or by shutting off some of the cold air supply by partly closing the door to the muffle. If the cupels are running very cold it will be necessary to start raising the temperature some five minutes before the end. The fire should be under good control at all times. As soon as the cupellation is finished remove the assay carefully from the muffle to avoid sprouting. All assayers agree that the best results are obtained by having a hot start, a cold drive, and a higher heat again at the finish.

Notes: 1. When a number of cupellations are carried on at one time, the buttons should be charged in the order of their size, i.e., largest first, so that all may start driving together.

A skilful assayer, with a large muffle, can run as many as fifty cupellations at one time and obtain feather crystals on all.

2. When a number of cupellations are carried on at one time, the cupels are not moved about after the lead is put in, but the temperature is regulated by means of the draft and firing and by the use of coolers, (cold scorifiers, cupels, crucible covers, etc.) which are put in toward the back of the furnace and replaced as soon as they become heated.

3. Bear in mind that although the temperature of the muffle may be as low as 650° or 700° C., the cupel itself should be slightly above the freezing point of litharge, to allow of its being absorbed. It has been found best, therefore, to protect the body of the cupel itself from the draft through the muffle, by placing an extra row of cupels or a low piece of fire-brick in front of the first row of cupels.

4. Buttons containing copper may be cupeled at a lower temperature than those consisting of pure lead and silver, owing to the fact that cupric oxide lowers the freezing point of litharge.

5. After the cupellation is finished, the cupel should be left in the muffle one or two minutes, depending on the size of the bead, to remove the last traces of lead. After this it should be withdrawn; otherwise a loss of silver ensues.

6. When the finishing temperature is too low, the beads will solidify without brightening. They retain lead and have a dull appearance and sometimes show flakes of litharge on the surface. Under certain conditions they flatten out, leaving a gray, mossy bead.

7. When the button contains only gold, a higher finishing temperature is required than when working for silver.

8. When gold is present in considerable amounts the bead will not sprout even if taken directly out of the muffle.

9. Besides gold and silver, the bead may contain platinum, palladium, rhodium, iridium, ruthenium, osmium, and iridosmium.

10. If the upper surface of the bead appears to be frosted this indicates the presence of tellurium or some member of the platinum group.

11. Buttons which contain a large amount of platinum flatten out and will not blick. They have a steel-gray color and a dull surface.

SECOND EXERCISE. CUPELLATION ASSAY OF LEAD BULLION.

Procedure. — Weigh out carefully three portions of bullion of ½ A. T. each. Wrap each in 10 to 15 grams of silver-free lead foil so that the whole is very compact, having each piece of lead foil of the same size and weight.

Have a good fire so that the lead will melt, and start to drive without delay. Use cupels which weigh 35 grams or more and have them all in a row with an extra row in front. Drop the assays in as quickly as possible and close the door. As soon as the lead starts to drive, close the drafts and cool as soon as possible so that feather crystals of litharge form on at least the front half of the cupel. Finally open the draft and otherwise increase the temperature for the last minute or two of cupellation to drive off the last traces of lead. Have some hot cupels in the muffle and, as soon as the beads brighten, pull them forward in the muffle to chill and then put a hot cupel over them and withdraw both slowly from the muffle. All danger of sprouting is over when the inside of the cupel reaches a dull red or when the bead has become solid throughout. Remove from the furnace to the cupel tray and allow to cool. When the bead is cold, detach it from the cupel with the pliers and brush with a stiff brush to remove bone-ash, or place it on its side on a clean anvil and slightly flatten with a hammer. When the bead is free from bone-ash, weigh it, recording in the notebook the weight of gold and silver. Then part and weigh the gold; finally report the amount of gold and silver in ounces per ton.

Notes: 1. Have a sheet of clean white paper at hand and when transferring the bullion from the scale-pan to the lead foil do it over this so that in case any is spilled it will be seen and recovered. Do all of the wrapping and compressing over this paper for the same reason.

2. If the assay is not compact, it may overflow the cupel while melting, or else leave small particles on the sides of the cupel, which will not come down into the main button.

Loss of Silver in Cupeling. — There is always some loss in cupellation, the amount depending on many factors such as the nature and shape of the cupel, the temperature of cupellation, the proportion of lead to silver, the amount and character of impurities, the draft through the muffle, etc. Losses may be due to spurting, absorption of bullion by the cupel, oxidation and absorption of silver with litharge, and volatilization of silver either alone or accompanied by other metals.

The cupel surface may be regarded as a membrane permeable to molten litharge and impermeable to lead. The more nearly the material of the cupel surface approaches this condition the lower the losses may be made. Some cupels, particularly some of magnesite, present spots of material which are permeable to lead and consequently give a high loss of silver.

The most important factor relative to cupel loss, however, is the temperature. The higher the temperature, the higher the loss, is an invariable rule. The increased loss due to higher temperature seems to be due mostly to an increased oxidation of the silver and a consequent greater absorption loss. The volatilization loss is also increased by an increase of temperature. A loss of 1 per cent silver is allowable and the loss may usually be kept close to this figure by taking pains to cupel with abundant crystals of litharge. If this matter is overlooked a loss of 4 or 5 per cent may readily be obtained and this, of course, is entirely inadmissable.

The following table, taken from Lodge's "Assaying," illustrates this point and shows the importance of cupeling at the correct temperature. The temperature was taken with a Le Chatelier pyrometer, the junction being held about one-quarter inch above the button.

TABLE IX.
EFFECT OF TEMPERATURE ON LOSS OF SILVER IN CUPELLATION.

Silver milligrams	Lead grams	Temperature degrees centigrade	Silver loss per cent*	Remarks
200	10	700	1.02	Crystals of PbO all around button.
200	10	775	1.30	Crystals of PbO on cooler side of cupel.
200	10	850	1.73	No crystals.
200	10	925	3.65	" "
200	10	1000	4.88	" "

* Average figures.

CUPELLATION

The amount of lead and silver present in any button has a marked effect on the percentage loss of silver in cupellation. Rose,* in speaking of cupellation says, " The losses of silver at first are small, so long as large quantites of base metals protect it from oxidation. .... Later, when the percentage of silver is high it is freely oxidized .... and the oxidation is at its maximum when the silver is practically pure."

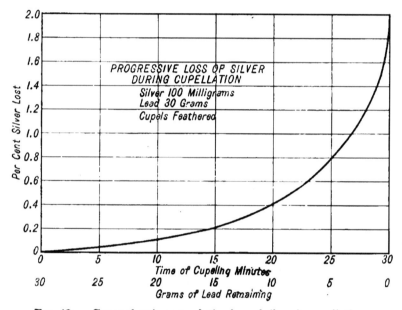

FIG. 40. — Curve showing cumulative loss of silver in cupellation.

This is well illustrated by the curve shown in Fig. 40 in which is plotted the cumulative, minute-to-minute, loss of silver in cupeling a 30-gram button containing 100 milligrams of silver. This is the result of considerable careful experimental work done in the fire assay laboratory of the Massachusetts Institute of Technology, several years ago.

Keeping the amount of silver constant and varying the lead, Lodge obtains the results shown in the following table:

* Trans. Inst. Min. Met., 14, p. 420.

TABLE X.
Effect of Lead on Loss of Silver in Cupellation.

Silver milligrams	Lead grams	Temperature degrees centigrade	Silver loss per cent[1]
200	10	685	1.39
200	15	685	1.38
200	20	685	1.52
200	25	685	1.85

[1] Average of two nearest together.

When the quantity of lead remains constant and the silver is varied the percentage loss of silver is found to increase as the silver is reduced. The following representative figures taken from Godshall's paper on "Silver Losses in Cupellation"[*] show this very clearly.

TABLE XI.
Effect of Varying Silver on Cupellation Losses.

Weight of Lead	1/2 A. T.	1/2 A. T.	1/2 A. T.	1/2 A. T.	1/2 A. T.	1/2 A. T.	1/2 A. T.
Weight of Silver	200 mg.	100 mg.	50 mg.	20 mg.	10 mg.	5 mg.	2 mg.
Silver Loss	1.73%	2.03%	2.65%	2.82%	3.44%	4.46%	6.90%

Loss of Gold in Cupeling. — There is always some loss of gold in cupeling, but owing to the greater resistance of this metal to oxidation this loss is smaller than the corresponding silver loss. The following table, taken from Lodge, shows the relation between the loss of gold and the temperature of cupellation.

TABLE XII.
Effect of Temperature on Loss of Gold in Cupellation.

Gold used milligrams	Lead grams	Temperature degrees centigrade	Gold loss per cent[1]	Remarks
200	10	700		Button froze.
200	10	775	0.155	
200	10	850	0.385	
200	10	925	0.460	
200	10	1000	1.435	
200	10	1075	2.990	

[1] Mean of two results nearest together.

[*] Trans. A.I.M.E. **26**, pp. 473-484 inc.

In the case of the gold with temperatures of 1000 degrees and above, the higher losses seem to be due in part to a lessening of the surface tension owing to the increased temperature, for when the cupels were examined with the microscope a large number of minute beads were found all over the inner surface. It would appear that small particles of the alloy were left behind to cupel by themselves.

As in the case of silver, the percentage loss of gold is found to increase as the quantity is reduced. Hillebrand and Allen [*] show that, contrary to the usual opinion, the loss of gold in cupeling is not negligible, and is greatly influenced by slight changes in temperature. They found that the most exact results were obtained when feather crystals of litharge were obtained on the cupels.

Effect of Silver on the Loss of Gold in Cupeling. — Lodge, in his "Notes on Assaying," states that the addition of silver in excess lessens the loss of gold, but gives no figures. Hillebrand and Allen [†] state that the loss of gold in cupeling is greater with pure gold and alloys poor in silver than with alloys rich in silver. Smith [‡] gives the following figures showing the protective action exercised by silver on gold during cupellation:

	Per cent of total gold recovered.	
	Tellurium added.	Without tellurium.
Without silver	94.9	98.2
With silver	97.0	99.5

In order to obtain more light upon this subject, Mr. A. B. Sanger, a student at the Massachusetts Institute of Technology, made a large number of careful experiments, using proof gold and C. P. silver. The work was done in a gas furnace and the temperature was measured by a thermo-electric pyrometer, the junction of which was placed in the center of a blank cupel in line with the cupels which were being used. Mr. Sanger used 10 milligrams of gold and various amounts of silver with 25 grams of lead, and with four different temperatures. His results [§] are shown in Fig. 41. The gold losses include any solution losses there may have been in parting, but these are extremely small, or nil. The results show a very decided protective effect of sil-

[*] Bull. No. 253 U. S. Geol. Survey. p. 20 et seq.

[†] Op. cit.

[‡] The Behavior of Tellurium in Assaying. Trans. Inst. Min. Met. **17**, p. 472.

[§] Thesis No. 492, M.I.T. Mining Department.

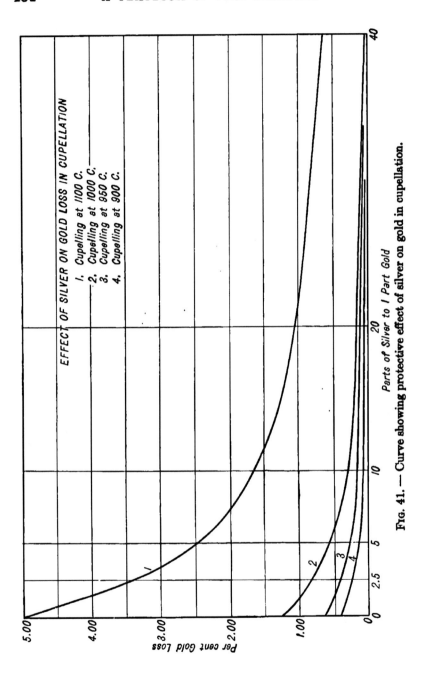

Fig. 41. — Curve showing protective effect of silver on gold in cupellation.

ver and confirm the statements of Lodge and others. A glance at the curves shows how important it is to run gold assays at a temperature close to that at which feather crystals are obtained. With smaller amounts of gold the percentage losses will be correspondingly greater.

Influence of Impurities on the Loss of Precious Metals during Cupellation. — According to Rose,* tellurium, selenium, thallium, bismuth, molybdenum, manganese, copper, vanadium, zinc, arsenic, antimony, cadmium, iron and tin, all induce extra losses of gold and silver in cupellation and should be removed before this stage is reached.

The behavior of tellurium in cupellation will be mentioned in the discussion of the assay of telluride ores. Copper is perhaps the most common impurity, and on account of the difficulty of removing it completely in scorification or crucible fusions, a knowledge of its behavior in cupeling is particularly important. Eager and Welch† give the following table showing the effect of copper on the loss of silver in cupellation.

TABLE XIII.
EFFECT OF COPPER ON SILVER LOSSES IN CUPELLATION.

No.	Silver used grams	Lead grams	Temperature degrees centigrade	Copper per cent of the silver	Per cent silver lost		Ratio of lead to copper
					Individual	Mean	
1	.20382	10	775	5	1.00		1000 to 1
2	.20256	"	"	"	1.15		"
3	.20036	"	"	"	0.93	1.03	"
4	.20618	"	"	10	1.19		500 to 1
5	.20193	"	"	"	1.09		"
6	.20118	"	"	"	1.06	1.11	"
7	.20146	"	"	15	1.35		333 to 1
8	.20138	"	"	"	1.27		"
9	.20432	"	"	"	[1]1.15	1.31	"
10	.20282	"	"	20	[1]1.15		250 to 1
11	.20100	"	"	"	1.45		"
12	.20338	"	"	"	1.46	1.46	"
13	.20224	"	"	25	1.05		200 to 1
14	.20496	"	"	"	0.95		"
15	.20420	"	"	"	1.07	1.02	"

[1] Disregarded.
* Jour. Chem. Met. and Min. Soc. of South Africa, 5, p. 167.
† Thesis No. 225, M.I.T. Mining Department.

When the results shown in this table are compared with those in Table IX, it appears that the presence of a small amount of copper, not more than 1 part to 500 of lead, and not more than 1 part to 10 parts of silver, reduces the loss of silver below that which results when no copper is used. This may be due to the protective action which copper is known to exert upon silver.*

With a ratio of 1 part of copper to 333 parts of lead and with 6.67 parts of silver, the loss is about the same as in the absence of copper.

With an increase in the amount of copper to 1 part to 250 of lead and 5 parts of silver the loss is greater than when no copper is used.

With a ratio of 1 part of copper to 200 parts of lead and 4 parts of silver the loss apparently becomes less, but this was found to be due to the retention of copper in the silver bead.

TABLE XIV.

Effect of Copper on Gold Losses in Cupellation.

No.	Gold used grams	Lead grams	Temperature degrees centigrade	Copper per cent of the gold	Per cent gold lost		Ratio of lead to copper
					Individual	Mean	
1	.20181	10	775	None	0.15		
2	.20104	"	"	"	0.16	0.16	
3	.20288	"	"	5	0.18		1000 to 1
4	.20110	"	"	"	0.20		"
5	.20318	"	"	"	0.10		"
(In the following the beads show a gain in weight.)							
6	.20102	"	"	10	−0.03		500 to 1
7	.20142	"	"	"	−0.03		"
8	.20138	"	"	"	−0.02	−0.03	
9	.20024	"	"	15	−0.11		333 to 1
10	.20060	"	"	"	−0.26		"
11	.20048	"	"	"	−0.18	−0.18	
12	.20100	"	"	20	−0.13		250 to 1
13	.20101	"	"	"	−0.56[1]		"
14	.20161	"	"	"	−0.20	−0.17	
15	.20422	"	"	25	−0.29		200 to 1
16	.20296	"	"	"	−0.21		"
17	.20284	"	"	"	−0.32	−0.27	"

[1] Disregarded.

* Rose, Trans. Inst. Min. Met. **14**, p. 422.

When the amounts of lead and copper in 10, 11 and 12 above are compared, it is found that the ratio of lead to copper should be at least 250 to 1 to ensure the removal of the copper, and at least 333 to 1 if the apparent loss of silver is not to be noticeably increased.

The effect of copper on the loss of gold is shown in the preceding table.

It appears that 5 per cent of copper with this lead ratio has no effect on the loss of gold. The gain in the weight of the gold beads with 10 per cent and over of copper shows clearly that copper is retained by the gold under these conditions. This was also indicated by the color of the gold beads. With a higher cupellation temperature the amount of copper retained would doubtless be smaller. It is interesting to note that with 10 per cent of copper the amount retained by the bead approximately neutralizes the loss of the gold itself. Apparently the ratio of lead to copper should not be less than 500 to 1 if the copper is to be completely removed.

Rule Governing Cupellation Losses. — As is well recognized in large-scale cupeling operations, the concentration of precious metal in the litharge increases as the concentration in the lead increases. W. J. Sharwood[*] after examining a large number of experimental results enunciated the following empirical rule connecting the actual or percentage loss with the weight of the bead: "When a given amount of silver (or of gold) is cupeled with a given amount of lead, under a fixed set of conditions as to temperature, etc., the apparent loss of weight sustained by the precious metal is directly proportional to the surface of the bead of fine metal remaining."

If the above is true the following are also true.

(1) "The loss of weight varies as the $\frac{2}{3}$ power of the weight, or as the square of the diameter of the bead."

(2) "The percentage loss varies inversely as the diameter of the bead, or inversely as the cube root of the weight."

As Sharwood points out it might be better to base the calculations on the original weight of metal taken, but in every day practice this is not known and we have to depend on the weight of the bead.

Inasmuch as small variations in the amount of lead have but

[*] T.A.I.M.E. **52**, p. 180.

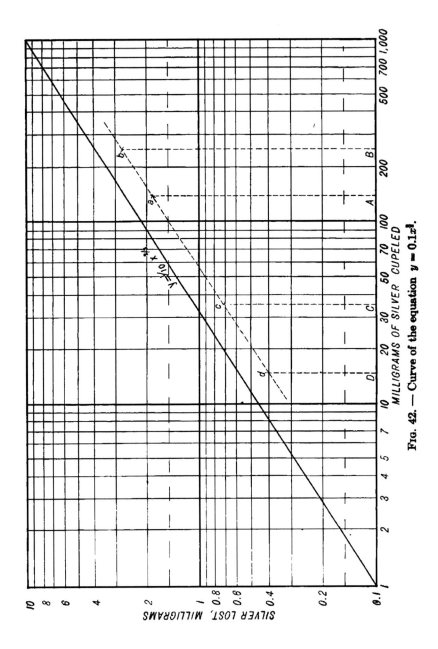

Fig. 42. — Curve of the equation $y = 0.1x^{\frac{2}{3}}$.

little effect on the cupellation loss, and as temperature conditions in a given row across a muffle are nearly uniform, we may apply this rule to determine the proper correction for a bead of any weight by a calculation applied to the loss observed in a proof of an entirely different weight, but cupeled at the same time under the same conditions. The simplest method of finding the amount of this correction for any particular case is by the use of a logarithmic plot of the equation $y = Cx^n$, which is a straight line, and on which, when the horizontal and vertical scales are equal, the tangent made by the line and the x axis is the exponent n.

In Fig. 42 is plotted the equation $y = 1/10x^{\frac{2}{3}}$ when the abscissa x equals the milligrams of silver cupeled and the ordinate y equals the silver loss in milligrams. To find a correction run one proof, as near the expected weight as possible in each row and plot the corresponding point (a) on the diagram, and draw through it a line parallel to the guide line $y = 1/10x^{\frac{2}{3}}$. Note the points on the line corresponding to the weights B, C, and D of other beads weighed, and read the correction for each from the scale.

Dewey, in discussing Sharwood's results, warns against placing too much reliance on this rule, however, because as he says, " It is so easy to say ' if all other conditions remain the same ' but it is so extremely difficult, and in practical work impossible, to actually maintain equal conditions."

Testing Cupels for Absorption of Silver. — An occasional test of cupels and especially of each new lot of bone-ash is desirable. Select some standard amount of lead and silver and always use the same amounts so that results may be comparable. One hundred milligrams of silver and 25 grams of lead is a convenient quantity.

Indications of Metals Present. — The lead buttons obtained from the assay of ores ordinarily give but little trouble in cupellation but occasionally the ore may contain some unsuspected impurity which makes its appearance during the cupellation process. In addition to all sorts of ores the assayer often has submitted to him various kinds of bullion, numerous by-products of the mining and metallurgical industries, as well as such material as jeweler's sweeps, dental alloys, etc. All of the latter may and do usually contain considerable amounts of base-metal impurities as well as occasional rare metals, many of which may exert considerable influence on the results of the assay if provision is not made for them. It is always important to determine the nature of the constituents of the material which is being assayed; and the behavior of the cupeling lead and the appearance of the cupel and bead during and after cupellation will often give much valuable information concerning the elements present. When the character of the constituents is ascertained, the skilful assayer will know exactly what to do, and when he again comes to the cupellation stage everything will go smoothly. All that is known about qualitative analysis is not found in books devoted to that subject, as assayers well know; and in the case of certain rare elements at least, the fire assayer has a decided advantage over the ordinary chemist.

As soon as the button melts any slag which may not have been removed in cleaning it, together with sulphides or arsenides of some of the base metals, if present, will come to the surface of the alloy as a dark-colored pasty dross. If not too great in amount this will go to the side of the cupel and cupellation may be continued. If zinc, tin, iron, nickel, cobalt, antimony or arsenic are present these will oxidize and come off in the order named. The oxides of zinc, tin, iron, nickel and cobalt are but slightly soluble in molten litharge and, if present in any considerable amount, give infusible scoria which float on top of the lead and interfere with cupellation.

ZINC if present will burn with a brilliant greenish-white flame and emit dense white fumes. A considerable part of the oxide condenses on the cupel and may cover over the lead thus preventing cupellation.

TIN if present in the button, is quickly oxidized, forming SnO_2, which, if present in sufficient quantity, covers the lead with infusible yellow scoria and stops cupellation.

IRON gives brown or black scoria if present in large amounts, as do also cobalt and manganese. Small amounts of iron oxide dissolve in the litharge and stain the cupel dark red.

NICKEL in small quantities gives dark green scoria and greenish stains. Larger amounts cause the button to freeze.

ANTIMONY is readily soluble in lead in almost all proportions, and for this reason the button may contain a large amount of it. It comes off in the first stages of cupellation, giving dense fumes of

Sb_2O_3 and yellow scoria of antimonate of lead around the cupel. This scoria appears when 4 per cent or more of antimony is present. It solidifies almost as soon as formed and expands in so doing. If much antimony is present the cupel will be split open by this action, allowing the lead to run out into the muffle. If present in smaller amounts it may simply crack the cupel and leave a characteristic ridge of yellow scoria.

ARSENIC acts much like antimony but is not so often carried into the lead button. The scoria from arsenical lead is light yellow and the fumes are less noticeable.

BISMUTH is less readily oxidized than lead and thus tends to remain with the silver until most of the lead has gone. It is finally oxidized and absorbed by the cupel and leaves a ring of orange-yellow around the silver bead. For purposes of comparison it should be noted that pure lead gives a brown-yellow cupel. Bismuth is the only other metal which behaves like lead in cupeling; this, however, makes it possible to cupel argentiferous bismuth directly.

COPPER, like bismuth, is less readily oxidized than lead, but it differs from bismuth in that its oxide alone is not liquid at the temperature of cupellation. Cuprous oxide, however, is readily soluble in molten litharge and the mixed oxides are absorbed in the cupel, giving a stain which ranges from dirty green almost to black according to the amount present. The intensity of the green coloration may be taken as an indication of the amount of copper present in the button. Even very small amounts may be detected in this way. Owing to the relative difficulty with which it oxidizes, copper tends to concentrate in the button and if too large in amount causes it to freeze. Sometimes it will go down to a small amount and then flatten out, leaving a copper-colored bead.

TELLURIUM gives the surface of the cupel a pinkish color most of which fades away upon cooling. If much tellurium is present it gives a frosted appearance to the bead. In an experiment with 200 milligrams of silver and 10 grams of lead, the frosting made its appearance when 40 milligrams of tellurium were added. Tellurium reduces the surface tension of the lead alloy and thus increases the loss of the precious metals, and, as it is less readily oxidized than lead, most of it remains with the precious metals until a large part of the lead is removed.

In attempting to determine the presence of various elements in the lead by the color of the cupel it must be remembered that one constituent, particularly if it has an intense coloring power and more particularly if the color produced is dark, will tend to mask other constituents producing lighter and less intense colors.

Indications of Rare Metals. — The members of the platinum group of metals practically all yield evidence of their presence either in the appearance of the surface of the finished bead or, in some cases, during the later stages of the cupellation process. We are indebted mostly to Lodge* and to Bannister† for information relative to the appearance of the surface of the finished bead. Lodge worked with relatively large amounts of rare metals and small amounts of silver, and depended on the unaided eye for his observations. Bannister worked with very much smaller quantities of rare metals and large amounts of silver and gold and used a low-power microscope. These indications, which should be recognized by all skilful assayers, may be made an important contribution to our knowledge of the qualitative analysis of these metals. At least they should serve to put the assayer on his guard and cause him to suspect the presence of rare metals in samples of ores and bullion submitted without request for their determination. In general, where the presence of any of these metals is suspected, the cupels should be finished at a reasonably high temperature and the beads allowed to cool slowly in order to fully develop their crystalline structure.

PLATINUM. — As little as 1.6 per cent of platinum gives a characteristic frosted appearance to a silver bead which is visible to the naked eye. Under a low-power microscope as little as 0.4 per cent may be detected in beads weighing only 0.1 gram. The effect of platinum on gold beads is not so marked as in the case of silver. The presence of 8 per cent of platinum seems to give a maximum amount of roughness and frosting to the silver bead. Buttons which contain a large amount of platinum flatten out when near the finishing point and refuse to drive, leaving a gray, mossy-appearing bead which sticks to the cupel. Such beads usually retain considerable lead. The only other metal of this group which gives a structure approaching that of platinum is palladium, the effect of which is dealt with later.

* Notes on Assaying, 1907.
† Trans. Inst. Min. Met. **23**, pp. 163–173.

IRIDIUM. — Iridium is but slightly soluble in silver or gold at the temperature of cupellation, and most of it sinks to the bottom of the bead, where it will appear as black specks. These specks are more readily distinguished after the bead has been rolled into a cornet for parting. On the surface, crystal boundaries are clearly visible, the roughness being, according to Lodge, of finer texture than that produced by platinum. Bannister notes that beads containing iridium were more nearly spherical than normal beads. Under the microscope, the crystal faces were strongly marked with lines, crossing one another after the manner of slip-bands. This strained appearance seemed to be caused by internal stresses.

RHODIUM. — The presence of mere traces of rhodium may be detected. As little as 0.004 per cent in silver beads was found to cause a distinct crystallization, visible to the naked eye. The facets of the crystals give the appearance of a cut gem.

With 0.01 per cent of rhodium this appearance is more distinct. The presence of 0.03 per cent of rhodium in silver causes the bead to sprout and spit in spite of all precautions. With this and larger amounts, the surface of the bead assumes a bluish-gray color.

RUTHENIUM. — The presence of ruthenium is always indicated by a black, crystalline deposit firmly attached to the bead, usually on the bottom edge. This is distinctly visible to the naked eye even with as little as 0.004 per cent. Under the microscope the surface shows a distinct herringbone structure.

OSMIUM. — Osmium is partly oxidized and volatilized during cupellation. According to Lodge, if the osmium is not completely volatilized, small black spots appear on the silver bead when nearly finished. These flash off and on, but finally disappear when the bead brightens. Bannister found no specific indications of the presence of osmium in his tests.

PALLADIUM. — According to Lodge, palladium gives the surface a raised and embossed appearance. According to Bannister, it is much like platinum. Fortunately its presence is indicated by a coloration of the solution in the parting operation.

Molten gold beads have a beautiful green color and when pure may be cooled considerably below the true freezing-point and still remain liquid. On solidification they " flash " as do silver beads and in solidifying they emit an apple-green light. According to Reimsdijk,* copper promotes the surfusion of gold. He also points out the curious fact that gold fused on a cupel without the addition of lead is not subject to surfusion and sets gradually without flashing. Fulton† measured the amount of surfusion of silver beads obtained from cupellation and found it to be as much as 77° C. He found that beads weighing more than 750 milligrams would not flash.

Very small quantities of iridium, rhodium, osmium, ruthenium and iridosmium prevent this flashing‡ in gold beads and probably also in silver beads. This gives us another indication of the presence of the more uncommon metals of the platinum group. It should be noted in this connection that small amounts of platinum and palladium do not hinder flashing. Over 6 per cent of platinum, however, does prevent it.

In cupeling pure gold or silver with pure lead it is found that the part of the cupel occupied by the bead as the last of the lead was going off will be stained green. The higher the temperature and consequently the higher the loss of precious metals, the larger this green area becomes. Certain brands of patent cupels give a large amount of this green stain, and whenever this is found a serious loss of silver is found to have occurred.

Retention of Base Metals. — It has already been mentioned that a plus error may be incurred because of the retention of lead in the silver bead. If the bead contains much lead, it will appear dull or slightly yellow, being thinly coated with litharge; the part resting against the cupel will be smooth, and it will not blick. Occasionally a bead will show the play of colors and even flash, and still retain as much as 1 or 2 per cent of lead. Sprouting, however, is considered proof of the absence of all but traces of impurities. When the alloy contains copper, the silver beads may retain from 1 to 2 per cent of copper without showing any unusual symptoms.

All gold and silver beads cupeled in the absence of copper probably retain small amounts of other impurities, and in beads cupeled in the presence of copper there is probably always some copper left. Hillebrand and Allen§ found gold beads retaining from 0.30 to

---

* Chem. News, **41**, pp. 126, 266.
† West Chem. and Met. **4**, p. 50.
‡ Reimsdijk, loc. cit
§ Bulletin No. 253 U. S. Geological Survey.

0.37 per cent of lead. Keller* reports the results of analysis of 30 grams of beads resulting from scorification assays. This showed 0.16 per cent of lead and 0.15 per cent of bismuth, the latter having been concentrated from the granulated lead used for scorification, which at the time contained approximately 0.02 per cent of that metal. Another series of tests by Keller† showed total impurities averaging 0.45 per cent. It also appears from Keller's work that large beads are of slightly lower fineness than small ones.

The persistency with which a small amount of copper is retained by gold and silver beads is taken advantage of in the gold bullion assay to toughen the beads so that they can be rolled thin without cracking. A small amount of lead, which is invariably retained in the absence of copper, causes the fillet to crack. Copper does not have this effect. It is, therefore, customary to add copper when none is present in the bullion. Being less readily oxidized than lead, it serves as an oxygen carrier and permits the entire elimination of lead from the bead.

These retained metals tend to compensate for the cupellation losses but do not do so entirely, so that ordinary assay results are still at least 1 or 2 per cent low. Experiments with fine silver, however, reveal the interesting fact that by assaying slags and cupels and adding the metal recovered to the weight of the original bead, a very close check on the original silver is obtained, provided the assay was carefully made and cupeled with crystals. This shows that the impurities in the assay beads balance the volatilization and other miscellaneous losses. This is only true, however, when cupellations and scorifications are run at a low temperature. Keller‡ gives figures which show that if scorifications and cupellations are run hot a decided volatilization loss occurs and corrected figures are still far too low.

Portland Cement and Magnesia Cupels. — Cupels of Portland cement and calcined magnesia have found favor in some localities, the former mostly in the United States and Canada, the latter principally in England and South Africa. Portland cement cupels are made from neat cement with from 6 to 10 per cent of water, in the usual way. If properly made and handled, they do

---

* Trans. A.I.M.E. **60**, p. 706.
† Trans. A.I.M.E. **46**, p. 783 (1913).
‡ Trans. A.I.M.E. **60**, p. 706.

not crack, and they absorb nearly their own weight of litharge. The silver loss due to absorption is greater than for bone-ash.

J. W. Merritt* compared the results obtained with bone-ash and cement cupels and found two essential points of difference: 1st, Beads from a bone-ash cupel were well rounded and stood on a small base, while those from Portland cement cupels were flatter and stood on a base as wide as the broadest diameter of the bead; 2nd, The cement sticks tenaciously to the beads from Portland cement cupels but hardly at all to those from bone-ash cupels.

Mann and Clayton,† in a study of cupellation losses, found cement cupels to give very high silver losses even under the most favorable conditions. They also found it very hard to clean the bottom of the bead without danger of loss.

Cement cupels are very much cheaper and more durable than bone-ash, but on account of the above disadvantages should not be used for careful, uncorrected silver assays. One disadvantage of cement cupels for gold assays is the extra care which must be taken in cleaning the bead. This is necessary because, in parting, a considerable amount of the cement would remain insoluble as gelatinous silica and would be weighed as gold. Bone-ash, on the other hand, is practically entirely dissolved.

Magnesia cupels are very hard, which is an advantage in that they do not suffer so much breakage in shipment. They are always factory-made and are decidedly more expensive than bone-ash cupels, which may be home-made. Certain brands of magnesia cupels give an apparently lower loss of silver in cupeling than can be obtained with bone-ash cupels but it is a question how much of this is real and how much due to an increase in the amount of impurities retained in the silver beads.

Magnesia cupels behave quite differently from ordinary bone-ash cupels, and the assayer who is accustomed to bone-ash cupels will have to learn cupeling over again when he starts using those made of magnesite. This difference in behavior is due mainly to the different thermal properties of the two materials. Both the specific heat and the conductivity of magnesite are decidedly greater than those of bone-ash, so that with cupels of both kinds running side by side, the lead on the magnesia cupel is comparatively dull while that on bone-ash is very bright. This is due to

* Min. and Sci. Press. **100**, p. 649.
† Technical Bulletin, Vol. II, No. 3, Missouri School of Mines, p. 33.

the greater conductivity of magnesite, which allows a more rapid dispersion of the heat of oxidation of the lead, with the result that magnesia cupels require a higher muffle temperature than do bone-ash cupels. An especially high finishing temperature is required for magnesite cupels, to insure the elimination of the last 1 or 2 per cent of lead. A bone-ash cupel will finish in a muffle, the temperature of which is sufficient to cause uncovering, but this is not true of the magnesia cupel, because in this case the heat of oxidation of the lead is diffused too rapidly and is not conserved to help out at the finish.

Magnesia cupels absorb about two-thirds of their own weight of litharge, those of cement about three-fourths of their weight of litharge.

Color Scale of Temperature. — Starting from the lowest visible red the temperatures of incandescent bodies can be approximated by the color impressions produced on the eye. Such estimates are, of course, dependent upon individual judgment and the susceptibility of the eye, also upon the amount of illumination of the locality in which the observation is made and upon the nature of the heated body itself. The following color-temperature scale[*] will be found convenient for reference in cupellation.

	Degrees Centigrade
Lowest red visible in the dark	470
Dark red, blood-red	550
Dark cherry	625
Cherry-red, full cherry	700
Light red	850
Orange	900
Light orange	950
Yellow	1000
Light yellow	1050
White	1150–1200

[*] Howe, Eng. and Min. Jour., **69**, p. 75.

CHAPTER VI.

PARTING.

Parting is the separation of silver from gold by means of acid. In gold assaying nitric acid is almost exclusively used, although sulphuric acid is usually employed for parting large lots of bullion. Nitric acid cannot be used successfully to separate silver from gold unless there is present at least three times as much silver as gold. With this ratio the alloy must be in a thin sheet and it requires a long-continued heating with acid of 1.26 specific gravity to effect a separation. In parting beads from ore assays it is best to have at least eight or ten times as much silver as gold present, and for ease of manipulation this ratio of silver to gold is preferable to a greater one. With much less silver than this a long-continued treatment with acid is necessary, while with much more silver than this, special precautions have to be taken to prevent the gold from breaking up into small particles which are difficult to manage. The idea of parting is to so manipulate that the gold will, if possible, remain in one piece.

The nitric acid for parting must be free from hydrochloric acid and chlorine in order to have no solvent action on the gold and also because any chlorides present would precipitate insoluble silver chloride on the gold. The acid strength is of great importance and the proper strength to be used depends upon the composition of the alloy. The higher the ratio of silver in the alloy, the less the acid strength should be.

Great care is necessary in parting to avoid breaking up the gold and subsequently losing some of the small particles, as well as to insure complete solution of the silver.

Different authorities recommend different vessels for parting; but for ore assays, and especially for beginners in the art, the use of a porcelain crucible or capsule is recommended and will be described first. Parting in flasks or test-tubes with the use of annealing cups will also be discussed so that either method may be used.

PARTING

Parting in Porcelain Capsules. — A glazed porcelain capsule 1⅜ inches in diameter and 1 inch high is preferable for this work on account of its broad flat base, but a small porcelain crucible does very well if care is taken not to upset it. Many different strengths of acid and other details of manipulation have been recommended, but the procedure given below is one which has given uniformly satisfactory results to the author in his laboratory. The strength of acid which may be used depends on the proportion of gold and silver in the alloy; the less the ratio of silver to gold, the stronger the acid may be without danger of breaking up the gold. It is not necessary that the method to be described should be followed in every case, but this method is a safe one for the treatment of beads having almost any proportion of silver to gold, from 3 to 1000 or more parts of silver to 1 of gold.

PROCEDURE. — Pour into the capsule about half an inch of dilute nitric acid of 1.06 sp. gr., made by diluting 1.42 acid with seven times its volume of water. Put on the hot-plate and heat until vapor can be seen rising from it, and then drop in the bead which should be f ee from adhering bone-ash. In case the alloy has only 3 or 4 parts of silver to 1 of gold it must be hammered or rolled out to the thickness of an ordinary visiting card, say to 0.01 inch. The bead should begin to dissolve at once, giving off bubbles of nitrogen oxides. If it does not begin to dissolve, add nitric acid, 1.26 sp. gr., a few drops at a time until action starts. The solution should be kept hot but not boiling. The action should be of moderate intensity. Continue the heating until action ceases and then decant the solution into a clean white evaporating dish in a good light, taking care not to pour off any of the gold. Then add a few cubic centimeters of 1.26 sp. gr. acid, made by diluting strong nitric acid, 1.42 sp. gr., with an equal volume of water, and heat almost to boiling for from two to ten minutes. Decant this solution and then wash three times with warm distilled water, decanting as completely as possible after each washing. Apply the stream of water from the wash bottle tangentially to the sides of the capsule, rotating it meanwhile to prevent direct impact of the stream on the gold. After the final washing manipulate the particles of gold so as to bring them together, decant off the last drops of water as completely as possible and set the cup on a warm plate to dry the gold, but avoid too high a temperature as the sputtering of the last drop of water would tend to break up and possibly throw out the gold. Finally "anneal" the gold by putting the cup in the muffle or over the open flame until the bottom is bright red, when the gold will change from its black amorphous condition to the true yellow color of pure gold. It is now ready to cool and weigh. To transfer the gold from the cup to the scale-pan, bring the scale-pan to the front part of the balance. Gradually invert the cup over the pan, tapping it meanwhile with a pencil. When this is done the gold will usually slide out without difficulty. If any small particles stick to the cup they may be detached by touching them gently with the point of the forceps or a small camel's-hair brush.

The gold should be pure yellow throughout and may be compared with parted gold of known purity. If it is lighter-colored than pure gold it is probable that all of the silver has not been dissolved. If it is dark in spots or if the cup is stained, it indicates incomplete removal of the silver nitrate. The "annealing" causes the gold to stick together, making it easier to handle, tends to burn out any specks of organic matter which may have fallen into the cup, allows the assayer to observe the color of the parted gold and to determine its purity in that way and to distinguish and separate any specks of foreign matter such as fire brick, coke dust etc., which may have found their way into the cup. The "annealing" at a red heat is also necessary in order that the gold may contract and lose most of its porosity, since otherwise it would condense a considerable quantity of gas during weighing.

After the silver has been dissolved from a doré alloy by the acid, the gold remains as a porous mass which is more compact the larger the proportion of gold the alloy contained, the thicker the alloy and the less the mechanical disturbance of the bead during solution. In treating a bead which is near the limiting ratio of silver to gold it is sometimes difficult to determine whether or not it is parted. This may be ascertained by touching it with a glass rod drawn down to a rather small diameter, (approximately 1/32 inch). If it feels soft throughout and can be broken up it is practically parted, but it should be heated almost to boiling with 1.26 sp. gr. acid for at least ten minutes to ensure dissolving the last of the silver. Such a mass of parted gold will require a longer and more careful washing, for on account of its density a longer time is required for the silver nitrate to diffuse through its minute pores. In parting the ordinary bead containing ten, twenty or more times as much silver as gold, it is easy to see when parting is complete by the considerable shrinking of the mass.

Notes: 1. The nitric acid solution should be hot before dropping in the bead as in cold acid the gold tends to break up into extremely fine particles.

2. The violent mechanical disturbance due to boiling or too rapid solution may cause the gold to break up, causing difficulty or actual loss in washing and subsequent handling.

3. If there remain only a few tenths of a milligram of porous gold the ten minutes heating with 1.26 sp. gr. acid is unnecessary.

4. Strong nitric acid (1.46 sp. gr.) should not be used at any time, as gold is slightly dissolved by it.

5. If in doubt at any time as to the purity of the parted gold, wrap it up six times its weight of silver foil and carefully cupel with lead, then repart and weigh.

6. If a small particle of gold is seen floating on the surface of the liquid, it may be made to sink by touching it with a glass rod.

7. The black stain occurring in parting cups after heating is due to metallic silver reduced from silver nitrate by the heat, showing insufficient washing.

Inquartation. — When the bead contains too little silver to part, it is necessary to alloy it with more silver. This process is called inquartation. It originated from the custom of the old assayers of adding silver until the gold was one-quarter of the whole. They considered a ratio of 3 parts of silver to 1 of gold to be necessary for parting. At present, in assaying gold bullion, a ratio of only 2 or $2\frac{1}{4}$ parts of silver to 1 of gold is used, mainly to avoid all danger of the gold breaking up in the boiling acid. In this case some little silver remains undissolved, even though the alloy is rolled out to about 0.01 inch in thickness.

To inquart a bead wrap it with six to ten times its weight of silver in 4 or 5 grams of sheet lead and cupel. Rose[*] considers that different proportions of silver should be used according to the weight of the gold, and gives the following suitable proportions:

Weight of Gold	Ratio of Silver to Gold
Less than 0.1 mg.,	20 or 30 to 1
About 0.2 mg.,	10 to 1
About 1.0 mg.,	6 to 1
About 10 mg.,	4 to 1
More than 50 mg.,	$2\frac{1}{4}$ to 1

[*] Metallurgy of Gold, Sixth Ed., p. 511.

Many assayers, when working for both gold and silver and suspecting an ore to be deficient in silver, add silver to the crucible or to the lead button before cupeling, part directly and then run separate assays to determine the silver in the ore.

Preparing Large Beads for Parting. — Large beads, especially those which approach the maximum ratio of 25 per cent gold, must be flattened on an anvil and rolled out to a thickness of about 0.01 inch before parting. During this process the alloy will require frequent annealing to prevent it from cracking. It should finally be rolled up into a little " cornet " before parting. (See " Assay of Gold Bullion.")

Parting in Flasks, etc. — Parting in flasks, test-tubes, etc. is, up to the completion of the washing of the gold, exactly similar to parting in porcelain capsules. From this point on, however, the manipulations are different, as the annealing is not done in the same vessel, but in an annealing cup. The annealing cup is a small unglazed crucible made of fire clay and very smooth on the inside.

PROCEDURE. — After washing the gold, fill the flask or test-tube with distilled water, invert over it an annealing cup and then quickly invert the two so that the gold may fall into the cup. This operation should be done in a good light and preferably against a white background. Tap the flask if necessary, to dislodge any gold which may have caught on the side, and after all the gold has settled, raise the flask slowly until its lip is level with the top of the annealing cup. Now, when all the gold is at the bottom of the cup, slip the flask quickly from the cup and invert it. Drain the water from the cup, cover it and set it on the hot-plate to dry. When fully dry, it is ready to be annealed and weighed. Examine the flask once more to make sure that no gold has been left in it.

This method of parting has the advantage that the acid may be boiled, if necessary, with less danger of its boiling over and causing loss of fine gold. It is well suited for the parting of large beads where the porcelain cup would not contain enough acid to dissolve all of the silver, and also to the parting of alloys where the ratio of silver to gold is only 2 or 3 to 1, and which therefore require a long-continued heating at or near boiling temperature. The method is therefore recommended for use in the assay of gold bullion. The clay cups have the advantage of porosity so that they can absorb the last drops of water and give it off again slowly, thus preventing spattering if they are set on a hot iron plate to dry. They also stand sudden changes of temperature somewhat better than the glazed porcelain cups.

This method has the disadvantage that if all the parted gold does not remain in one piece, there is greater danger of loss, because the fine gold settles with difficulty and because it cannot be watched so well through all stages of the process. There is also danger of small particles of the cup, and especially the cover, being broken off and mixed with the gold.

Influence of Base Metals on Parting. — Pure gold-silver alloys of almost any proportions not exceeding 30 per cent of gold, with a proper strength of nitric acid and the right degree of heat, will part and leave the gold in a coherent mass similar in shape to the original alloy, although very much reduced in size when but little gold is present. While a relatively strong acid may be used directly on alloys containing large proportions of gold, this same strength of acid cannot be used on those alloys containing but little gold, without producing disintegration. Heating of the parting acid is more necessary, too, when but little gold is present. The fact that the gold holds together under these circumstances, and contracts, following the retreating surface of silver, very much simplifies the determination. When the gold breaks up, it increases the difficulty for the assayer and causes unavoidable losses in decantation. The high temperature of the parting acid increases the mobility of the gold, and in the case of pure alloys prevents it from breaking up.

Keller[*] states that, although assay beads of not less than 997 parts gold plus silver fineness offer no difficulty in parting, yet when the fineness falls to 990 or lower the gold cannot be obtained in any form other than powder, no matter what acid and heat combinations are employed. The explanation of this difference may be that the whole gold-silver series form solid solutions, in which the molecules of gold, even when in dilute solution, are uniformly distributed and almost if not quite in contact, or at least within spheres of mutual attraction. It may be imagined that impurities forming compounds or eutectic mixtures may so disrupt the uniformity of texture of the alloy, and

[*] Trans. A.I.M.E. 60, p. 706.

therefore the continuity of the gold, as to prevent its cohesion during the acid treatment.

There is naturally a gradation in the degree of gold disintegration, from its almost complete cohesion when derived from practically " fine " beads, to its completely pulverulent form when derived from beads of 990 fineness.

Indications of Presence of Rare Metals. — As has been indicated in the chapter on cupellation, the assay beads may contain, in addition to traces of lead, bismuth, copper and tellurium, practically all of the platinum, palladium, iridium, iridosmium, as well as more or less of the rhodium, osmium and ruthenium contained in the original material which was assayed. Most of these rare metals make their presence known by the appearance of the bead. If they are not discovered in the bead, indications of their presence may be found during parting.

In nitric acid parting a considerable part of the platinum, palladium and osmium are dissolved, the amount depending on various conditions such as the amount of silver present, the strength of acid, etc.

According to Rawlins,* PLATINUM has a disintegrating effect upon the gold, when the latter does not make up more than 5 per cent of the weight of the bead. As platinum is only partly soluble, the remaining insoluble platinum discolors the gold, leaving it steel-gray instead of yellow. Furthermore, platinum gives the parting acid a brown or blackish color according to the amount present, but small amounts might not be detected this way. If, however, the appearance of the bead leads one to suspect the presence of platinum the above indications would help to confirm its presence.

PALLADIUM yields an orange-colored solution in nitric acid parting. This test is very delicate, so that even 0.05 milligrams in a small bead gives a distinct coloration to the solution.

IRIDIUM appears in the parted gold as detached black specks retaining their color after annealing.

Errors Resulting from Parting Operations. — In addition to platinum, iridium, and other of the rare metals which may be retained and weighed as gold there is always a small amount of silver which persistently resists solution. The amount depends upon a number of factors, chief of which are the ratio of silver to

* Trans. Inst. Min. and Met. 23, p. 177.

gold in the original bead, the strength of acid used and the time of acid treatment. Under ordinary conditions this silver retained probably amounts to about 0.05 per cent of the weight of the gold.

When gold disintegrates in parting on account of the presence of impurities in the bead, part of it is invariably lost in decantation. This decanted gold is often so finely divided as to be invisible.

If the parting acid contains impurities, particularly chlorine in any form, some of the gold is sure to be dissolved. Even pure nitric acid, if concentrated and boiling, dissolves a small amount, according to Rose* about 0.05 per cent. The silver retained and the gold dissolved in pure acid produce errors so small as to be negligible, but the loss resulting from the use of impure acid and the decantation loss must be carefully guarded against.

There are a number of errors in the determination of gold which should be obvious and which can be either avoided or corrected. Such errors need not be discussed here.

Recovery of Gold Lost in Decantation. — Because of the effect of impurities in the bead or for other reasons, some of the gold may disintegrate in parting and be lost in decantation. This decanted gold is often so finely divided as to be invisible, and is therefore lost in ordinary commercial work. It may be readily collected, however, by the precipitation of a small amount of silver chloride which carries it down in settling. The precipitate containing the gold is then filtered off, dried and scorified with lead. The button is cupeled and the bead parted.

Testing Nitric Acid for Impurities. CHLORIDES. — To test for the presence of hydrochloric acid take about 10 c.c. of acid and pour a few c.c. of silver nitrate solution cautiously down the side of the tube, so that the two liquids do not mix. If chlorides, bromides or iodides are present, a precipitate in the form of a ring will appear where the two liquids come together. This test is more delicate than mixing the two solutions. It is not necessary to try to distinguish between the three haloids, as, if any precipitate is found, the acid must be either rejected or purified.

* Metallurgy of Gold, Sixth Ed., p. 541.

CHLORATES. — Nitric acid often contains chlorine in the form of chloric acid, and this does not give a precipitate with silver nitrate. The chloric acid must first be decomposed before the chlorine will precipitate as silver chloride. To test nitric acid for chlorates take about 250 c.c. in a beaker and add 1 c.c. of silver nitrate solution. In the absence of any precipitate which would indicate the presence of chlorides, etc., add about 5 grams of some metal to reduce the chloric salt. Silver, zinc or copper will do. Heat nearly to boiling to dissolve the metal. If chloric acid is present a precipitate of silver chloride will form. To confirm, observe solubility in water and in cold dilute ammonia, also effect of sunlight.

Testing Wash Water, etc. — The water used for washing the parted gold and for diluting the nitric acid should be distilled to ensure its purity. Any chlorides in the wash water will of course precipitate in the parting vessel as silver chloride and if not removed will be weighed as gold. The wash water should be carefully tested by slightly acidifying with nitric acid and then pouring in silver nitrate as in testing the nitric acid. If distilled water is not available and water at hand contains a small amount of chlorides the proper combining proportion of silver nitrate may be added, the whole well mixed and then allowed to stand until the silver chloride settles out. Care must be taken to avoid adding an excess of silver nitrate, for obvious reasons. If by any chance silver chloride has been precipitated in the parting cups, the addition of a little ammonia will cause it to dissolve, after which the washing may be completed with pure water.

Testing Silver Foil for Gold. — It is never safe to assume that so-called C. P. silver is free from gold, until it has been tested and proven so. A simple dissolving of the foil in nitric acid is hardly sufficient as small amounts of gold might escape recognition in this way. A better method is to fuse about a gram into a bead and dissolve this slowly in hot dilute nitric acid. The best method is to dissolve about 10 grams in nitric acid, dilute slightly and add a small quantity of a solution of sodium chloride. This will precipitate some silver chloride which will collect any finely divided gold. Allow this precipitate to settle, then filter it off, dry and scorify with lead. Cupel the button and part the small bead obtained. This should give all the gold in one piece.

CHAPTER VII.

THE SCORIFICATION ASSAY.

The scorification assay is the simplest method for the determination of gold and silver in ores and furnace products. It consists simply of an oxidizing muffle fusion of the ore with granulated lead and borax-glass. The lead oxide formed combines with the silica of the ore and also to a certain extent dissolves the oxides of the other metals. The only reagents used other than lead are borax-glass and occasionally powdered silica, which aid in the slagging of the basic oxides.

The scorifier is a shallow, circular fire-clay dish 2 or 3 inches in diameter. The sizes most commonly used are $2\frac{1}{2}$, $2\frac{3}{4}$ and 3 inches in diameter.

The amount of ore used varies from 0.05 A. T. to 0.25 A. T., the amount most commonly used being 0.10 A. T. With this is used from 30 to 70 grams of test lead and from 1 to 5 grams of borax-glass, depending on the amount of base metal impurities present. Sometimes powdered silica and occasionally litharge are also used. With nearly pure galena, or a mixture of galena and silica, a charge of 30 to 35 grams of test lead and 1 gram of borax-glass will suffice for 0.10 A. T., of ore, but when the ore contains nickel, copper, cobalt, arsenic, antimony, zinc, iron, tin, etc., a larger and larger amount of lead and borax-glass must be used according to the relative ease with which the metals are oxidized and the solubility of their oxides in the slags formed. Of the above, copper especially is very difficultly oxidized and when much is present in the ore the lead button from the first scorification will have to be rescorified once or twice with added lead. Iron, on the other hand, is comparatively readily oxidized, and except for the necessity of adding an extra amount of lead and borax-glass to make a fluid slag the ore is as readily assayed as galena. Lime, zinc, and antimony require especially large amounts of borax-glass to convert their refractory oxides into a fusible slag.

Solubility of Metallic Oxides in Litharge. — Litharge although a strong base, has the power of holding in igneous solution certain quantities of other metallic oxides. This has an important bearing on the ease or difficulty with which various metals may be slagged in scorification. According to Berthier and Percy, the solubilities of the various metallic oxides in litharge are as shown in the following table:

One part of	Cu_2O	CuO	ZnO	Fe_2O_3	MnO	SnO_2	TiO_2
Requires parts of PbO	1.5	1.8	8	10	10	12	8

Antimony trioxide (Sb_2O_3) dissolves in litharge in all proportions.

Heat of Formation of Metallic Oxides. — Another important factor having to do with the elimination of impurities by scorification is the relative heat of formation of the various metallic oxides. In a mixture of various metallic sulphides, (assuming for a moment the ignition temperature to be the same for all), that reaction in which is evolved the greatest amount of heat would naturally proceed at the fastest rate. The heat of combination of various metals each with 16 grams of oxygen is shown in the following table. This basis is used on the assumption that the amount of oxygen is limited.

TABLE XV.

HEAT OF FORMATION OF METALLIC OXIDES.

Reaction.	Heat of comb. with 16gO	Reaction.	Heat of comb. with 16gO
Zinc to ZnO	84,800	Bismuth to Bi_2O_3	$\frac{139,200}{3} = 46,400$
Tin to SnO_2	$\frac{141,300}{2} = 70,650$	Copper to Cu_2O	43,800
Iron to FeO	65,700	Sulphur to SO_2	$\frac{69,260}{2} = 34,630$
Cobalt to CoO	64,100		
Nickel to NiO	61,500	Tellurium to TeO_2	$\frac{38,600}{2} = 19,300$
Antimony to Sb_2O_3	$\frac{166,900}{3} = 55,600$	Silver to Ag_2O	7,000
Arsenic to As_2O_3	$= \frac{156,400}{3} = 52,100$	Gold to Au_2O_3	$-\frac{11,500}{3} = -3,800$
Lead to PbO	50,800		

Ignition Temperature of Metallic Sulphides. — The ignition temperature of the metallic sulphides may also be of interest in this connection.

TABLE XVI.

Ignition Temperatures[1] of Metallic Sulphides when Heated in Air.

Material	Formula	Ignition Temp. °C.	Material	Formula	Ignition Temp. °C.
Stibnite	Sb_2S_3	290–340	Galena [2]	PbS	554–847
Pyrite	FeS_2	325–427	Millerite	NiS	573–616
Pyrrhotite	Fe_xS_{x+1}	430–590	Argentite	Ag_2S	605–873
Chalcocite	Cu_2S	430–679	Sphalerite	ZnS	647–810

[1] Friedrich, Metallurgie, 6, p. 170 (1909).
[2] In Oxygen.

The metals in Table XV are arranged in order of their heats of combination with oxygen, expressed in terms of a unit weight of oxygen. This is the order in which they will be removed in scorification or cupellation. In general it may be said that the metals in a molten alloy, such as a lead button on a cupel, or the lead alloy in a scorifier, are oxidized in succession, each partly protecting those which are less easily oxidized than itself. This separation is not quantitative however, owing to the effect of mass action, and in the case under discussion, where we have a large amount of lead and small amounts of other metals, a considerable amount of lead would be oxidized during the complete oxidation of the metals above it in the table.

Those metals which lie below lead in the table will be but slowly slagged in scorification and only at the expense of a large amount of lead. Thus, during scorification or cupellation, bismuth, copper and tellurium are concentrated in the residual unoxidized lead and this explains why it is so difficult to separate these metals from silver by scorification and cupellation. This can only be done by repeated scorification with fresh lead and, as might be expected, this will result in a considerable loss of silver.

From their positions in the table, it is evident that silver is not easily oxidized and that gold is protected by all other metals.

To one who has a knowledge of the mineral character of the ore, a glance at the ignition temperature of the sulphides shown in Table XVI will afford an idea of the initial temperature required for scorification. From a comparison of the heats of oxidation of the metals present with that of lead, the relative ease or difficulty of their elimination in scorification may be determined; and a knowledge of the solubility of the metal oxides in litharge and in borax will indicate the relation between ore, lead and flux which will give the most satisfactory results.

A small amount of nickel will cause more trouble in scorification and cupellation than any other metal. This is largely due to the insolubility of its oxide in litharge. The presence of copper seems to increase the difficulty of eliminating it from the lead. In scorifying ores containing nickel but no copper, practically all of the nickel comes out in the first slag, making it lumpy, to be sure, but leaving the lead practically clean. When copper is also present the button will require rescorification and much nickel scoria is found in the second scorifier. Brown[*] calls attention to a similar action of nickel in converting copper-nickel matte. In this case the nickel does not behave like iron, as it might be expected to do by reason of its heat of oxidation, but like copper, which has a much lower heat of oxidation. It was found impossible to slag off the nickel without at the same time removing a large part of the copper. In fact the nickel-copper alloy acts like one metal and follows the same laws that govern the behavior of copper alone. No adequate explanation of this behavior is known.

SCORIFICATION ASSAY OF SILVER ORE.

Procedure. — Empty the bottle or envelope of ore on to a sheet of glazed paper or oilcloth and mix thoroughly by rolling.

Take three scorifiers, $2\frac{1}{2}$, $2\frac{3}{4}$, and 3 inches in diameter respectively. Weigh out on the flux balance three portions of granulated lead 35, 45, and 55 grams respectively. Divide each lot of lead approximately in halves, transfer one-half of each to the corresponding scorifier and reserve the remaining portions. Weigh out three portions of exactly 0.1 A. T. of ore on the pulp balance and place on top of the lead in the scorifiers. Mix thoroughly with the spatula and cover with the remaining portions of lead. Scatter 1 or 2 grams of borax-glass on top of the lead. The scorifiers are now ready for the muffle, which should be light red or yellow before the charges are put in. This temperature should be maintained during the first part of the roasting period.

[*] Trans. A.I.M.E., **41**, p. 296.

FUSION PERIOD. — Place the scorifiers about midway in the muffle, close the door and allow the contents to become thoroughly fused.

ROASTING PERIOD. — When thoroughly fused, open the door to admit air to oxidize the ore and lead. If the ore contains sulphides these will now be seen floating on the top of the molten lead. The sulphur from these is burned going off as SO_2 and the base metals are oxidized and slagged. The precious metals remain unoxidized and are taken up by the lead bath. These patches of ore grow smaller and soon disappear, after which the surface of the melt becomes smooth, consisting of a bath of molten lead surrounded by a ring of slag.

The vapor rising from the assays will often indicate the character of the ore. Sulphur gives clear gray fumes, arsenic grayish-white and antimony reddish. Zinc vapor is blackish and the zinc itself may be seen burning with a bright white flame.

SCORIFICATION PERIOD. — The lead continues to oxidize and the ring of slag around the circumference of the scorifier becomes larger as more of the lead is oxidized. Finally the whole of the lead is covered with slag and the scorification is finished. The ore should be completely decomposed and practically all of the gold and silver should be alloyed with the metallic lead.

LIQUEFACTION PERIOD. — Close the door of the muffle and increase the heat for a few minutes to make the slag thoroughly liquid and to ensure a clean pour. Then pour the contents of the scorifiers into a dry, warm, scorifier mold which has been previously coated with chalk or iron oxide. Pour into the center of the mold, being careful to see that the lead does not spatter and that all of it comes together in one piece. The inside surface of the scorifiers should be smooth and glassy, showing no lumps of ore or undecomposed material.

When the slag is cold examine it and the sides of the mold carefully for shots of lead. These are most likely to occur at the contact of the slag with the mold, and if found should be saved and added to the main button. Next separate the main lead button from the slag, hammer it into the form of a cube and weigh to the nearest gram on the flux balance.

If the lead is soft and malleable, and the color of the scorifier does not indicate the presence of large amounts of copper, nickel or cobalt, the button is ready for cupellation. If it is hard or brittle it may contain impurities which must be removed by re-scorifying with an additional amount of granulated lead.

Finally cupel and weigh the resultant silver or doré beads. Report in your notes the weight of ore and reagents used, the weight of lead button obtained, as well as the weight and assay in ounces per ton of gold and silver. Note also the time of scorification and cupellation and describe the appearance of the scorifier and cupel.

Notes: 1. The ore must be so fine that a sample of 0.1 A. T. will truly represent the whole; 100-mesh may be fine enough for some ores, 170-mesh may be necessary for some others.

2. In weighing out the ore, spread the sample which has been thoroughly mixed, into a thin sheet on the glazed paper at one side of the pulp balance. Place the weight on the right-hand pan and the ore on the left-hand pan. With the spatula mark the ore off into squares 1 inch or so on a side, and then take a small portion from every square for the sample, being sure to take a section from top to bottom of the ore. During this first sampling the scale-pan should be held over the paper in one hand and the spatula in the other. When what is judged to be the right amount of ore is obtained the pan is put back on the balance and the hand with which it was held is used to turn the balance key.

The balance should be turned out of action each time ore is put on or taken off the scale-pan and the pointer need move only 1 or 2 divisions to indicate whether too much or too little ore is on the pan. To obtain the final balance, have a little too much ore in the pan, take off enough on the point of the spatula to reverse the condition of balance. With the balance key lift the beam only enough to allow the pointer to swing 1 or 2 divisions to the left of the center and then hold the key in this position. Hold the spatula over the pan and by tapping it gently with the first finger allow the ore to slide off onto the scale-pan a few grains at a time, until the balance is restored and the needle swings over to the center. By repeating this process, rejecting the ore retained on the spatula each time, an exact weight can soon be obtained.

3. The value of the results depends upon the care which is taken in mixing, sampling and weighing out the charges. Do not attempt to save time by slighting the mixing, for if a true sample is not obtained at this point no amount of subsequent care will avail to give reliable results.

4. Instead of being weighed, the granulated lead may be measured with sufficient accuracy by the use of a shot measure or small crucible. The borax-glass may also be measured.

5. The size of scorifier to be used depends upon the amount of ore, lead, borax-glass and silica used, and should be such as to give a button of approximately 15 to 18 grams. If a large scorifier is used with a small amount of lead the resulting lead button will be very small and a high loss of silver will result. Again, the larger the amount of borax-glass that is used the more slag there will be and the sooner the lead will be covered.

6. If the contents of the scorifiers do not become thoroughly liquid and show a smooth surface of slag after ten or fifteen minutes, the assays require either more heat, more borax-glass or more lead.

7. If the ore contains much tin, antimony, arsenic, nickel or large amounts of basic oxides such as hematite, magnetite,. etc., an infusible scoria is almost certain to form on the surface of the slag or on the sides of the scorifier which neither a high temperature nor extra borax-glass will remove. As this scoria is likely to enclose particles of undecomposed ore the only safe procedure is to make a fresh assay with less ore, and with such other changes in charge and manipulation as the experience of the first assay may suggest.

8. Ores containing pyrite require a higher temperature during the roasting period than those containing galena.

9. Some assayers add litharge to the scorification charge, especially with pyritic ores. On heating, the litharge is reduced to metallic lead, the sulphur of the pyrite being oxidized.

10. Litharge, being a strong base, has a great affinity for the silica of the scorifier and, especially when mixed with copper oxide, it attacks this silica readily. When scorifying matte and copper bullion it is often necessary to add powdered silica to the charge to prevent a hole being eaten through the scorifier.

11. The lead button should weigh from 12 to 20 grams. If it is much smaller than this there is danger of a loss of silver due to oxidation, especially when the ore is rich. If the button is too large it may be rescorified in a new scorifier to the size desired.

12. Hard buttons may be due to copper, antimony or in fact almost any metal alloyed with the lead. Brittle buttons may be due to one of many alloyed metals, or to the presence of sulphur or lead oxide.

13. The scorifier slag should be homogeneous and glassy. If non-homogeneous it probably contains undecomposed ore.

14. The white patches occasionally found in the slag are made up mostly of lead sulphate which is formed when the scorification temperature is low.

15. Scorifier slags are essentially oxide slags and consist of metallic oxides dissolved in an excess of molten litharge, together with smaller amounts of dissolved silicates and borates.

16. If too low an initial temperature is employed or if the muffle door is opened too soon, the scorification losses may be considerable, owing to the retention in the slag, or on the sides of the scorifier, of undecomposed silver minerals.

The scorification assay is simple, inexpensive and reasonably rapid. For the determination of silver in sulphide ores having an acid gangue, it is generally satisfactory and widely used. It is particularly suited for the determination of silver in ores containing considerable amounts of the sulphides, arsenides or antimonides of the difficultly oxidizable base metals, particularly copper, nickel and cobalt. It is used in many localities for silver in all sulphide ores, as well as for gold and silver in copper bullion, impure lead bullion, copper and nickel mattes and speiss.

It is not to be recommended for pure ores, low in silver, because of the difficulty of handling and weighing the small beads obtained. Rich ores have to be weighed more carefully for scorification assays, than for crucible assays where usually two and a half to five times as much ore is used, in order to obtain the same precision. The ordinary charge using 0.10 assay-ton of ore, does not give a close enough approximation on a gold ore for commercial purposes. Therefore, in the case of ores, this method is restricted to those containing only silver. Ores containing both silver and gold will ordinarily be assayed by the crucible method so as to obtain gold results of the necessary precision.

There is no good reason for scorifying ores or products which do not require oxidation, and scorification is entirely unfitted for those ores carrying higher oxides such as magnetite, hematite, pyrolusite, etc. It is not suitable for ores having any considerable amount of basic gangue as but a small quantity of acid reagents can be used. It should not be used on ores containing volatile constituents such as carbonates and minerals containing water of crystallization which tend to cause spitting and consequent loss of alloy. Volatile compounds of the precious metals are more likely to escape from a scorifier than from a crucible because of the exposed conditions of the ore in the former.

Chemical Reactions in Scorification. REACTIONS DUE TO HEAT ALONE.—Various chemical changes may be caused by heat alone, so that during the fusion period, even in the absence of oxygen, the hydrates give up their water, most of the carbonates give up their carbon dioxide and are converted into oxides and even some of the sulphates are decomposed.

Chalcopyrite breaks up as follows when heated to 200° C.:

$$2 \, Cu \, FeS_2 = Cu_2S + 2 \, FeS + S.$$

As soon as the temperature rises above 540° C. the iron and copper sulphides melt, forming matte.

Pyrite, when heated to redness, is decomposed about as follows:

$$7 \, FeS_2 = Fe_7S_8 + 6 \, S.$$

The exact composition of the residual iron sulphide depends upon the temperature and the partial pressure of the sulphur vapor. For all practical purposes the reaction may be written

$$FeS_2 = FeS + S.$$

During the fusion stage the lead melts and reacts with any silver sulphide which may be present, as follows:

$$Ag_2S + Pb = 2\,Ag + PbS.$$

The metallic silver is immediately dissolved by the excess of molten lead.

SLAG FORMING REACTIONS. — According to the evidence of freezing-point diagrams a few simple combinations of silica and the various metallic oxides form compounds. So we are justified in writing reactions such as the following:

$$2\,PbO + SiO_2 = Pb_2SiO_4.$$

This may be termed a slag-forming reaction but, in general, slags, as far as we know, are igneous solutions of one constituent oxide in another. In the molten state they follow the laws of solutions and should be so considered.

Most chemical reactions cause either an evolution or an absorption of a considerable quantity of heat, but, from what little evidence we have, the heats of formation of silicates and borates from their component oxides is very small and it is doubtful whether these combinations should be termed reactions.

SIMPLE OXIDATION. — As soon as the air is admitted to the muffle, the lead begins to oxidize to PbO, and this oxidation continues through the whole scorification period.

ROASTING REACTIONS. — The sulphides in the ore are roasted as indicated by the following reactions:

$$FeS + 3O = FeO + SO_2,$$
$$PbS + 3O = PbO + SO_2,$$
$$2PbS + 7O = PbO + PbSO_4 + SO_2,$$
$$ZnS + 3O = ZnO + SO_2,$$
$$Sb_2S_3 + 9O = Sb_2O_3 + 3SO_2.$$

Part of the Sb_2O_3 is volatilized, and part of it is oxidized to Sb_2O_5 and combines with litharge, forming lead antimonates, $xPbO.ySb_2O_5$. Arsenic behaves much like antimony.

The roasting reactions shown above are exothermic and, owing to the escape of the sulphur dioxide, proceed rapidly in a right-handed direction.

REACTIONS BETWEEN SULPHIDES AND OXIDES. — After enough PbO has been formed to slag the siliceous gangue, the litharge which is formed reacts on the partially decomposed sulphides, aiding in the elimination of sulphur, thus:

$$PbS + 2PbO = 3Pb + SO_2,$$
$$ZnS + 3PbO = 3Pb + ZnO + SO_2,$$
$$Ag_2S + 2PbO = 2Pb.Ag + SO_2,$$
$$As_2S_3 + 9PbO = As_2O_3 + 3SO_2 + 9Pb.$$

Lead sulphate also reacts with lead sulphide as indicated by the following reactions:

$$PbS + PbSO_4 = 2Pb + 2SO_2,$$
$$PbS + 2PbSO_4 = Pb + 2PbO + 3SO_2,$$
$$PbS + 3PbSO_4 = 4PbO + 4SO_2.$$

The double reactions shown above are endothermic, and hence are probably relatively unimportant in scorification.

If Cu_2S were present in the ore, part of it would be oxidized to CuO, and then the cuprous sulphide and the cupric oxide would tend to react as follows:

$$Cu_2S + 2CuO = 4Cu + SO_2.$$

A similar reaction between the litharge and the cuprous sulphide would probably take place as follows:

$$Cu_2S + 2PbO = 2CuPb + SO_2.$$

A prolonged scorification is required to remove the copper thus reduced and alloyed with the lead. The last two reactions are more pronounced at high temperatures, so that for the elimination of copper in the scorification assay it is evident that a low muffle temperature should be maintained.

Indications of Metals Present. — The color of the thin coating of slag on the scorifier is an indication of the amount and kind of metal originally present in the ore, and taken in connection with the mineralogical examination of the ore it gives a very good approximation as to its composition.

COPPER gives a light or dark green, depending on the amount present. If there is much iron in the ore this color may be wholly or in part obscured by the black of the iron oxide. Practically all of the iron is removed in the first scorification, so that in assaying a copper matte the first scorifier may appear black while the second one will be green. The green color is said to be due to a mixture of blue cupric silicate and yellow lead silicate.

IRON. — A large amount of iron makes the scorifier black, from which the color ranges from a deep red through various shades of brown to a yellow brown.

LEAD, in the absence of other metals, makes the scorifier lemon-yellow to a very pale yellow.

COBALT gives a beautiful blue if other metals do not interfere.

NICKEL colors the scorifier brown to black depending on the amount present. When much nickel is present the cupel becomes covered with a thick film of green nickel oxide.

MANGANESE colors the scorifier brownish-black to a beautiful wine-color.

ARSENIC and ANTIMONY, if present in large amounts, will leave crusts on the inner surface of the scorifier even if much borax-glass is used. In the absence of other metals the scoria will be yellow in color.

If a scorifier is colored dark green, indicating much copper, dark blue, indicating much cobalt, or black with infusible scoria, indicating nickel, the button should be scorified again with more lead.

Rescorifying Buttons. — When it is necessary to rescorify buttons to remove copper or other impurities, or when bullion is assayed by scorification, a good plan is to place the scorifiers containing the right amount of test lead in a hot muffle. When the molten lead has ceased spitting, the button, or bullion, is dropped in. This precaution is suggested to prevent loss of bullion by spitting which occurs quite often in rescorifying, probably because of moisture in the scorifier. Another method is to place the scorifier in the muffle and heat for ten or fifteen minutes and then drop in the buttons and the proper amount of lead.

Buttons weighing over 35 grams should be scorified to 15 or 20 grams before being cupeled. If this is carefully done, the loss of silver should be less by the combined method than by direct cupellation.

Spitting of Scorifiers. — Occasionally small particles of lead are seen being projected out of the scorifier. This is due to decrepitation of the ore or to the action of some gas given off by the ore or scorifier itself. If the particles of lead do not all fall back into the scorifier a loss of precious metal will result. The direct cause may be found among the following and a proper remedy applied:

1. Dampness of scorifier.
2. Presence of carbonates in clay from which scorifier was made.
3. Imperfect mixing of charge, resulting in ore being left on the bottom of the scorifier and covered with lead.
4. Too high a temperature at the start, resulting in too rapid oxidation of sulphides, evolution of CO_2 or violent decrepitation.
5. Admittance of air into the muffle too soon, resulting in too rapid oxidation. (Especially to be avoided in the case of ores or products carrying zinc.)
6. Character of the ore itself. (Ores containing carbonates etc., are not suited for scorification.)

Assaying Granulated Lead. — Almost all assay reagents contain traces of gold and silver, but the lead and litharge are especially likely to contain these metals in appreciable amounts. Each new lot of granulated lead which is obtained should be sampled and assayed before it is used, and in case any silver or gold is found a strict account must be kept of the lead used in each assay and a correction for its precious metal contents made.

PROCEDURE. — Scorify 2 or 3 portions of 120 grams each in $3\frac{1}{2}$ or 4 inch scorifiers. If necessary rescorify until the buttons are reduced to 15 or 20 grams. Cupel, weigh and part. This correction must be made even if extremely small, as any error thus introduced would be multiplied by 10 in reporting the results in ounces per ton.

Scorification Assay for Gold. — The silver in an ore can be determined with a sufficient degree of accuracy by taking 0.1 A. T. for each assay, since we may thus determine the contents of the ore to 0.1 of an ounce, or its value to 5 or 10 cents a ton. When, however, we determine gold to 0.1 ounce per ton by this same method, we have determined its value to only $2.00 per ton, which is not sufficiently accurate for any but very high-grade ores. For this reason the scorification assay is not usually chosen for gold ores unless they contain impurities which interfere seriously with the crucible assay.

SCORIFICATION ASSAY OF COPPER MATTE.

Procedure. — Take three portions of 0.1 A. T. of matte, mix with 45 grams of granulated lead and 1 gram powdered silica in a 3-inch Bartlett scorifier, and cover with 60 grams more of lead. Put half a gram of borax-glass and 1 gram of silica on top. Scorify hot at first and then at a low temperature to facilitate slagging the copper.

When the lead eye covers, pour as usual and separate the lead from the slag. Weigh each button and add sufficient granulated lead to bring the total weight to 60 grams and drop into three new scorifiers which have been heated in the muffle. Add about 1 gram of silica and scorify at a low temperature.

If necessary, repeat this second scorification until the cool scorifiers are light-green. Cupel as usual. The color of the cupel should be greenish and not black. The latter color indicates insufficient scorification.

Weigh the combined silver and gold and part, weighing the gold.

Notes: 1. For matte containing not more than 30 per cent of copper two scorifications are sufficient.

2. This method gives rather high slag and cupel losses and for exact work the slags and cupels are reassayed and a correction made for their silver and gold contents.

3. The final silver beads will often contain from 2 to 4 per cent of copper.

4. When accurate results in gold are desired, as many as 10 portions of 0.1 A. T. each of matte are scorified and the buttons combined for parting and weighing.

Losses in Scorification. — Losses in scorification may be due to "spitting," volatilization, oxidation and slagging as well as to shots of alloy lost in pouring. Some loss due to oxidation and slagging is unavoidable, but it should be low. If there is any decided loss by volatilization it shows that the process is unsuited to the ore.

The tendency of scorification assays to "spit" is one of the most serious objections to the process. Ores which decrepitate or contain volatile constituents such as CO_2, H_2O, etc., ($CaCO_3$, $CaSO_4.2H_2O$) are unsuited to the process and should be assayed by crucible methods. Very often a preliminary glazing of the scorifier with a mixture of sodium carbonate and borax-glass will prevent spitting. The scorifiers should always be kept in a warm, dry place.

Losses of alloy, due to failure of all the lead to collect in one piece, may be caused by careless pouring, in which case some of the lead may splash on the side of the mold and solidify there, or by a poor slag, or a cold pour, resulting in shots of alloy being left in the scorifier or scattered through the slag in the mold.

As scorification is an oxidizing process it is only reasonable to expect some loss due to oxidation of the precious metals, and this will naturally be greater the longer the scorification is continued and the more intense the oxidizing action. Silver is more easily oxidized than gold, therefore we should expect a much greater loss of silver than of gold. To keep this loss at a minimum let the liquefaction period be thorough. The molten lead tends to reduce and collect some of the silver previously slagged. Some assayers recommend sprinkling a small amount of charcoal over the slag in the scorifier just before closing the door of the muffle for the liquefaction period, with the idea of reducing some lead from the slag and thus collecting most of the oxidized silver by the rain of lead shot thus induced. English authorities almost invariably recommend this practice which they term "cleaning the slag."

Keller* gives average figures for corrected assays on anode mud known to contain 3750 ounces of silver per ton. Assays were by scorification and in one series scorifications and cupellations were run hot while in the other they were run cool. The results, each representing an average of twenty individual assays, are shown in the following table:

TABLE XVII.
Assays of Copper Anode Residues.

Origin	Hot scorification and cupellation		Cool scorification and cupellation	
	Silver oz. per ton	Gold oz. per ton	Silver oz. per ton	Gold oz. per ton
In beads...........	3613.12	28.030	3688.85	27.815
In slag.............	55.38	0.010	56.44	0.020
In cupels..........	21.64	0.045	20.93	0.025
In decantation....	....	0.075	....	0.225
Total.............	3690.14	28.160	3766.22	28.085

* Trans. A.I.M.E., 60, p. 706.

The greatest difference between hot and cool assays is shown in the uncorrected assay results. The other figures agree surprisingly well. The loss of silver shown by these figures is very high, due to the repeated scorifications necessary and the effect of copper in increasing the loss. The loss of gold is extremely small and serves to illustrate the protective action of silver on gold.

The difference in temperature of hot and cool cupellations could not have been great, or else the cool scorification gave purer buttons for cupellation, as the cupel losses differ very little.

Because of the low results of the corrected assays, in the case of hot scorifications and cupellations, compared with the known silver content of 3750 ounces per ton, Keller concludes that there must have been a decided loss of silver by volatilization. This is a good argument for cool scorification in copper work as well as for cool cupellation.

The gold lost in decantation, in the case of beads resulting from cool work, is three times that for beads resulting from hot work. This difference he claims to be due to increased disintegration of the gold, because of the presence of added impurities retained in the beads resulting from cool cupellation.

Use of Large Ore Charges in Scorification. — While the usual charge for a scorification assay is 0.1 assay-ton, Simonds* claims to be able to obtain good results on practically all classes of sulphide ores using 0.5 assay-ton of ore, 75 grams of lead and 2.5 grams of borax-glass in a 3-inch shallow scorifier. This should certainly cause no difficulty with mixtures consisting only of galena and quartz.

Scorification Charges for Different Materials. — The following charges have been found generally satisfactory:

* California Mines and Minerals, p. 226 (1899).

TABLE XVIII.
Scorification Charges.

Material	Charge					Heat high at first then
	Ore Assay Tons	Granu- lated lead Grams	Borax- glass Grams	Silica Grams	Scorifier Inches	
Galena............	0.1	35	½–1	—	2¼	Low
Half galena, half silica............	0.1	35	½–1	—	2¼	Low
Low grade galena.	0.2	45	½–1	—	2½	Low
Pyrite............	0.1	50	2–3	—	2¾	Medium
Half pyrite, half silica............	0.1	45	1–2	—	2½	Medium
Stibnite..........	0.1	50–60	1–2	—	2¾–3	High
Sphalerite........	0.1	60	3–5	1–2	3	High
Arsenical ore....	0.1	45–60	1–2	—	2¾–3	High
Cobalt ore........	0.1	60	3	—	3	High
Nickel ore........	0.05–0.1	60	3	—	3	High
Chalcopyrite.....	0.1	60	1–2	1	3	Low
Tin ore	0.1	60–70	2–3	1	3–3½	High
Lead matte.......	0.1	50	½	—	2¾	Low
Copper matte.....	0.1	60	1	1	3	Low

CHAPTER VIII.

THE CRUCIBLE ASSAY.

Theory of the Crucible Assay. — The majority of ores are, by themselves infusible, or nearly so, but if pulverized and mixed in proper proportion with suitable reagents, the mixture will fuse at an easily attained temperature. The finer the ore is crushed, the better and more uniform are the results obtained. We assume in considering a crucible assay that there is such a thorough mixture of ore and fluxes that each particle of ore is in contact with one or more particles of litharge and reducing agent. As the temperature of the mass is gradually raised, part of the litharge is reduced to lead (commencing at 500° to 550° C.) by the carbon of the charge, and these reduced shots of lead, alloy and take up the gold and silver from the surrounding particles of ore, so far at least as the precious metals are free to alloy.

At about this same temperature, 560° C., the borax of the charge begins to melt and to form fusible compounds with some of the bases of the flux and ore charge. In the absence of borax or other fusible constituents, lead oxide and silica commence to combine at about 700° C., and from this point the slag begins to form rapidly. The conditions should be such that the slag remains viscous until the ore particles are thoroughly decomposed and every particle of gold and silver has been taken up by the adjacent suspended globules of lead. After this point has been passed, the temperature may be raised until the slag is thoroughly fluid, when the lead particles combine and, falling through the slag, form a button in the bottom of the crucible in which are concentrated practically all of the precious metals originally present in the ore.

To make an intelligent crucible assay it is necessary to know the mineral character of the ore, for a siliceous ore requires a different treatment from one which is mostly limestone and a sulphide requires to be treated differently from an oxide. For the purpose of the assayer, ores should be considered from two standpoints, first according to the character and quantity of their slag-forming constituents, and second according as they are oxidizing, neutral or reducing in the crucible fusion with lead and lead oxide.

Ores Classified According to Slag-forming Constituents. — The principal slag-forming constituents of ores and gangue minerals, arranged approximately in the order of their occurrence in the earth's crust are as follows:

Silica	SiO_2	⎫ Acids
Alumina	Al_2O_3	⎬
Ferrous oxide	FeO	
Manganous oxide	MnO	
Calcium oxide	CaO	
Magnesium oxide	MgO	⎬ Bases
Sodium oxide	Na_2O	
Potassium oxide	K_2O	
Zinc oxide	ZnO	
Lead oxide	PbO	
Cuprous oxide	Cu_2O	⎭

These oxides, with the exception of those of sodium, potassium and lead, are infusible at the temperature of the assay-furnace. To get them into the molten condition we add fluxes. All of the common assay fluxes with the exception of silica are readily fusible by themselves. In general it may be said that to flux the acid, silica, it is necessary to add bases and to flux any of the basic oxides, acids must be added. To flux alumina it is best to add both acids and bases.

Ores Classified According to Oxidizing or Reducing Character. — According to their oxidizing or reducing character in the crucible assay, ores may divided into three classes as follows:

CLASS 1. NEUTRAL ORES. — Siliceous, oxide and carbonate ores or ores containing no sulphides, arsenides, antimonides, tellurides, etc., *i.e.*, ores having no reducing or oxidizing power.

CLASS 2. ORES HAVING A REDUCING POWER. — Ores containing sulphides, arsenides, antimonides, tellurides, carbonaceous matter, etc., or ores which decompose litharge with a reduction of lead in the crucible fusion.

CLASS 3. ORES HAVING AN OXIDIZING POWER. — Ores containing ferric oxide, manganese dioxide, etc., or ores which when fused with fluxes oxidize lead or reducing agents. Ores with any considerable oxidizing power are comparatively rare.

Determining the Character of a Sample. — The mineral character of an ore can be most readily determined when the ore is in the coarse condition. However, as a large proportion of the samples received by the assayer are already pulverized, it becomes

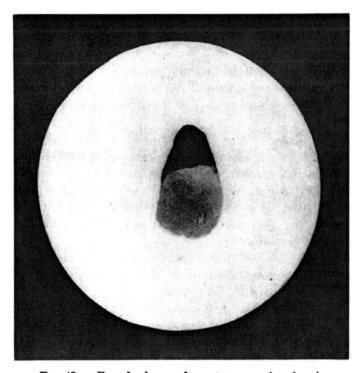

FIG. 43. — Fan of galena and quartz on vanning-shovel.

necessary for him to be able to form a close estimate of their composition in this condition. This may be best accomplished by washing a small sample on a vanning-plaque or shovel.

Place one or two grams of the ore on the vanning-shovel, cover it with water and allow it to stand until the ore is thoroughly wet, then shake violently in a horizontal plane until the fine slime is in suspension and all lumps are broken up. Allow to settle a moment, decant some of the water if necessary and then separate the ore according to the specific gravity of its different minerals by a combined washing and shaking. The water should be made to flow over the ore in one direction only and the velocity of the shaking motion should be accelerated in a direction opposite to the flow of the water. The shaking tends to stratify the ore, heaviest next the pan, lightest on top, while the water tends to wash everything downward, the material on top being most affected because of its position, and also because of its lesser specific gravity. Finally, if there are a number of minerals present, they should appear spread out in fan shape in the order of their specific gravity, for instance, galena, pyrite, sphalerite and quartz.

Figure 43 shows a fan of galena and quartz on a vanning-shovel. If account is taken of the specific gravity of the different minerals, an experienced operator can make a reasonably good estimate of the percentage of each of the common minerals present in an ore.

Crucible Slags. — The slags obtained in the crucible assay may be regarded as silicates and borates of the metallic oxides dissolved in one another and in litharge. They also often contain dissolved carbon dioxide. The acid constituents of rocks, other than silica, so seldom play an important part in the formation of slags that they may be omitted at least from a preliminary discussion of the subject.

Assay slags high in litharge and low in silica, borax and other acids are sometimes called oxide slags. Very little is known about the constitution of these slags.

Very acid slags are sometimes emulsions and not true solutions. That is, they may contain suspended solid or molten globules of other minerals.

A slag suitable for assay purposes should have the following properties:

1. It should have a comparatively low formation temperature readily attainable in assay-furnaces.

2. It should be pasty at and near its formation temperature, to hold up the particles of reduced lead until the precious metals are liberated from their mechanical or chemical bonds and are free to alloy with the lead.

3. It should be thin and fluid when heated somewhat above its melting-point, so that shots of lead may settle through it readily.

4. It should have a low capacity for gold and silver, and should allow a complete decomposition of the ore by the fluxes.

5. It should not attack the material of the crucible too violently.

6. Its specific gravity should be low, to allow a good separation of lead and slag.

7. When cold, it should separate readily from the lead and be homogeneous, thus indicating complete decomposition of the ore.

8. It should contain all the impurities of the ore and should be free from the higher oxides of the metals.

9. Except in the case of the iron-nail assay it should be free from sulphides.

Color of Crucible Slags. — As is also the case in scorification, the color of the slags resulting from crucible assays is often indicative of the metals present. Due to the larger proportion of silica and borax and the smaller amount of litharge in crucible slags the significance of the coloring is not always the same. Thus in crucible slags various shades of green may usually be ascribed to the presence of ferrous silicates and not of copper as is the case in scorification slags, while in the absence of iron, copper gives the crucible slag a brick-red color, due to the presence of cuprous silicate or borate.

Calcium, magnesium, aluminum and zinc give white or grayish-white slags, usually more or less opaque. The acid silicates of pure soda and lead are clear, colorless glasses. Cobalt gives the well-known cobalt blue. Iron and manganese in large quantities make the slag black. A small amount of manganese may, in the absence of interfering elements, yield a purple to a light pink; and as is well known by all glass-makers, a small amount serves to neutralize the color effect of iron.

Classification of Silicates. — Silicates are classified according to the proportion of the oxygen in the acid to oxygen in the base. Thus, a mono-silicate has the same amount of oxygen in the acid as in the base. A bi-silicate has twice as much oxygen in the acid as in the base and so on.

The silicates which have been found to behave satisfactorily as assay slags lie within the following limits:

TABLE XIX.
Classification of Silicates.

Name	Oxygen ratio Acid to base	Formula. R_1 = bivalent base
Sub-silicate	½ to 1	$4RO.SiO_2$
Mono- or singulo-silicate	1 to 1	$2RO.SiO_2$
Sesqui-silicate	1½ to 1	$4RO.3SiO_2$
Bi-silicate	2 to 1	$RO.SiO_2$
Tri-silicate	3 to 1	$2RO.3SiO_2$

The formation temperature and melting-point of the different silicates depend not only on the relation of the silica to base, but also on the nature of the bases present. Thus we may say that within the above range the silicates of lead and the alkalies are all readily fusible, the iron and manganese silicates are difficultly fusible and the silicates of calcium, magnesium and aluminum are infusible at the temperature of the assay-furnace. Note that so far we are referring to the individual silicates of the different bases and not to mixtures of the same.

Of these slags the bi- and the tri-silicates have but little effect on the ordinary assay crucible while the sub-silicates attack it strongly to satisfy their affinity for silica.

The student should distinguish between the formation temperature of a slag and the melting-point of the same slag when already formed. It has been shown by Day,* that when the constituents of a slag are finely crushed and intimately mixed as in an assay fusion, the formation temperature of the slag is decidedly lower than the melting temperature. That is to say, the slag forms without melting and actually passes through a pasty stage before coming to perfect fusion.

Action of Borax in Slags. — Borax ($Na_2B_4O_7 + 10H_2O$) melts at about 560° C. and gives up its water of crystallization forming borax-glass. Borax-glass when molten is decidedly viscous, and on account of its excess of boric oxide acts as an acid flux.

Although primarily an acid flux, borax exerts considerable solvent power upon the silicates as well. It lowers the temperature of slag formation and in the case of non-sulphide ores helps to make the slag viscous during the reduction period. In the

* Jour. Am. Chem. Soc., **28**, p. 1039 (Sept. 1906).

case of basic ores particularly, it reduces the temperature of final complete fluidity. According to Steel* it seems to protect the crucibles from the solvent action of litharge, probably by coating them with a viscous aluminum boro-silicate.

To determine what relation it bears to silica as regards its acid fluxing quality we may consider the matter first from a theoretical standpoint, and then from the results of experiments.

Considering the borates according to their metallurgical classification, i.e., according to the amount of oxygen in the acid to that in the base, we may compute the weight of borax-glass necessary to form a mono-borate with a unit weight of sodium carbonate and compare this with the amount of silica required to form a mono-silicate with the same amount of base. From the rational formula for borax-glass ($Na_2O.2B_2O_3$) we see that to form the mono-borate ($6Na_2O.2B_2O_3$), borax-glass requires five additional molecules of Na_2O. The equation may be written as follows:

$$5Na_2CO_3 + Na_2O.2B_2O_3 = 6Na_2O.2B_2O_3 + 5CO_2.$$

Whence we may write the following proportion to find the amount of borax-glass necessary to form a mono-borate with 100 grams of soda:

$$5Na_2CO_3 : Na_2O.2B_2O_3 = 530 : 202 = 100 : x,$$

solving, x is found to equal 38.1. In the same way we may find the amount of silica necessary to form a mono-silicate with 100 grams of sodium carbonate,

$$2Na_2CO_3 : SiO_2 = 212 : 60 = 100 : y,$$

solving, y is found to equal 28.3. Whence, from the theoretical standpoint we may say that in the case of a mono-silicate slag, 38.1 grams of borax-glass is equivalent to 28.3 grams of silica, or when borax-glass is used to replace silica in a mono-silicate slag one gram has the same effect as 0.743 grams of silica.

For a bi-silicate slag the relation is different owing to the molecule of Na_2O already in the borax-glass. The amount of borax-glass required to form a bi-borate with 100 grams of sodium carbonate is 95.3 and the silica for a bi-silicate is 56.6. Thus, in the case of a bi-silicate slag, 1 gram of borax-glass is equivalent to 0.584 grams of silica.

* Eng. and Min. Jour., 87, p. 1243.

Experiments* on the size of lead buttons obtained in reducing power fusions, with varying amounts of silica in some instances, and borax-glass in others, give results approaching the theoretical values obtained above. They show that 10 grams of borax-glass has the same effect in preventing the reduction of lead from litharge as between 6 and 7 grams of silica.

Rose,† in a discussion of the refining of gold bullion with oxygen gas, made a number of experiments to determine the best proportions of borax, silica and metallic oxides. Borax alone was found to be unsatisfactory on account of the rapid corrosion of the crucible. Silica alone gave a pasty, very viscous, slag. The best slag found corresponded nearly to the formula $\frac{2}{3}$ (Na_2O, B_2O_3) + $3RO$, $\frac{2}{3}B_2O_3$, $3SiO_2$. This is made up according to the following formula, $9RO + 2Na_2B_4O_7 + 9SiO_2$, where R = Ca, Mg, Pb, Zn, Cu, $\frac{2}{3}$Fe, $\frac{2}{3}$Ni. Leaving out of account the meta-borate of soda $Na_2B_2O_4$, it is a boro-silicate in which the relation of oxygen in acids to oxygen in bases is 2.66 to 1. This slag melts at a low temperature and is very fluid at between 1000° and 1100° C. It has only a slight corrosive action on clay crucibles. The flux contains 3 parts by weight of borax-glass to 4 parts of silica.

Charles E. Meyer‡ in fluxing zinc-box slime, made zinc into a bi-silicate with silica and added $Na_2B_4O_7$ for other bases. The other bases were all assumed to be Fe_2O_3 and borax-glass was added pound for pound, i.e., 1 pound $Na_2B_4O_7$ for 1 pound Fe_2O_3.

Fluidity of Slags. — It is also necessary to distinguish between the melting-point and the fluidity of slags. Many slags of low melting and formation temperature are entirely unsuited for assay purposes on account of their viscous nature when melted. As a rule, the higher the temperature the more fluid a slag will become, but different slags vary much in this respect. All slags are viscous at their freezing-point, yet one slag will be thinly fluid 200° C. above its melting-point and another will be decidedly viscous at this degree of superheat. The viscosity of silicates increases with the percentage of silica above that required for the mono-silicate, and the same may be said for borates.

* Lodge, Notes on Assaying, 2nd Ed. p.
† Inst. Min. and Met., **14**, p. 396, (1905).
‡ Jour. Chem. Met. and Min. Soc. of South Africa, **5**, p. 168, (1905).

Acidic and Basic Slags. — Slags more acid than the mono-silicate are generally termed acid, while those approaching a sub-silicate are called basic. The acid slags are all more or less viscous when molten and can be drawn out into long threads. They cool slowly and are usually glassy and brittle when cold. The basic slags are usually extremely fluid when molten; they pour like water, with no tendency to string out; in fact they may even be lumpy where the bases are in too great excess. They solidify rapidly and usually crystallize to some extent during solidification. Basic slags are dull and tough when cold. They are often of a dark color and on account of the large proportion of bases they contain they usually have a high specific gravity.

Mixed Silicates. — The mixture of two or more fusible compounds usually fuses at a lower temperature than either one taken alone, just as, for example, a mixture of potassium and sodium carbonate fuses at a lower temperature than either one of them alone. For this reason assayers always provide for the presence of a number of easily fusible substances, although their presence is not always necessary for the decomposition of the ore. For instance, even in the assay of pure limestone, which is a base, a certain amount of sodium carbonate, also a base, is always added.

Use of Fluxes. — For the sake of economy in material and time it is best to limit the amount of fluxes to the needs of the ore. The great saving to be made in this way may be illustrated as follows: If we use twice as much flux as necessary, we have to use twice as large a crucible which cuts down the furnace capacity very considerably. Besides this, the large charges require a longer time in the furnace to fuse and decompose the ore and this again reduces the furnace capacity.

The Lead Button. — In every gold and silver assay, a carefully regulated amount of the litharge is reduced. This results in the formation of a great number of minute globules of lead which serve to collect the gold and silver. When the charge becomes thoroughly liquid these collect in the bottom of the crucible forming the lead button. There is considerable difference of opinion as to the proper size for the lead button. Many assayers hold that it should be proportional to the total volume of charge; others vary the lead-fall according to the quantity of precious metals to be collected. Both of these ideas appear to have merit and agree in general with the experience of lead blast-furnace operators, who insist that the charge shall contain not less than 10 per cent of lead, all of which, of course, they attempt to reduce.

Miller[*] and Fulton, in experimenting on an ore containing 2260 ounces of silver per ton, found that the silver recovered from the lead button increased regularly with the increase in size of the lead button to a maximum of 28 grams. They concluded that the collecting power of a given weight of lead was independent of the amount of the charge.

In most cases a 28-gram lead button will collect all the gold and silver in the ordinary crucible charge, and the assayer is advised to figure for a button of this size unless some good reason for change is shown.

The Cover. — In practically all crucible assay work it was formerly customary to place a cover of some fusible substance on top of the mixed charge in the crucible. Different assayers advocate different materials, as salt, sodium sulphate, borax, borax-glass and soda, as well as different flux mixtures.

The idea which leads to the use of the cover is that, melting early, it makes a thick glaze on the sides of the crucible above the ore charge and that, if particles of ore or lead globules are left on the sides of the crucible by the boiling of the charge, the cover tends to prevent them from sticking there. As the fusion becomes quiet and the temperature rises, most of this glaze runs down to join the main charge and carries with it any small particles of ore or lead which may have stuck to it in the early part of the fusion.

The salt cover is thinly fluid when melted. It does not enter the slag but floats on top of it, thus serving to keep out the air and to prevent loss by ebullition.

The borax cover fuses before the rest of the charge. It is thick and viscous when melted and serves to prevent loss of fine ore by " dusting," as well as to stop loss by ebullition. It finally enters the slag and so ceases to be a cover after the fusion is well under way.

Some assayers object to the use of salt on the ground that it is likely to cause losses of gold and silver by volatilization. It is a well-known fact that gold chloride is volatile at a comparatively low temperature, commencing at 180° C. and that silver chloride

[*] School of Mines Quarterly, 17, pp. 160–170.

is volatile in connection with the chlorides of arsenic, antimony, copper, iron, lead, etc. When an ore contains substances such as manganese oxide, basic iron sulphate etc., capable of generating chlorine upon being heated with salt, it would seem wise to omit the use of salt. If it is not desired to use salt a good cover may be made from a mixture of borax-glass and sodium carbonate in the proportion of 10 parts of the former to 15 parts of the latter.

The present tendency is to do away with the cover altogether. For muffle fusions, at any rate, a salt cover is entirely unnecessary and even objectionable, in that it fills the room with chloride fumes at the time of pouring. Salt assists in the volatilization of lead compounds and these are most injurious to health.

REDUCTION AND OXIDATION.

Reducing and oxidizing reactions are common in fire assaying as in other chemical work, and practically all fusions are either reducing or oxidizing in nature. For instance, the scorification assay is an oxidizing fusion in which atmospheric air is the oxidizing agent, while the crucible fusion of a siliceous ore is a reducing fusion in which argols, flour or charcoal act as the reducing agents.

By the term "reducing power," as used in fire assaying, is meant the amount of lead that 1 gram of the ore or substance will reduce when fused with an excess of litharge. For instance, if we use 5.00 grams of ore and obtain a lead button weighing 16.50 grams the reducing power of the ore is

$$\frac{16.50}{5.00} = 3.30.$$

By the term "oxidizing power" is meant the amount of lead which 1 gram of the ore or substance will oxidize in a fusion, or more exactly it is the lead equivalent of a certain amount of reducing agent or ore which is capable of being oxidized by 1 gram of the ore or substance.

Reducing Reactions. — The reduction of lead by charcoal is shown by the following reaction:

$$2PbO + C = 2Pb + CO_2,$$

from which it is seen that 1 gram of pure carbon should reduce $\frac{2 \times 207}{12} = 34.5$ grams of lead. However, as charcoal is never pure carbon the results actually obtained in the laboratory will be somewhat less, usually from 25 to 30. All carbonaceous materials have more or less reducing power. Those most commonly used as reducing agents in assaying are charcoal, R. P. $\pm$ 27.5; argols, R. P. 8–12; cream of tartar, R. P. 5.5; flour, R. P. 10–12.

Besides carbonaceous matter many other substances and elements are capable of reducing lead from its oxide. The most important of these are metallic iron, sulphur and the metallic sulphides. The reduction of lead by iron is shown by the following reaction:

$$PbO + Fe = Pb + FeO,$$

whence the reducing power of iron is $\frac{207}{56} = 3.70$.

The reducing power of sulphur and the metallic sulphides will vary according to the amount of alkaline carbonate present. For instance, the reduction of lead by sulphur in the absence of alkaline carbonates is shown by the following reaction:

$$2PbO + S = 2Pb + SO_2.$$

The reducing power of sulphur under these conditions would be

$$\frac{2 \times 207}{32} = 12.9.$$

In the presence of sufficient alkaline carbonates the sulphur is oxidized to sulphur trioxide which combines with the alkali to form sulphate. The reaction is as follows:

$$3PbO + S + Na_2CO_3 = 3Pb + Na_2SO_4 + CO_2,$$

from which we see that the reducing power of sulphur, under these conditions, should be

$$\frac{621}{32} = 19.4.$$

In the same way we find that the reducing power of the metallic sulphides varies according to the amount of available alkaline carbonate present. For instance, in the absence of alkaline carbonates and with a small amount of silica to slag the iron oxide and to hold it in the ferrous condition, the following equation expresses the reaction between iron pyrite and litharge:

$$FeS_2 + 5PbO + SiO_2 = FeSiO_3 + 5Pb + 2SO_2.$$

This last statement is not strictly true, as in the entire absence of alkaline carbonate the reaction is not quite complete. Miller* found that under the above conditions the lead button and slag always contained sulphides and the actual results fell slightly below those called for by the above equation. According to this equation the reducing power would be

$$\frac{5Pb}{FeS_2} = \frac{1035}{120} = 8.6.$$

With an excess of sodium carbonate and in the absence of silica, the sulphur is oxidized to trioxide and the iron to the ferric condition, as shown by the following equation:

$$2FeS_2 + 15PbO + 4Na_2CO_3 = Fe_2O_3 + 15Pb + 4Na_2SO_4 + 4CO_2,$$

and this gives a reducing power of $\frac{3105}{240} = 12.9.$

With a small amount of silica present the iron may be left in the ferrous condition, which is much to be preferred. Then the reaction becomes:

$$2FeS_2 + 14PbO + 4Na_2CO_3 + SiO_2 =$$
$$Fe_2SiO_4 + 14Pb + 4Na_2SO_4 + 4CO_2,$$

which gives a reducing power of 12.07.

All of the above reactions may take place simultaneously in the same fusion, and therefore it will be obvious that there may be obtained for pyrite any reducing power between 8.6 and 12.9, according to the amount of sodium carbonate, litharge and silica present. Unfortunately it is somewhat difficult to control the oxidation of the sulphur, and this makes it hard to obtain a lead button of the right size. What the assayer wants to know is the "working reducing power" of the ore, which always lies somewhere between the two extremes indicated, and this he determines by a preliminary fusion with a small quantity of ore, an excess of litharge and a carefully regulated amount of soda.

The accompanying table gives the reducing power of some of the common sulphides. The theoretical figures are computed

* Trans. A.I.M.E., 34, p. 395.

for sulphur oxidized to both SO_2 and SO_3. In the last column is given the reducing power of the pure minerals using the following charge Na_2CO_3 5 gms., PbO 80 gms., SiO_2 2 gms., ore to yield an approximate 25 gram button.

TABLE XX.

REDUCING POWER OF MINERALS.

Mineral	Formula	Computed		Actually determined
		S to SO_2	S to SO_3	
Galena	PbS	2.6	3.46	3.41
Chalcocite	Cu_2S	3.9	5.2	
Arsenopyrite	FeAsS	5.7	6.96	8.18[1]
Stibnite	Sb_2S_3	5.5	7.35	6.75
Chalcopyrite	$CuFeS_2$	6.2	8.44	7.85
Sphalerite	ZnS	6.37	8.5	7.87
Pyrrhotite	Fe_7S_8	7.35	9.9	10.00[1]
Pyrite	FeS_2	8.6	12.07	11.05

[1] The sample used probably contained pyrite.

As is the case with sulphur and the metallic sulphides the amount of lead reduced by the carbonaceous reducing agents also depends upon the nature of the charge, particularly upon the amount of silica present. Other things being equal, the more basic the charge, the greater the amount of lead which will be reduced by a unit quantity of the reducing agent. Thus, a certain sample of argols showed a reducing power of 11.04 when silica for a sub-silicate was added, 10.93 for a mono-silicate, 10.62 for a bi-silicate and only 9.26 for a tri-silicate. The rate of fusion and the final temperature both have a good deal to do with the amount of this reduction, for the reason that the silicates of lead more acid than the mono-silicate are but little reduced by carbon below 1000° C. With a limited amount of litharge present, part is bound to be converted into silicate before it can be reduced by carbon, and naturally the greater the proportion of silica, the larger the amount of litharge which will combine and thus be rendered unavailable for reduction by carbon.

Oxidizing Reactions. — Certain metals, notably iron, manganese, copper, cobalt, arsenic and antimony, are capable of existing in two states of oxidation. When fused with a reducing agent the higher oxides of these metals are reduced to the lower state of oxidation at the expense of the reducing agent. Ores containing these higher oxides are said to have an oxidizing power on account of this property of using up reducing agent. For convenience this oxidizing power is measured in terms of lead, although the bulk of the oxidizing reaction in any assay fusion is probably accomplished against the reducing agent of the charge.

For instance if in an assay fusion containing silica we have ferric oxide, sufficient for a bi-silicate, and carbon, the following reaction takes place:

$$2Fe_2O_3 + C + 4SiO_2 = 4FeSiO_3 + CO_2,$$

from which we find that 1 gram of Fe_2O_3 requires 0.037 gram of carbon to reduce it to FeO. Expressed in terms of lead the relation would be as follows:

$$Fe_2O_3 + Pb = 2FeO + PbO.$$

That is to say the oxidizing power of Fe_2O_3 is $\frac{207}{160} = 1.31.$

Similarly

$$MnO_2 + Pb = MnO + PbO.$$

The oxidizing power of MnO_2 is $\frac{207}{87} = 2.4$, which means that each gram of MnO_2 present in a fusion with litharge and a reducing agent will prevent the reduction of 2.4 grams of lead. It is easily seen, therefore, that this oxidizing power of ores must be taken account of in computing assay charges. The method of determining the oxidizing power of ores will be discussed later.

In the crucible assay of high sulphide ores it is frequently necessary to add some oxidizing agent to the charge to prevent the reduction of an inconveniently large lead button. A 28-gram lead button is usually sufficiently large to act as a collector of the precious metals, and were a larger button obtained, it would entail an extra loss due to scorification, or a prolonged cupellation, as well as consuming extra time in this treatment. When, therefore, the ore charge would of itself reduce more than 28 grams of lead we ordinarily add potassium nitrate or some other oxidizing agent. Niter is almost exclusively used in this country for oxidizing. Its action with carbon is shown by the following equation:

$$4KNO_3 + 5C = 2K_2O + 5CO_2 + 2N_2,$$

from which the theoretical oxidizing power of niter expressed in terms of lead is found to be 5.12. The theoretical oxidizing power may also be figured from its reactions with sulphur, or any of the metallic sulphides and will always give substantially the same result when the degree of oxidation of the sulphur is kept the same in the reducing and oxidizing reactions.

The actual oxidizing effect of niter is always found to be lower than this, partly because the niter ordinarily used for this purpose is not 100 per cent KNO_3 and partly because in the actual fusion some oxygen is likely to escape unused. This loss of oxygen increases as the acidity of the charge increases. The loss is also probably influenced by the depth of the charge, the rate of fusion and the temperature. In the case of actual assay fusions with sulphides, the oxidizing power will be found to vary between 3.7 and 4.7, the lower figure being approached when the charge contains considerable silica and borax-glass and but little litharge, the upper figure prevailing when no silica or borax is used and in the presence of an excess of sodium carbonate and litharge.

With both the reducing power of the sulphides and the oxidizing power of the niter varying with different proportions of sodium carbonate, litharge, borax and silica, as well as with variations of temperature, the problem of obtaining a lead button of the right size in niter assays is not a simple one. The only solution is so to control the conditions that the state of oxidation of the sulphur in the final assay shall be the same as that in the reducing power fusion. This is the first essential; the second is to decide on some slag of definite silicate degree and always use it; then the proportion of oxygen which escapes unused will be nearly constant and the oxidizing power of the niter, once determined, may be depended on to remain constant.

With the type of charge recommended in the latter part of the chapter, the oxidizing power of niter will be found to lie between 4.0 and 4.2 and with this minor variation but little trouble should be found in properly controlling the size of the button.

Just as we may obtain several reactions between any of the

sulphides and litharge according to the degree of oxidation of the sulphur and occasionally also of other constituents of the mineral, so we may also obtain several different reactions between niter and the sulphides. For instance, in the absence of alkaline carbonates and in the presence of silica, the sulphur can be oxidized only to the dioxide, and the reaction between niter and pyrite would be as follows:

$$2KNO_3 + FeS_2 + SiO_2 = K_2O.FeO.SiO_2 + 2SO_2 + N_2.$$

In the presence of an excess of alkaline carbonate and litharge with little or no silica, both the iron and the sulphur would be oxidized as highly as possible and the following reaction would result:

$$6KNO_3 + 2FeS_2 + Na_2CO_3 = Fe_2O_3 + 3K_2SO_4 + Na_2SO_4 + 3N_2 + CO_2.$$

Ferric oxide is a most undesirable component of assay slags and its formation must be avoided. To prevent the iron from going to the ferric condition enough silica should be present to hold and slag it as ferrous singulo-silicate. If this is provided the reaction then becomes

$$28KNO_3 + 10FeS_2 + 6Na_2CO_3 + 5SiO_2 = 5Fe_2SiO_4 + 14K_2SO_4 + 6Na_2SO_4 + 14N_2 + 6CO_2.$$

A slight oxidizing effect may be obtained by using red lead in place of litharge, and this is sometimes done, especially in England and the British colonies. The oxidizing effect of red lead is shown by the following reaction:

$$Pb_3O_4 + Pb = 4PbO.$$

The oxidizing power in terms of lead is $\frac{207}{685} = 0.30$.

TESTING REAGENTS.

Each new lot of litharge and test lead should be assayed for silver and gold so that when any is found to be present a proper correction may be made. Different lots of argols, and flour are also found to vary in reducing power, and their reducing powers should also be determined.

The following procedure is designed, first, to allow the student to determine the reducing power of flour, charcoal or other reducing agents and at the same time to determine the silver correction for litharge, and, second, to familiarize him with the principal operations connected with the crucible method of assay.

Procedure. — Take two E or F pot-furnace crucibles, or 12 or 15 gram muffle crucibles.

Weigh into them, in the order given, the following:

No. 1			No. 2		
Sodium carbonate	5	grams	Sodium carbonate	5	grams
Silica	5	"	Silica	5	"
Litharge	60	"	Litharge	60	"
Flour	2.50	"	Charcoal	1.00	"

Weigh the flour and charcoal on the pulp balance as exactly as possible, the others on the flux balance. Mix thoroughly with the spatula by turning the crucible slowly with one hand while using the spatula with the other. When finished tap the crucible several times with the handle of the spatula to settle the charge and to shake down any material which may have lodged on the sides of the crucible above the charge. Finally put on a half-inch cover of salt.

Pot-Furnace Fusion. — Have a good bright fire in the pot-furnace which should not, however, be filled with coke more than halfway to the bottom of the flue. Place the crucibles so that their tops shall not be much above the bottom of the flue. Place a piece of cold coke directly under each crucible as it is put into the furnace. Cover the crucibles and pack coke around them, being careful to prevent the introduction of any coke or dust. Close the top of the furnace, open the draft if necessary and urge the fire until the charges begin to fuse. Then close the draft and continue the melting slowly enough to prevent the charges from boiling over. When the charges have finished boiling, note the time and open the draft if necessary, to get a yellow heat and continue heating for ten minutes.

Pour the fusions into the crucible mold, which has been previously coated with ruddle, thoroughly dried and warmed. When the material is cold, a matter of five or ten minutes for a small fusion, break the cone of lead from the slag and hammer it into a cube to thoroughly remove the slag. Weigh the buttons on the pulp balance to the nearest tenth of a gram and record the weights and reducing powers in the notebook.

Save the lead buttons and cupel them. The beads should

contain all of the gold and silver in the 60 grams of litharge used. Weigh the beads and part to see if gold is present. Record the weights of the beads and compute the correction for silver in 30 grams of litharge.

Muffle Fusion. — If the fusions are to be made in the muffle have the muffle light red and the fire under such control that the muffle can be brought to a full yellow in the course of half an hour. Place a row of empty 30-gram crucibles in the front part of the muffle so as to close the space as completely as possible. These serve to keep the assays hot by reflection of heat and so prevent loss of heat by conduction through the door. See that the muffle door is tightly closed to prevent admission of air. Melt at sufficiently low temperature to avoid violent boiling and then when the sound of bubbling is no longer heard, raise the temperature and pour as in the case of the pot-furnace fusion.

Notes: 1. So-called silver-free litharge can now be purchased but even this often carries traces of gold and silver.

2. In assaying samples of litharge low in silver 120 to 240 grams may be required to give a bead of sufficient size to handle and weigh.

3. It is convenient to use litharge in multiples of 30 grams and therefore the silver correction is based on 30 grams of litharge.

4. The temperature which the muffle should have before the crucibles are introduced depends upon the number of charges which are to be put in at one time. If only one or two the temperature should be low to avoid danger of boiling over. However, if the muffle is to be filled with crucibles the initial temperature may be higher, as the crucibles can be depended upon to decidedly lower the temperature.

5. Pour the fusions carefully into the center of the molds and do not disturb until the lead has had time to solidify.

The following are the reducing powers of some of the common reducing agents:

Charcoal	25–30	Corn-starch	11.5–13
Argols	8–12	Sugar	14.5
Flour	10–12	Cream of tartar	4.5–6.5

ASSAY OF CLASS 1 ORES. GOLD OR SILVER.

This is the most common class of ores and as it is also the one which presents the fewest difficulties for the assayer, it is considered first. Actually, ores with no traces of sulphides are somewhat of a rarity, but the methods given below may be adapted to ores containing moderate amounts of sulphides by simply decreasing the amount of reducing agent used.

Slags for Class 1 Siliceous Ores. — To fuse a siliceous ore, basic fluxes must be added, the alkaline carbonates and litharge being the ones available. The bi-silicates of soda and lead are readily fusible and sufficiently fluid for the purpose; therefore, the basic fluxes may be limited to the amount necessary to form these silicates. Sodium carbonate and litharge combine with silica to form bi-silicates in proportions indicated in the following equations:

$$Na_2CO_3 + SiO_2 = Na_2SiO_3 + CO_2,$$
$$PbO + SiO_2 = PbSiO_3.$$

From a comparison of the molecular weights of the left-hand members of these equations, it may be determined that one assay-ton of pure silica will require either 51.2 grams of sodium carbonate, or 108 grams of litharge to form a bi-silicate.

As the mixed silicate of soda and lead is generally more satisfactory than either one alone, it is common to use both of these basic fluxes in every fusion, thus making a double, or bi-basic silicate. It is customary to use at least as much sodium carbonate as ore in every assay. On this basis it appears that approximately three-fifths of the silica is fluxed with soda, leaving two-fifths of it to be fluxed with litharge. Taking these proportions, then, there will be required for one assay-ton of pure silica exactly 30.7 grams of sodium carbonate and 43.2 grams of litharge.

In assaying an ore provision must also be made for a lead button to act as a collector of the precious metals. A 28-gram button is usually sufficient. To allow for this it will be necessary to add 30 grams more of litharge and also some reducing agent, say $2\frac{1}{3}$ grams of flour (R. P. 12).

The charge will now stand as follows:

Ore....................................	1	A. T.
Sodium carbonate......................	30.7	grams
Litharge for slag 43 grams Litharge for button 30 grams }	73	grams
Flour (R. P. 12).......................	$2\frac{1}{3}$	grams

The ore so far considered has been an ideal one, pure silica, which is rarely if ever found in practice. The ordinary siliceous ore almost invariably contains small amounts of iron oxide, various silicates of alumina, pyrite and other sulphides, as well as occasionally more or less calcite, all of which reduce the amount of silica for which basic fluxes must be supplied. It is obvious that for such an ore it is possible to make a bi-silicate slag with a somewhat smaller amount of basic reagents than those in the ideal charge shown above. It will be advisable also to use a small amount of borax in almost every fusion, as this helps both in fluxing silica and in slagging the basic oxides. So that, by rounding out the above charge and adding borax, the following practical bi-silicate charges for siliceous ores are obtained:

Ore	½ A. T.	1 A. T.	2 A. T.
Soda (Na$_2$CO$_3$)	15 grams	30 grams	60 grams
Borax	3–5 "	5–10 "	10–15 "
Litharge	50 "	70 "	110 "
Flour (R. P. 12)	2⅓ "	2⅓ "	2⅓ "

The larger the amount of ore used the more necessary it becomes to keep down the quantity of fluxes. The following charges, more acid than the bi-silicate, are regularly used by the author for the assay of siliceous tailings.

Ore	1 A. T.	2 A. T.	5 A. T.
Soda (Na$_2$CO$_3$)	30 grams	60 grams	150 grams
Borax	3 "	6 "	15 "
Litharge	60 "	90 "	180 "
Flour for a	28 gram	30 gram	35 gram lead button.

The results obtained with the last mentioned charges are good; the slags, of course, are more viscous than the bi-silicate slags but they pour well even when fusions are made in the muffle furnace. The crucibles are practically unattacked and if of good quality, can be used for many such fusions, especially if care is taken to cool them slowly.

The following table gives the amounts of the different common basic reagents required to form bi-silicates with pure silica. This will be found useful in calculating assay charges for various quantities of siliceous ores.

TABLE XXI.
Bi-Silicate Slag Factors No. 1.

SiO$_2$	Quantity of bases required			
	PbO	Na$_2$CO$_3$	K$_2$CO$_3$	NaHCO$_3$
1 assay-ton	108. gm.	51.2 gm.	66.8 gm.	81.2 gm.
10 grams	37.0 gm.	17.6 gm.	22.9 gm.	27.9 gm.

One gram of FeO neutralizes 0.84 grams SiO_2 or requires 1.4 grams borax-glass. One gram of $CaCO_3$ neutralizes 0.60 gram SiO_2 or requires 1.0 gram borax-glass.

All assayers do not agree on the use of bi-silicate slags for siliceous ores, and even if they did agree they might prefer different proportions of sodium carbonate and litharge than those mentioned above. Many assayers consider it better to make the slag less acid than the bi-silicate; in fact there are certain advantages in making what is approximately a sesqui-silicate. The quantity of basic fluxes required for this silicate may be determined by increasing the figures found in the last table by one-third.

Where a large number of assays are to be made on ore of about the same character it is neither necessary nor desirable to weigh out each individual unit of flux, as this would take too much time. Instead, a flux mixture is made up and then a unit weight of this mixture is weighed out for each assay, or better still a measure is used which delivers the proper amount. There are innumerable formulas for such mixtures and even for the same ore many different mixtures are advocated. A good flux for the assay of siliceous ores consists of 3.5 parts of sodium carbonate, 0.5 parts of borax and 6 parts of litharge. If an assayer uses 100 grams of this mixture per assay-ton of quartz and reduces a 28-gram lead button he will have what is approximately a bi-silicate slag. If he prefers he may use 125 grams of flux which gives practically a sesqui-silicate. The latter proportion is somewhat more popular with assayers, and the student is advised to try both. It should be noted, however, that half of this quantity of flux will not give a sesqui-silicate with half an assay-ton of ore, unless at the same time the reducer is limited to the amount required for a 14-gram lead button. This latter procedure is not commonly followed, so that for half an assay-ton of ore approximately 75 grams of this flux should be used, if a sesqui-silicate and a button of reasonable size are to be obtained.

Slags for Class 1 Basic Ores. — In the assay of basic ores it is necessary to add acid fluxes, silica and borax to obtain a fusible slag. Also, on account of the fact that the silicates of iron, manganese, calcium and magnesium are by themselves infusible, or nearly so, at the temperature of the assay-furnace, it is customary to add some soda and excess litharge to the charge. These latter, combining with some of the silica and borax, form readily fusible compounds which help to take into solution the silicates of the basic oxides and by diluting them give more fusible and fluid slags. A weight of soda equal at least to that of the ore is generally taken as a starting point, and very often a quantity of litharge equal to that of the ore is also allowed for the slag.

The silicate-degree of the slag will depend on the character of the bases. For Class 1 ores, consisting principally of iron, manganese, calcium, or magnesium it has been found best to approximate a sesqui- or a bi-silicate slag.

If the silica and borax are cut down so as to make mono-silicates, the slags from limestone and dolomite will be lumpy when hot and full of lead shot when cold. Those from iron oxide will be lumpy when hot, and when they are poured the crucible will be left full of lead shot which refuse to collect. When cold, the slag will be found full of shots of lead and will be magnetic. This is due to the formation of the magnetic oxide of iron, which, being infusible, floats around in the lower part of the slag and interferes with the settling of the reduced lead.

The following table of bi-silicate slag factors will facilitate the calculation of charges for basic ores.

TABLE XXII.
BI-SILICATE SLAG FACTORS No. 2.

Quantity of bases	Quantity of acid required
1 A. T. FeO	24.5 grams SiO_2
1 A. T. $CaCO_3$	17.4 " "
1 A. T. $MgCO_3$	20.8 " "
10 gms. PbO	2.7 " "
30 " $NaHCO_3$	10.8 " "
30 " Na_2CO_3	17.0 " "
10 " K_2CO_3	4.4 " "

For sesqui-silicates use three-quarters of the above quantities of silica. When borax-glass is substituted for silica, 1 gram of borax-glass may be considered equivalent to 0.6 gram of silica.

The amount of silica which should be replaced by borax has not been determined, but on account of the greater fusibility and fluidity of boro-silicates it is well to replace at least a quarter to a third of the silica with its equivalent of borax or borax-glass. When the calculated amount of borax-glass falls below 5 grams, this quantity is generally used as a minimum.

The following example will illustrate the use of the table. Take 1 assay-ton of an ore consisting of 50 per cent $CaCO_3$ and 50 per cent SiO_2. Start with 30 grams of sodium carbonate and 60 grams of litharge, 30 for the slag and 30 for the lead button, and plan for a bi-silicate slag. Under these conditions the silica requirements of the different bases are as follows:

The $CaCO_3$ of the ore requires $0.5 \times 17.4 =$ 8.7 grams SiO_2
30 grams of soda require.................17.0 " "
30 grams of litharge require .... 8.1 " "

    Total..........................33.8 " "
Deducting the silica of the ore, ½ A. T. = 14.6

Silica or equivalent borax necessary........19.2

If two-thirds of this is put in as silica, there remains $19.2 - 12.8 = 6.4$ grams of silica, for which we must substitute the equivalent amount of borax-glass, which is $\frac{10}{6} \times 6.4 = 10.7$ grams.

The final charge stands

    Ore.......................................1 A. T.
    Sodium carbonate........................30 grams
    Borax-glass..............................10.7 "
    Litharge.................................60 "
    Flour (R. P. 12).........................2⅓ "
    Silica...................................12.8 "

This charge contains 17.0 grams of $CaSiO_3$ and 34.6 grams of Na_2SiO_3, or about twice as much sodium bi-silicate as calcium bi-silicate. Figure 3 shows that such a combination will melt at a reasonably low temperature. The lead silicate and the borax-glass will, of course, reduce this melting temperature materially.

Following the procedure outlined above it may readily be determined that for pure calcium carbonate the charge shown below should be used:

    Ore.......................................1 A. T.
    Sodium carbonate........................30 grams
    Borax-glass..............................23.6 "
    Litharge.................................60 "
    Flour....................................2⅓ "
    Silica...................................28.3 "

This charge contains approximately equal amounts of the bi-silicates of sodium and calcium, as well as litharge and borax-glass. It fuses without difficulty and gives a glassy slag and a good separation of lead.

Figure 44 gives at a glance the quantity of reagents other than flour required to flux one assay-ton of any mixture of limestone and silica.

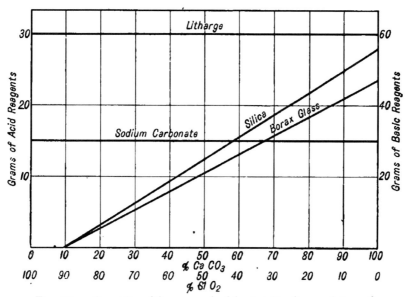

FIG. 44. — Quantity of fluxes required for 1 A.T. of any mixture of limestone and silica.

Magnesium silicates are somewhat more difficult to fuse than the corresponding calcium silicates; but the same method of procedure should be followed for ores containing magnesite or dolomite as for limestone. Precious metal ores containing large quantities of magnesium carbonate are not likely to be found; but the assayer may have to determine the quantity of silver contained in a magnesia cupel, and for this bi-silicate slags are the best.

Ores containing much calcium or magnesium carbonate cause considerable boiling in the crucible, due to their dissociation into oxide and carbon dioxide at a temperature about the same as that required to melt the charge. The assayer should bear this in mind in selecting a crucible for such an ore.

The charges for ores consisting mainly of iron or manganese oxides are figured in the same way as for those containing calcium carbonate. In assaying ores containing iron or manganese oxides, more than the ordinary amount of reducing agent must be added to counteract the oxidizing effect of these minerals.

Slags for Alumina. — Alumina is the most difficult to flux of any of the common metal oxides. Fortunately, pure alumina is never found associated with gold and silver, and the assayer is not likely to encounter anything worse than ores containing a good deal of alumina in the form of clay. Pure china-clay, or kaolinite, which has the following composition, $H_4Al_2Si_2O_9$, contains only 39.5 per cent of alumina. Ordinary clays contain more or less quartz and other minerals, so that even the above-mentioned content of alumina will not have to be dealt with. Small amounts of combined alumina are found in many ores but these cause no trouble in the fusion.

Metallurgists have never entirely agreed as to the behavior of alumina in slags. The work of Day, Shepherd, Rankin, Wright, Bowen and others has thrown much new light on the subject of the constitution and thermal properties of the ternary system $CaO - Al_2O_3 - SiO_2$. The melting-point curve of the $CaO - SiO_2$ series was shown in Chapter I. Figures 45 and 46 give the melting-point diagrams[*] of the $Al_2O_3 - SiO_2$ and the $CaO - Al_2O_3$ series respectively.

The $Al_2O_3 - SiO_2$ curve is almost a straight line between the melting-point of silica, 1625° C. and that of alumina, 2050°, the silicate of lowest melting-point being the eutectic containing 87 per cent of silica, which melts at 1610°. This curve is not at all like that of the $CaO - SiO_2$ series, as it might be expected to be if alumina were a base. It shows but one compound, $Al_2O_3.SiO_2$.

The $CaO - Al_2O_3$ curve, on the other hand, shows a number of compounds and, what is more important to the metallurgist, a very decided reduction of melting temperature at about the point where the components are of equal weight. The compound $5CaO.3Al_2O_3$, which contains 47.8 per cent of CaO, lies just between two eutectics, both of which melt at about 1400° C. It would seem from the above, that alumina behaves more like an acid than a base, and it is suggested that it be so treated.

Alumina makes slags viscous, no matter how it is treated, and

[*] Am. Jour. Sci., **39**, pp. 9 and 11.

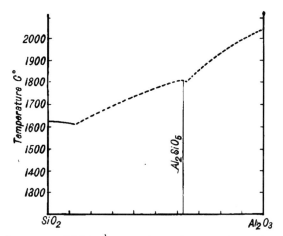

FIG. 45. — Melting points of the alumina-silica series.

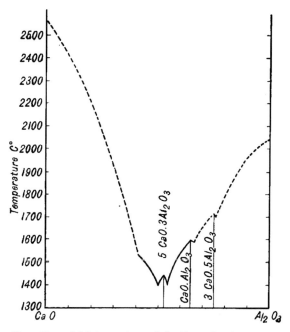

FIG. 46. — Melting points of the lime-alumina series.

it should not be allowed to exceed 10 or 15 per cent of the weight of the slag. Borax-glass should be increased as the alumina in a siliceous ore increases. The addition of lime has been found helpful in fluxing alumina, as might be expected from a study of the last curve. The following charge gives good results with pure china-clay:

Clay	½ A. T.
Lime (CaO)	6 grams
Sodium carbonate	20 "
Borax-glass	10 "
Litharge	45 "
Flour (R. P. 12)	$2\frac{1}{3}$ "
Silica	12 "

Cryolite is the best flux for alumina and dissolves it readily. Cryolite melts at about 1000° and dissolves more than 20 per cent of its weight of Al_2O_3. Either sodium fluoride or fluorite may be substituted if desired. The fluorides are all very liquid when fused and because of this property are particularly helpful as fluxes for ores containing alumina. The addition of 5 or 10 grams of any of the fluorides will be found beneficial with ores containing large quantities of alumina.

Procedure. — Carefully van some of the ore, estimate and record in the notebook the amount and character of each of the slag-forming constituents and also of any sulphides present. If the ore is mainly siliceous weigh out one of each of the following charges:

Charge (a)		Charge (b)	
Ore	0.5 A. T.	Ore	0.5 A. T.
Sodium carbonate	30 grams	Sodium carbonate	15 grams
Borax	5 "	Borax	5 "
Litharge	30 "	Litharge	50 "
Flour	*	Flour	*

Use F pot-furnace crucibles or if the work is to be done in the muffle 15- or 20-gram muffle crucibles.

Weigh out the fluxes and place in the crucible in the order given, adding the ore and flour last of all. Weigh the flour and ore on the pulp balance, the others on the flux balance. Mix

* Enough combined with the reducing material of the ore to give a 28-gram button.

thoroughly and if the fusion is to be made in the pot-furnace place a half-inch cover of salt or soda-borax mixture on top. Muffle fusions, except those for reducing power, do not require any covers.

Fuse at a moderate red heat to avoid danger of the charge boiling over and when quiet raise the heat to a bright yellow. In muffle fusions the assayer must depend upon the sound to tell when the bubbling has ceased. Allow fifteen minutes of quiet fusion. Pour as usual, tapping the crucible gently against the mold if necessary to make sure of getting out the last globules of lead.

When the material is cold, separate the lead buttons from the slag, keeping them in order (a) (b). Record in the notebook the character and appearance of the slags, the ease or difficulty of the separation of each from the lead buttons, the appearance of the lead buttons and their degree of malleability.

Weigh the lead buttons on the flux balance and cupel carefully to obtain feather crystals of litharge. Weigh the silver beads, correct for silver in the litharge used, part and weigh any gold found and finally report the value of the ore in ounces per ton.

Both of these charges should give good results on a siliceous ore. Charge (a) is a little less expensive, but charge (b) is more commonly used, as the slag contains two bases and the excess litharge will hold a moderate amount of impurities in solution. Charge (b) also gives a better separation of lead button and slag and has the further advantage that if the ore contains slightly more sulphide than was estimated the litharge will take care of it, giving a lead button free from matte. If in charge (a), there is more carbonaceous reducing agent plus sulphide mineral than the 30 grams of litharge can oxidize, some of the sulphur will combine with various metals of the charge, principally lead, and form a matte which will appear immediately above the lead button.

Approximately 30 grams of litharge from each charge will be reduced to give the 28-gram lead button and is therefore not available to combine with the silica. The active* fluxes are then in charge (a), 30 grams of soda, and 5 of borax, totaling approximately two and a half times the ore. In charge (b), the active fluxes are 15 grams of soda, 5 of borax and 20 grams of litharge,

* By an active flux is meant a flux which is to appear in the slag and therefore does not include the litharge which goes to form the lead button.

totaling approximately three times the ore. A very good rule to follow in making crucible charges is always to use at least two and a half times as much active flux as ore.

Borax in the charge should be increased as the bases increase. For an ore with 10 or 20 per cent of iron or manganese oxide, limestone or clay, add up to 10 or 15 grams of borax or 5 to 8 grams of borax-glass. For ores containing larger amounts of bases, work out a charge from the data given under the discussion of "slags for basic ores."

For high-grade ores and those containing considerable quantities of such common impurities as oxides of tellurium, copper, bismuth, arsenic, antimony, or nickel, the quantity of litharge must be increased in proportion to the amount of impurity present. Some idea as to the quantity of litharge required may be found in the chapter on Special Methods of Assay.

Notes: 1. Some assayers prefer to omit the borax from the charge and use a cover of crude borax or borax-glass in place of the salt. A borax cover may be used to advantage with ores which "dust" in the crucible, as the borax swells and melts early, tending to catch and hold down the fine particles of ore which are projected upward from the charge.

2. The crucible should never be more than two-thirds full when the charge is all in.

3. If a silver assay alone is asked for, it is customary to omit parting and report the combined precious metals as silver.

4. In assaying for gold alone, if sufficient silver for parting is not known to be present, a piece of proof silver should always be added to the crucible or to the lead button before cupeling. If the approximate amount of gold is known, about eight times its weight of silver should be allowed.

5. The slag should be fluid on pouring and should be free from lead shot. If it is pasty or lumpy, either the fusion has not been long enough to thoroughly decompose the ore, or the charge is too basic and more borax and silica should be added. The crucible should have a thin glaze of slag and should be but little corroded. It should show no particles of undecomposed ore or "shots" of lead. These latter can best be seen immediately after pouring, and the student should make it a point to examine his crucible immediately after every pour. Neither the cover nor the outside of the crucible should show any glazing, as this indicates that the fusion has boiled over. The cold slag should be homogeneous, as otherwise it indicates incomplete decomposition of the ore. Glassy slags are usually preferred by assayers but are not essential for all ores.

6. A brittle slag is to be preferred, particularly one which separates easily and completely from the lead button. If too acid, particularly if too much borax has been used, the slag is apt to be tough and to adhere tenaciously to the lead button so that when separated some of the lead comes off

with the slag. This causes a great deal of annoyance and is bound to result in some loss of alloy. By setting the mold in cold water just after the red has disappeared from the slag, the latter may be made more brittle. The water must not be allowed to enter the mold, which must be handled carefully to avoid disturbing the still liquid lead.

7. If the button is hard or brittle or weighs more than 30 grams it should be scorified before cupeling. Hard buttons indicate the presence of copper, antimony, or nickel. Brittle buttons may be due to antimony, arsenic, zinc, sulphur, litharge or may be rich alloys of lead and the precious metals.

8. Examine carefully the line of separation of the slag and lead. The separation should be clean with no films of lead adhering to the slag. There should be no third substance between the slag and lead, nor should the surface of the lead show any disposition to crumble when hammered. Any lead-gray, brittle substance between the lead and slag or attached to the lead button is probably matte. This indicates incomplete decomposition of the ore, due to incorrect fluxing or too short a time of fusion. If the former is the cause, decreasing the silica and increasing the soda and litharge will usually prevent the formation of this substance in a subsequent fusion.

ASSAY OF CLASS 2 ORES.

Ores of this class containing only small amounts of sulphides are assayed in exactly the same manner as Class 1 ores but with lesser amounts of flour. However, when sulphides are present in such amounts as to reduce a lead button too large to cupel a different method of procedure must be followed. The most important methods for the assay of these ores follow:

1. SCORIFICATION. — This method has already been considered. It is not well suited for gold ores and fails for many silver ores.

2. LITHARGE-NITER METHOD. — The reducing power of the ore is first determined by means of a preliminary assay. Using the figure thus obtained, the assayer adds a certain amount of niter to the regular fusion to oxidize a part of the sulphur of the ore, thus preventing the reduction of too large a lead button. This is the most common method for the assay of sulphide ores. The sulphides are decomposed partly by litharge and partly by the niter.

3. SODA-IRON METHOD. — The litharge added to the charge is kept low so that the lead from it, plus that in the ore, will yield a button of suitable size for cupeling. The sulphide minerals of the ore are decomposed by means of the metallic iron. This is a good method for many ores and is commonly used.

174   A TEXTBOOK OF FIRE ASSAYING

4. ROASTING METHOD — A carefully weighed portion of the ore is roasted to eliminate sulphur, arsenic, antimony etc., and the roasted ore is then assayed as a Class 1 ore.

5. COMBINATION WET-AND-FIRE METHOD. — The sulphides, etc. of the ore are oxidized with nitric acid, the silver is precipitated as chloride and combined with the insoluble residue containing the gold. This is filtered off and assayed either by scorification or crucible.

The Litharge-Niter Assay.

With half-assay-ton charges of ore in fusions containing an excess of litharge, there may be as much as 18 per cent of pyrite or proportionately larger amounts of other sulphides, de-

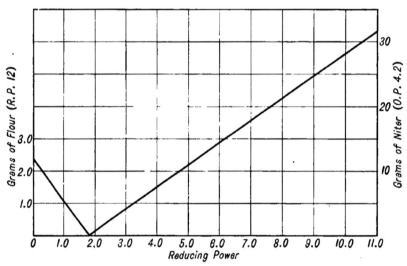

FIG. 47. — Quantity of flour or niter required per 0.5 A.T. of ore of any reducing power.

pending on their reducing power, and lead buttons of the right size for cupellation may still be obtained by cutting down or entirely eliminating the flour or other reducing agent. With ores containing more than 18 per cent of pyrite the lead buttons obtained will be too large, unless some oxidizing agent is added to counteract this extra reducing effect. For this purpose potassium nitrate is commonly used. Figure 47 shows the quantity of flour; R. P. 12, or of niter, O. P. 4.2, which must be added to half an assay-ton of sulphide ore of any reducing power to obtain a 28-gram lead button.

To perform an intelligent niter assay it is also necessary to know whether the ore is a simple sulphide of lead, iron, or zinc or whether it contains considerable amounts of metal impurities such as tellurium, copper, bismuth, arsenic, antimony, nickel or cobalt. In the latter case special measures have to be taken to eliminate these so-called "impurities." In the discussion of the process the simple case of the assay of "pure ores" will be taken first.

Slags for Pure Ores. — When an ore contains so large a proportion of sulphide minerals that it is necessary to add niter to prevent the reduction of too much lead, it will be found that the charges recommended for Class 1 ores will not allow a satisfactory decomposition of the ore. Instead of two products, slag and lead, a third intermediate product, matte, is often obtained as the result of the fusion. This amounts to an incomplete decomposition of the ore and as matte is a good collector of precious metals its presence is a sure indication of low results. A matte is much less likely to be formed, however, with a less acid charge and it has been found best, therefore, to make a slag approaching a monosilicate for all sulphide ores, as by this means more uniformly satisfactory results are obtained.

A moderate excess of litharge is always desirable in this method as it assists in the oxidation of the sulphides and also tends to keep the metal impurities out of the lead button. For this reason no less than 60 grams of litharge per half assay-ton should be used. Fifteen grams of sodium carbonate should be provided for the slag, as well as a small amount in addition, to combine with the SO_3 not taken care of by the K_2O of the niter.

In calculating a charge, the silica requirements of the various bases are determined, just as in the case of Class 1 basic ores, and the silica in the ore is deducted. A minimum of 5 grams of borax-glass is generally used; in the case of ores containing much zinc this should be increased to 10 grams. The silica equivalent of the borax-glass is deducted from the calculated amount of silica required.

Slags for Impure Ores. — When the ore consists mainly of sulphides or nickel, antimony, arsenic, bismuth, copper or tellurium the type of charge mentioned above does not contain enough uncombined litharge to keep the impurities out of the lead button. The remedy is to increase the litharge without increasing the silica, thus increasing the amount of uncombined litharge in the slag and thereby having it available for the solution of the base metal oxides. R. W. Lodge* recommends the use of from 15 to 25 per cent of litharge in excess of that called for by the reducing power of the ore and this yields satisfactory results with most impure ores. It calls for an increase in litharge as the reducing power of the ore increases. In the case of impure ores, this is equivalent to an increase of litharge with an increase of impurities. It is desirable in this case to figure for a sub-silicate slag. More detailed instructions for the assay of impure ores will be found in the following chapter.

Disadvantages of Excess Litharge. — Owing to its property of dissolving and forming easily fusible mixtures with oxides of the metals which are in themselves difficultly fusible, and particularly because of its property of keeping the impurities out of the lead button, litharge has become the assayers "cure-all." The student should have in mind, however, the possible disadvantages of the use of too much litharge. These include the extra cost of the added reagent and the more rapid destruction of crucibles, which most assayers prefer to use for a number of fusions. More important than the latter, is the damage which is done in case a crucible is eaten through, thus allowing this corrosive slag to run out on the muffle floor. It has long been recognized, also, that an increase of litharge increases very slightly the quantity of silver which is held in the slag, so that no more litharge than is necessary to ensure a pure lead button and proper decomposition of the sulphide should ever be used.

Conduct of the Fusion. — It was formerly believed that charges containing niter require very slow and careful heating to prevent loss due to boiling-over, and in some quarters this impression still prevails. This danger of loss due to boiling is a real one if fusions are made in coke pot-furnaces, as was formerly the custom; but to-day, in this country at least, practically all regular assay fusions are made in large muffles. In the coke-fired pot-furnace the charge is unevenly heated, the bottom melts while the top is still cold. Somewhere between the two is a zone of viscous semi-melted material which tends to be lifted

* Notes on Assaying, 2nd Ed., p. 105.

bodily out of the crucible by the ascending gases. In the muffle, on the other hand, the crucibles are evenly heated from all sides and because of the heat-retarding effect of the bottom and sides of the crucible, fusion probably begins at the top and proceeds downward. This provides a fluid slag through which the gases may readily escape, so that the charge boils up only very little.

For the best results in niter fusions the crucibles should be introduced into a hot muffle and brought rapidly to fusion, the whole fusion process not taking more than ten or fifteen minutes. This method of procedure ensures a complete decomposition of the sulphide minerals of the ore and prevents the formation of a matte which is likely to result if the fusion takes a long time. The crucibles should be in the furnace not more than thirty, or at the most forty minutes. If a number of crucibles are to be charged at one time the furnace should be at a light yellow heat. The cold crucibles will lower the temperature materially and it need not be heated above a yellow heat, about 1000° C., to finish. In fact a higher finishing temperature, particularly if maintained for some time, will cause low silver results, probably due to volatilization.

To obtain good results, particularly when a large amount of litharge is used in the charge, the muffle door should be closed tightly and a reducing atmosphere maintained in the muffle. If coal-fired muffles are used for fusions, the holes in the back of the muffles should be closed and several crucibles containing bituminous coal placed in the front part. This latter precaution is unnecessary with gas, gasoline, or oil-fired furnaces as these ordinarily have a reducing atmosphere in the muffle or crucible chamber.

The quick fusion which occurs in properly conducted niter assays effects a rapid and apparently complete decomposition of the ore, but, except in the most skilful hands, the slag losses are higher than for Class 1 ores of corresponding grade. The rapid fusion and very liquid slag do not permit globules of lead to remain in suspension for more than a few moments and the high slag losses common with this method may be due partly to the less complete collection of the precious metals by the lead. For this reason it is essential to reduce a generous amount of lead in this assay, not less than 25 grams and even 35 grams in the case of large charges. The use of the large quantity of litharge and niter required in the assay of impure sulphide ores is thought to give high slag losses, due to oxidation of silver and its solution in the heavy litharge slag.

Perkins* finds that the excessive silver loss in this kind of a slag may be largely prevented by maintaining a reducing atmosphere in the furnace throughout the fusion period.

Physical and Chemical Changes Taking Place in Niter Fusions. — When the crucibles are placed in the furnace the temperature of the charge immediately begins to rise, and soon any hydroscopic water contained in the reagents is driven off. When the temperature reaches 339° C., at which point niter melts, the charge begins to frit and some of the sulphides commence to react with the niter, although the action is slow at this temperature. At about 450°, silica begins to react on the niter with the evolution of oxygen, nitrogen and the formation of potassium silicate. The oxygen evolved reacts with some of the more readily oxidized sulphides, particularly pyrite which begins to oxidize readily at about this temperature.

Borax-glass begins to soften and combine with litharge at about 500°, and the fritting of the charge increases. At 530° niter begins to dissociate and the oxygen evolved helps to roast the still solid sulphides and probably converts some of the litharge into Pb_3O_4, thus making of it an oxygen carrier. Any pyrite remaining begins to decompose at 575° forming pyrrhotite and sulphur, but this reaction is slow until the temperature reaches 665°. Even in the absence of other fluxes, litharge and silica begin to combine at about 700° C. to 750° and at this temperature the charge becomes decidedly pasty, particularly in the presence of sodium carbonate and borax. If the temperature were to be held at this point the charge might boil over on account of its pasty consistency, but the properly conducted fusion is heated rapidly to 900° or 1000° C., and at this temperature it is entirely fluid and bubbles escape freely. The rate of oxidation of the sulphides increases rapidly as the temperature rises and these reactions evolve a large amount of heat.

At about 750° some of the metallic oxides and sulphates begin to react with the undecomposed sulphides and these reactions are endothermic. The following are examples:

$$PbS + PbSO_4 = 2Pb + 2SO_2 - 92,380 \text{ cal.},$$
$$PbS + 2PbO = 3Pb + SO_2 - 52,540 \text{ cal.}$$

* Trans. A.I.M.E., **33**, p. 672.

The last reaction is only one of many similar ones, which might be written, showing the direct reduction of sulphides by litharge. In the presence of sufficient silica, any ferric oxide which is present will be reduced to the ferrous state by sulphides with the liberation of sulphur dioxide, as for example:

$$3Fe_2O_3 + FeS + xSiO_2 = 7FeO.xSiO_2 + SO_2 - 81,640 \text{ cal.}$$

This reaction is of importance above 900°.

In this assay the niter is limited to less than that required to entirely decompose the sulphides of ore, the amount of undecomposed sulphide left being just enough to react with litharge and give a lead button of the right size for cupellation. No one knows in just what order the reactions take place, but the net result is the same as if the niter continued to react until entirely consumed and then the remaining sulphide was oxidized by litharge.

It is noteworthy that all authorities recommend the use of an excess of litharge for the niter assay, although it may be recalled that it is possible to decompose the sulphides entirely by fusion with sodium carbonate and niter alone, as in the Fresenius method for the determination of sulphur in pyrite. This brings up the question, "Why, and how much, excess litharge is needed?" Beringer[*] answers the first half of the question by explaining, as is now well known to all assayers, that "when metallic sulphides are present in the ore, an excess of oxide of lead helps to keep the sulphur out of the button of metal," in other words, helps to prevent the formation of a matte. Lodge[†] calls for an excess above that required for the reducing power of the ore, but this is only necessary with impure ores when the litharge is required to hold these impurities in the slag.

It is obvious that every reagent has some influence on the result, but with enough litharge to provide a lead button and some small excess to help in making a fusible slag, the quantity of silica present and the rate of fusion have the greatest effect on the result. The presence of too much silica in proportion to the bases, or too slow a fusion, will result in the formation of a matte, and this means incomplete decomposition of the ore. The reason for this is not difficult to find. In the slow fusion at a low tem-

---

[*] A Textbook of Assaying, 13th Ed., p. 93.
[†] Notes on Assaying, 2nd Ed., p. 105.

perature in the presence of an excess of silica, the litharge will be entirely converted into silicate before the completion of the reactions resulting in the oxidation of the sulphur, which require a comparatively high temperature. The litharge contained in the lead silicate is no longer available for the decomposition of the sulphides, the niter is all used up and hence sulphide sulphur remains and a matte results. The slower the fusion, the more excess litharge there must be, and the more basic the slag must be, to ensure the presence of enough undecomposed litharge to complete the oxidation of the residual sulphides. With only enough silica present for a sub-silicate, the fusion may be relatively slow and yet afford complete decomposition of the ore. This type of slag is destructive of crucibles and for this reason it is better to use a more acid slag whenever possible. It would be unwise, however, to make a slag much more acid than the mono-silicate, for the mono-silicate of lead is only partly reduced by metallic sulphides at the highest temperature of the assay-furnace. With this silicate degree, however, rapid fusions are found to result in complete decomposition of the ore.

The silica which is added in the assay of high sulphide ores helps to slag the metallic oxides which are derived from the oxidation of the sulphides; it helps to keep the iron in the ferrous condition and it serves to protect the crucibles. If possible, no reaction between it and the litharge of the charge should be permitted until all the niter has been consumed and the remaining sulphide has been decomposed by litharge. It is impossible to realize this ideal entirely but it may be approached by using comparatively coarse silica, perhaps 40- or 60-mesh, so that an appreciable time will be required for its complete solution in the slag.

Preliminary Fusion. Procedure. — Van some of the ore and estimate the character and amount of the different sulphides present, as well as the amount and character of the slag-forming constituents. Take from 3 to 10 grams of ore according to the amount of sulphide present, 3 grams for pure pyrite, and correspondingly greater amounts for ores containing less sulphides. If the ore is mostly galena as much as 10 grams may be taken, the idea being always to get a button of about 30 grams. (See "Reducing Power of Minerals.") Take twice as much sodium carbonate as ore, 60 grams of litharge and up to 5 grams of silica. If the ore contains silica a proportionately smaller amount should be added. Use an E crucible for the pot-furnace or a 12- or 15-gram crucible for the muffle. Weigh out the fluxes first, in the order given and place the ore on top, mixing thoroughly with a spatula. Place a half-inch cover of salt on top.

Fuse for ten or fifteen minutes, finishing at a good yellow heat. Pour into crucible mold, allow to cool, separate the lead from the slag and weigh on the pulp balance to tenths of grams. Divide the weight of the lead by the weight of the ore taken.

It should be noted that this reducing power is not an absolute thing but depends upon many factors, such as the ratio of sodium carbonate to ore, the amount of borax, litharge and silica added, as well as the temperature at which the fusions are conducted. Reducing power fusions made in the soft-coal muffle furnace are likely to give low results on account of oxidation of the sulphides and reduced lead during the fusion.

Estimating the Reducing Power of Ores. — In many instances it is possible to estimate the reducing power of an ore within close limits. This requires a knowledge of the reducing powers of the common sulphide minerals as well as the knack of vanning. The ore is vanned and the per cent of the various sulphides estimated. From these data the reducing power is found. For instance, if the ore is 50 per cent pyrite and the rest gangue, the reducing power will be about 5.5, 50 per cent of R. P. of pure pyrite. If it is 40 per cent galena and 10 per cent sphalerite, the reducing power will be 40 per cent of 3.4 + 10 per cent of 7.9 = 2.15 approximately. The reducing power of the ore is equal to the sum of the products of the reducing powers of the different constituents, multiplied by the percentage of each in the ore, divided by 100. For example, with an ore having three constituents, A, B, and C, whose reducing powers are respectively, a, b, and c and which are present in the ore to the extent of x, y, and z per cent respectively, the reducing power of the ore would be $\dfrac{ax + by + cz}{100}$.

In general if the amount of sulphides in the ore is comparatively small and especially if only 0.5 assay-ton of ore is used, it is a very simple matter to obtain a lead button of suitable size for cupeling, by this means. If, for example, a mixture of galena and gangue mineral contains 50 per cent of galena the reducing power of the ore will be $\frac{3.40}{2} = 1.70$. Half an assay-ton of this ore would give a lead button weighing 24.8 grams without either flour or niter. If the galena had been estimated at 40 per cent, half a gram of flour (R. P. 12) would have been added and the result would have been a 30.8-gram button which could still be cupeled. In a similar manner, if the galena had been estimated at 60 per cent about 1 gram of niter would have been added and the resulting button of about 20.8 grams could also have been cupeled.

Again, in dealing with practically pure sulphides, as in the case of pyrite or galena concentrates, it is easy to estimate the reducing power and properly control the size of the lead button.

Determining the Oxidizing Power of Niter. — The oxidizing power of niter is found by fusing a weighed amount with an ore whose reducing power is known. To obtain comparative results the slags must be exactly like those used for the reducing-power fusion and, moreover, to give lead buttons of the proper size in the final assay, the slag that is made there must be similar as regards acidity, litharge excess, etc. to that made in the preliminary fusion.

The following example illustrates the method of finding the oxidizing power of niter:

Ore	5 grams	5 grams
Sodium carbonate	10 "	10 "
Litharge	60 "	60 "
Niter		4 "
Silica	5 "	5 "
Lead obtained	24.31 grams	6.61 grams

Reducing power of ore $\frac{24.31}{5} = 4.86$

Lead oxidized by 4 grams of niter $24.31 - 6.61 = 17.70$

Oxidizing power of niter $= \frac{17.70}{4} = 4.42$

Quantity of Sodium Carbonate Converted to Sulphate. — When the reducing power of the ore, its character and the oxidizing power of niter are known the charge for the regular assay can be made up. Assume that it is desired to make a slag containing 15 grams of sodium carbonate and 30 grams of litharge for 0.5 assay-ton of ore, and that enough silica should always be present to hold and slag the iron as ferrous singulo-silicate, thus preventing it from becoming converted to ferric oxide. With pure pyrite, the reducing power of which may be assumed to be 12, and with the further assumption that all of its sulphur is oxidized to SO_3, it is evident that if the soda in the slag is to be kept constant the soda which is added to the charge will have to be increased as the reducing power of the ore increases, because one of the products of the reaction of niter upon sulphides in the presence of soda is sulphate of soda, and because the soda thus used up no longer serves as a flux.

The reactions governing the decomposition of the pyrite under the assumed conditions are the following:

(a) $2FeS_2 + 14PbO + 4Na_2CO_3 + SiO_2 =$
$$F_2SiO_4 + 14Pb + 4Na_2SO_4 + 4CO_2,$$

(b) $10FeS_2 + 28KNO_3 + 6Na_2CO_3 + 5SiO_2 =$
$$5Fe_2SiO_4 + 14K_2SO_4 + 6Na_2SO_4 + 14N_2 + 6CO_2.$$

When the ore has a reducing power of 12, $\frac{28}{12} = 2.33$ grams of pyrite react according to equation (a), yielding a 28-gram lead button. From the proportion

$$FeS_2 : 2Na_2CO_3 = 120 : 212 = 2.33 : 4.12,$$

it may be seen that this reaction results in the conversion of 4.12 grams of Na_2CO_3 into sulphate.

Reaction (a) is actually the last to take place, but was considered first to determine the quantity of pyrite in excess of that required to furnish the lead button, as this is the amount which must be oxidized by niter. There remains to be decomposed by niter under the conditions of equation (b) $14.58 - 2.33$ grams $= 12.25$ grams of pyrite. The sodium carbonate required to satisfy this reaction may be found from the proportion

$$5FeS_2 : 3Na_2CO_3 = 620 : 318 = 12.25 : y,$$

solving, y is found to be 6.28. Adding these two quantities, it will be seen that 0.5 assay-ton of pyrite, under these conditions, causes the removal of 10.4 grams of Na_2CO_3 from the slag.

It is possible to generalize from these figures and say that each gram of pyrite in the charge, up to 2.33 grams, requires the addition of 1.75 grams of soda-ash, and every gram of pyrite above 2.33 grams requires 0.52 grams of soda-ash. The computations for the actual charges need not be carried out in such detail, but it is done here to illustrate the principle.

The potassium and sodium sulphates formed by these reactions are only slightly soluble in silicate slags and, being lighter than the slag, form a layer on top of it. This sulphate cover is very liquid when molten and serves to keep the air away from the fusion. In the mold it appears on top of the slag cone as a crystalline white layer.

Quantity of Niter Required. — The quantity of niter required for any charge is determined by multiplying the reducing power of the ore by the quantity of ore taken for assay, which gives as a result the quantity of lead which would be reduced from an excess of litharge if the latter were present and no niter were added. From this quantity is subtracted the weight of the lead button desired and the remainder is divided by the oxidizing power of niter, expressed in terms of lead. For instance, in the case referred to above, the reducing power of pure pyrite being assumed to be 12, the oxidizing power of niter in this type of charge to be 4.2, the quantity of niter required for 0.5 assay-ton of ore is determined as follows:

Total reducing effect of ore $14.58 \times 12.0 =$ 175.0 grams of lead
Lead button desired 28.0 "

Difference, pyrite equivalent of which must
be oxidized by niter 147.0 "

Niter required $\dfrac{147.0}{4.2} = 35.0$ grams.

This is a large amount of niter for 0.5 assay-ton of ore and considerably more than would actually be required. The writer has never found an ore requiring more than 25 grams of niter for 0.5 assay-ton.

Silica Requirements of Bases. — For ores which consist of the sulphides of iron, lead and zinc, together with gangue minerals, and which are here classified as pure ores, a singulo-silicate slag will give satisfactory results. The silica requirements for the different bases entering the charge in the example taken would be as follows:

For 8.65 grams of FeO resulting from the
oxidation of 0.5 assay-ton of pyrite
there is required.................... 3.64 grams SiO$_2$
For 15 grams of sodium carbonate in the
slag................................ 4.25 " "
For 30 grams of litharge............... 4.06 " "

Total........................11.95 " "

Completed Charge. — Combining these various quantities the charge for pure pyrite is found to be as follows:

Ore (Pyrite R. P. 12).................. 0.5 A. T.
Sodium carbonate......................25 grams
Litharge..............................60 "
Niter..................................35[1] "
Silica................................11.95 "

[1] About 10 grams more than would ever be required.

With the proper furnace treatment this charge will give a good decomposition of the ore with a clean lead button and greenish-black, glassy slag.

Most assayers would, however, add a minimum of 5 grams of borax-glass. If this is done the equivalent amount of silica should be omitted, and the charge would be

Ore................................... 0.5 A. T.
Sodium carbonate......................25 grams
Borax-glass........................... 5 "
Litharge..............................60 "
Niter..................................
Silica................................ 8 "

Zinc oxide is difficult to slag, and the zinc silicates fuse only at a very high temperature. Stein* states that ZnSiO$_3$ melts at 1479° C., and Zn$_2$SiO$_4$ at 1880° C. In the presence of much zinc the borax-glass may be increased to a maximum of 10 grams in case of pure sphalerite. It is interesting to note that the additions of borax increases the solubility of the sulphate salt in the slag. With pure sphalerite and no borax the slag is glassy and the weight of the sulphate cover closely approaches the theoretical amount. When 10 grams of borax-glass is added the

* Zeitschr. anorg. Chemie, **55**, p. 179 (1907).

solid slag appears slightly stony and a much smaller sulphate cover is obtained. The alkaline sulphates are dissolved in the superheated slag but tend to crystallize out on cooling, resulting in the stony appearance of the solid slag.

The following are examples of suitable charges for pure ores:

	No. 1 Pure Galena R. P. 3.45	No. 2 Pure Sphalerite R. P. 8.5	No. 3 Pure Pyrite R. P. 12.0
Ore..............	0.5 A. T.	0.5 A. T.	0.5 A. T.
Sodium carbonate.	19 grams	21 grams	25 grams
Borax-glass......	0 "	10 "	5 "
Litharge.........	50 "	60 "	60 "
Niter (O. P. 4.2)..	5 "	23 "	35 "
Silica............	5 "	6 "	8 "
Crucible.........	20-gram	25-gram	30-gram

Procedure. Regular Niter Fusion. — Make up charges according to the rules outlined above. The fusion should preferably be made in large muffle furnaces regulated so as to have a slight reducing atmosphere. It is best to close the holes in the back of soft-coal muffles with bone-ash, but this precaution is unnecessary with gas or oil-fired furnaces. Crucible-type furnaces heated by gas or gasoline are satisfactory if thoroughly preheated before the crucibles are introduced. Coke-fired crucible furnaces are the least satisfactory of all for niter fusions, because of the difficulty of careful temperature control, which is particularly necessary with this method. A salt cover is entirely unnecessary for muffle fusions.

Be sure that none of the reagents are lumpy and that the charges are thoroughly mixed. If this precaution is taken and the temperature is properly adjusted no trouble should be caused by boiling. However, if the soda and the niter are in lumps the results will be less satisfactory and the charges may boil over. Fuse at a high temperature so that the charges will be well melted in ten minutes and will have finished bubbling in from fifteen to twenty-five minutes. After audible bubbling has ceased allow to remain at a yellow heat for ten or fifteen minutes more. Then pour and finish as usual. Examine the crucibles while hot to see whether the fusion has been satisfactory and note particularly whether any lead shots have remained behind. Examine the button and line of separation between lead and slag, to be sure that lead buttons are free from matte. If matte or shotty lead is obtained, the assay should be repeated with such changes in manipulation of fire or of composition of charge as may be suggested.

An annoying situation occasionally encountered in assaying some sulphide ores, particularly those containing pyrrhotite and arsenical pyrite, is the behavior of the lead which refuses to collect and remains shotted throughout the slag. When the slag is poured, some clear slag comes first, then slag full of lead shot. The slag which is left in the crucible is also full of lead shot. This is usually due to too low a temperature of fusion or too little silica, but may also be caused by the oxidation of the iron to ferric oxide during the fusion. Ferric oxide is infusible at the temperature of the fusion and is insoluble in the ordinary slag at this temperature.

The best way of overcoming this difficulty is to increase the silica and run the new assay at a higher temperature. If sufficient silica is present to form bi-silicates with all of the bases, the iron will be held firmly in the ferrous condition and shots due to this cause are avoided. A high temperature favors the reduction of Fe_2O_3 to FeO or what amounts to the same thing, prevents the formation of Fe_2O_3 by the niter and litharge. This is in accordance with the well-known principle of physical chemistry, that "the change of heat energy into chemical energy takes place more readily at high than at low temperatures." According to data given by Richards[*] the thermal equations representing this type of reaction may be written as follows:

$$Fe_2O_3 + Pb = 2FeO + PbO - 13,400 \text{ cal.}$$
$$Fe_3O_4 + Pb = 3FeO + PbO - 22,900 \text{ cal.}$$

According to van't Hoff's law, when the temperature of such a system is raised, the equilibrium point is displaced in the direction which absorbs heat, that is to say, the above reactions will proceed in a right-handed direction.

Ferric oxide is soluble in an excess of litharge, and another way to avoid obtaining a slag containing lead shots is to use a large excess of litharge in the charge. This method of procedure is

[*] Metallurgical Calculations.

open to the objection that the recovery of silver and gold is more or less incomplete when the slag contains ferric oxide.*

The following table of mono-silicate slag factors may be found useful in determining the quantity of silica required for any niter fusion.

TABLE XXIII.

Mono-Silicate Slag Factors.

Quantity of bases	Quantity of acids required	
	Silica	Borax-glass
8.65 grams FeO from ½ A. T. FeS$_2$ requires...	3.64	4.89
11.3 " FeO " ½ A. T. Fe$_7$S$_8$ "	4.75	6.38
12.17 " ZnO " ½ A. T. ZnS "	4.51	6.06
13.6 " PbO " ½ A. T. PbS "	1.84	2.44
15 grams Na$_2$CO$_3$ .... "	4.25	5.72
30 grams PbO .... "	4.06	5.46

To avoid low results due to oxidation by niter, it is often advantageous to reduce the quantity of ore used. When silver alone is being sought, the niter may be entirely done away with by reducing the ore charge to a quantity sufficient to give a lead button weighing not more than 30 grams. In gold assays, however, a charge less than 0.5 assay-ton is undesirable, as it fails to give a sufficiently close valuation of the ore.

The Soda-Iron Method.

The soda-iron, or iron-nail method of assaying sulphide ores is radically different from any of the other methods so far described. It consists of a reducing fusion of the ore with a large amount of sodium carbonate, as well as a limited amount of litharge and borax and occasionally a small amount of silica, together with an excess of metallic iron, usually in the form of nails or spikes. The principal difference between this and the other crucible methods consists in the use of metallic iron as a reducing and desulphurizing agent. As iron reduces lead from litharge, as well as from the common lead minerals,

* Jour. Chem. Met. and Min. Soc. of South Africa, **2,** p. 465.

this latter reagent is limited to 30 or 35 grams and even less if the ore itself contains lead. Therefore, the only basic fluxes available are the alkaline carbonates, and the quantity of these to be used is at least two or three times the quantity of ore. Just before pouring, the excess of iron is removed.

Chemical Reactions. — The chemical reactions which take place in the crucible are entirely different from those of the other crucible methods. In the case of the niter and roasting methods of assaying, the sulphides of the ore are oxidized by litharge, niter, or the oxygen of the air and the sulphur either passes off as SO_2 or is converted into SO_3, which displaces the carbonic acid of the sodium carbonate, forming sodium sulphate. In the iron assay, part of the sulphur in pyrite and some of the other sulphides is volatilized, part of the sulphur is oxidized by the small amount of litharge used and the rest remains as sulphide, appearing either as an iron matte on top of the lead button or dissolved in the excess of basic slag.

The following reactions will serve to illustrate the chemical changes which take place:

$$FeS_2 = FeS + S,$$
$$PbS + 2PbO = 3Pb + SO_2,$$
$$Cu_2S + 2PbO = 2CuPb + SO_2,$$
$$FeS + 3PbO = 3Pb + FeO + SO_2,$$
$$Fe + PbO = Pb + FeO.$$

When the litharge is all reduced the following occur:

$$PbS + Fe = Pb + FeS \text{ (matte)},$$
$$FeS_2 + Fe = 2FeS \text{ (matte)},$$
$$Sb_2S_3 + 3Fe = 2Sb + 3FeS \text{ (matte)},$$
$$As_2S_3 + 13Fe = 2Fe_5As \text{ (speiss)} + 3FeS \text{ (matte)},$$
$$Cu_2S + Fe = Cu_2 + FeS \text{ (partial)}.$$

Finally, if a sufficient excess of alkaline flux is used, the iron matte is dissolved by this basic slag, probably as a double sulphide of iron and sodium or potassium.

From the equations it will be seen that copper, arsenic and antimony are reduced, at least in part, and either go into the lead button, or in the case of arsenic form a speiss which appears as a hard, white globule partly embedded in the top surface of the lead button.

In Table XXIV are shown the heats of formation of some of the common metallic sulphides expressed in terms of a unit weight of sulphur.

TABLE XXIV.

HEAT OF FORMATION OF METALLIC SULPHIDES.

Formula	Calories	Formula	Calories
K_2S	103,500	CoS	21,900
CaS	94,300	Cu_2S	20,300
Na_2S	89,300	PbS	20,200
MnS	45,600	NiS	19,500
ZnS	43,000	$\tfrac{1}{3}Sb_2S$	11,500
FeS	24,000	Ag_2S	3,000

A glance at this table points to the theoretical possibility of reducing the sulphides of cobalt, copper, lead, nickel, antimony and silver by metallic iron, and this is borne out by laboratory experience. From the thermochemical data it may also be predicted that but little zinc will be reduced, and therefore the lead button will be free from this metal.

Another reaction which is important in this connection is the oxidizing effect of alkaline carbonates on metallic sulphides. This reaction affords a considerable reduction of lead from galena when the latter is fused with alkaline carbonate alone, and was the basis of the Upper Harz method for the assay of lead in galena ores. The reaction as given by Kerl is as follows:

$$7PbS + 4K_2CO_3 = 4Pb + 3(K_2PbS_2) + K_2SO_4 + 4CO_2.$$

At first glance this reaction may not appear to be reasonable, but a simple trial fusion with these two substances will serve to convince the most skeptical that something very much like this does occur. Taken step by step, starting with the reversible reaction:

(1) $\quad 3PbS + 3K_2CO_3 \rightleftarrows 3K_2S + 3PbCO_3,$

the explanation is simple. Lead carbonate is readily dissociated by heat as follows:

(2) $\quad 3PbCO_3 = 3PbO + 3CO_2.$

The CO_2 escapes and this allows equation (1) to proceed in a right-handed direction.

The lead oxide resulting from equation (2), in the presence of alkaline carbonate, reacts with more lead sulphide as follows:

(3) $PbS + 3PbO + K_2CO_3 = 4Pb + K_2SO_4 + CO_2$.

A condition of equilibrium appears to be reached when the simple double sulphide of alkali and lead is obtained, *i.e.*:

(4) $3PbS + 3K_2S = 3(K_2PbS_2)$.

Adding equations (1), (2), (3) and (4) we have Kerl's reaction:

$7PbS + 4K_2CO_3 = 4Pb + 3(K_2PbS_2) + K_2SO_4 + 4CO_2$.

It is obvious that sodium carbonate will have the same effect as potassium carbonate.

Limitations of the Method. — The soda-iron method is an excellent one for suitable ores when the greatest accuracy is not desired, but is limited in its application to pure ores. It is known to give low silver results on high sulphide ores such as nearly pure pyrite, but if properly conducted the results should not be more than 2 or 3 per cent lower than those obtained by the niter method, while the gold results are but little different in the two cases. This loss of silver is attributed by Hall[*] to the solubility of the silver in the iron sulphide of the slag, although according to Fulton[†], " ferrous sulphide has practically no solvent action on silver or on gold." The slag obtained in the assay of pure pyrite contains a large amount of ferrous-alkaline-sulphide and this probably has a slight solvent action on silver, so that the silver is distributed between the slag and the lead button in proportion to the relative amounts of ferrous-alkaline-sulphide and lead present and according to its solubility in the one as compared with the other. If this is true, the less sulphide sulphur the slag contains and the greater the quantity of lead reduced, the higher the silver recovery and the more satisfactory the results should be. This points out one detail of the furnace manipulation of the iron-nail assay of pyritic ores which should be carefully regulated, *i.e.*, the temperature should be held at a dull red for some time to aid in the elimination of the first atom of sulphur from the pyrite, which breaks up at this temperature. It is also important to provide sufficient litharge to supply a good-sized lead button and more important still to reduce this as completely as possible.

[*] Assay of Gold and Silver by the Iron-Nail Method Trans. A. I. M. E., **47**, p. 37.

[†] Trans. A.I.M.E., **39**, p. 596.

A 35-gram lead button is needed for pure pyrite. The excessively high slag losses often reported for this method, are probably caused by too small a lead-fall and too short a time of fusion, which would result in leaving some lead sulphide, a good solvent for silver, in the slag.

In general it may be said that the method is not suited for ores carrying nickel, copper, cobalt, arsenic, antimony, bismuth or tellurium. Even when an ore contains several per cent of copper, this metal may not enter the lead button in sufficient quantity to interfere seriously with cupellation; but the presence of copper always gives low results, probably because of the solvent action of the copper sulphide, contained in the slag, upon the silver. Ores containing nickel are least of all suited to the method.

The Slag. — The slag made should not be more acid than a mono-silicate, and a sub-silicate is, perhaps, preferable. The slag does not attack the crucibles to any extent, and the latter may be used a number of times, if care is taken to see that they do not retain any lead shot.

Atmosphere. — A reducing atmosphere should be maintained in the furnace to prevent oxidation and corrosion of the nails. This may be accomplished by placing several crucibles containing soft coal in the front part of the muffle and renewing the coal in them if necessary. In an oxidizing atmosphere the nails are badly corroded. The ferric oxide scale formed causes the slag to become thick and pasty and this tends to cause the retention of lead shot in the crucible.

Procedure. — Van the ore, estimate and record its mineral composition. Note especially the amount of lead minerals. Use a 20-, 25- or 30-gram crucible according to the amount of reagents required. The following charges are suggested as capable of yielding better results than the customary 30 grams of sodium carbonate, 10 grams of borax-glass, and 25 grams of litharge.

	Galena	Half Galena Half Pyrite	Pyrite
Ore	0.5 A. T.	0.5 A. T.	0.5 A. T.
Sodium carbonate	30 grams	40 grams	50 grams
Borax	10 "	15 "	20–25 "
Litharge	20 "	27 "	35 "
Silica	2 "	2 "	2 "

Insert from 3 to 5 twenty-penny cut nails, or preferably one 3½ or 4 inch track spike, point downward.

Heat gradually to fusion, fuse from forty to sixty minutes. Examine the nails occasionally and if they are badly eaten add several fresh ones, leaving the old ones in the crucible if they cannot be removed free from lead. Fuse until the nails may be freed from lead by tapping them gently and washing them around in the slag. Remove all nails and pour as usual. The slag will be black and should separate easily from the lead button.

Notes: 1. If the ore contains two or more grams of silica none need be added.

2. If bicarbonate of soda is substituted for the normal carbonate use a correspondingly greater weight.

3. This fusion requires a somewhat longer time than the niter fusion, owing to the fact that time must be allowed for all of the charge to come in contact with the surface of the iron nails.

4. The lead may not start to drive in cupeling quite as rapidly as other buttons owing to a small amount of iron which is often present.

5. A matte indicates too much silica, too little alkaline carbonate or too short a time of fusion.

The Roasting Method.

This method of assaying sulphide ores is rarely used, but may be found of advantage for very low-grade pyritic ores, and will be briefly described.

Procedure. — Take from 0.5 to 5.0 assay-tons of ore and spread out in a well-chalked roasting dish of sufficient size to allow of stirring without loss. Have the muffle at a dull red only and the fire so low that the temperature of the muffle may be held stationary, or raised slowly. Place the dish in the muffle and, if the ore contains minerals which decrepitate, cover it and keep it covered until danger from this source is passed. The ore should soon begin to roast. When fumes are noticed coming from the ore, check the fire and hold it at this temperature for some time, stirring frequently. After all danger of fusing is over, gradually raise the temperature, stirring at intervals of twenty minutes or half an hour. Finally heat to about 700° C. for half an hour. If the ore contains only sulphides of iron and copper, practically all of the sulphur will be removed within this time. If there is any doubt about the roast being complete, remove from the muffle, add a small amount of charcoal and see if there is any odor of sulphur dioxide. If the ore contains zinc, a much higher temperature will be required to break up the zinc sulphate. It is not advisable, however, to carry the roasting temperature above 700° C. For ores which consist principally of pyrite, galena or stibnite, place a weighed amount of silica on the dish before introducing the ore. A weight of silica equal to that of sulphide may be used. This will serve to prevent the roasted material from adhering to the dish and will be found useful as a flux in the subsequent fusion.

If the ore contains arsenic or antimony, the roasting operation is more difficult. The best conditions for the elimination of these elements are alternate oxidation and reduction at a low temperature. The presence of sulphur aids in the elimination of these elements, because their sulphides are volatile. To obtain the reducing action necessary for the elimination of arsenic and antimony, take the partially roasted ore from the muffle, allow it to cool for a few moments, and then mix powdered charcoal or coal dust with it and roast at a dull red heat until the coal is burned off. Then add more coal and reroast. Repeat this until no more fumes of arsenic or antimony are noticed, then heat with frequent stirring to about 700° C.

After the ore is roasted, the dish is carefully cleaned out and the ore is charged into a crucible with fluxes and treated exactly as a Class 1 ore. If the sulphide mineral was mostly iron, the ore will probably be found to have a slight oxidizing power due to the formation of Fe_2O_3 and Fe_3O_4 in the roasting.

The roasting method of assaying is slow and takes up much muffle space. It is open to the liability of serious mechanical and volatilization losses. Its most useful field would seem to be the assay of low-grade pyritic gold ores where a very accurate determination of gold is desired. The method usually gives low results in silver.

The Combination Wet-and-Fire Assay.

The combination wet-and-fire assay is used principally for the determination of gold and silver in impure ores, matte, speiss and bullion. A description of the method, as applied to the assay of ores containing cobalt, nickel and arsenic, will be found in the chapter on "The Assay of Complex Ores," and the application of the method to the assay of copper bullion may be found in the chapter on "The Assay of Bullion."

ASSAY OF CLASS 3 ORES.

The principal ores belonging to this class are those containing some of the higher oxides of iron or manganese, *i.e.*, Fe_2O_3, Fe_3O_4, MnO_2. These are reduced by carbon and tend to enter the slag as ferrous and manganous silicates respectively. If the charge made up for these ores contained only the ordinary amount of flour, all of this might be used up in reducing the oxides of the ore and no lead button would result. To remedy this, the oxidizing power of the ore should be known before the charge is made up.

To determine the oxidizing power of an ore, fuse a known weight of it, say 10 or 20 grams, with a regular crucible charge for that amount of ore and a carefully weighed amount of argols or flour of known reducing power, more than sufficient to oxidize the ore. The weight of lead that the argols may be supposed to have reduced from an excess of litharge, minus the weight of lead obtained, is evidently the amount oxidized by the ore. This weight divided by the weight of ore taken gives the oxidizing power.

When the oxidizing power of the ore has been determined the assay is made in the same manner as for Class 1 ores, with the addition of the extra flour required.

CHAPTER IX.

THE ASSAY OF COMPLEX ORES AND SPECIAL METHODS.

THE ASSAY OF ORES CONTAINING NICKEL AND COBALT.

Ores from the Cobalt district of Ontario present unusual difficulties for the assayer, as well as for the metallurgist. The high-grade ore, which carries several thousand ounces of silver per ton, is an intimate mixture of the arsenides and sulphides of cobalt, nickel and silver with a large amount of what appears to be native silver, but actually consists of an alloy of silver with arsenic, nickel and cobalt.

The question of determining the amount of silver in a shipment of such ore is actually more of a sampling than an assaying problem. The accepted method of sampling consists in crushing the entire lot of ore to a relatively small size and separating the metallic from the non-metallic portions. Each portion is then assayed separately and the results combined to give the average silver content of the ore. For a more detailed account of the sampling of such an ore the student is referred to Volume 11, pages 287 to 293 inclusive, of the Journal of the Canadian Mining Institute where the practice at the Copper Cliff smelter is described. A later paper describing the method used at the Cobalt sampler may be found in the Transactions of the Canadian Mining Institute, Volume 17, pages 199 to 251 inclusive.

For low-grade ores containing but little nickel, the crucible method of assaying will give satisfactory results. For details reference may be made to an article on this subject in the Engineering and Mining Journal, Volume 90, page 809.

For high-grade ores, a properly conducted combination method will yield higher and more concordant results than can be obtained by any " all-fire " method. The following method of A. M. Smoot is taken from his discussion* of this problem.

* Trans. Can. Min. Inst. **17**, pp. 244-250.

The Combination Assay. — Quarter- or half- assay-ton portions of the pulp are taken, the former weight if the sample contains over 2000 ounces per ton, the latter if the silver is less than this. The pulp is treated in beakers with strong nitric acid, added a little at a time until danger of frothing is past. About 75 c.c. of acid is required for 0.25 A. T. portions and 100 c.c. for 0.5 A. T. portions. The solutions are heated on a steam bath until red fumes cease to be generated and are then diluted with 200 c.c. of distilled water and allowed to stand until cold, preferably over night. It is very important that the solutions be allowed to stand before they are filtered, because with certain ores containing much arsenic together with some antimony and lime, a white crystalline coating appears on the bottoms and sides of the beakers and cannot be detached by washing or even scraping. This coating contains a little silver, and if it is not allowed to form in the original nitric acid solution it forms later on in the process and makes trouble. Insoluble residues are filtered off and washed thoroughly. If there is any coating on the sides and bottoms of the beakers which cannot be readily detached with a piece of filter paper, it is treated in the beaker with a hot solution of caustic soda which quickly disintegrates it. The caustic soda solution is acidulated with a little nitric acid and washed into the filter with the insoluble residue. Most of the silver is dissolved by the original nitric acid treatment and passes through the filters as silver nitrate, but a little remains with the insoluble residue. If the insoluble residues are large in amount they are dried and burned in crucibles, fused with sodium carbonate, borax-glass, litharge and a reducing agent. If they are small they are dried and burned in scorifiers and scorified with test lead and borax-glass. In either case, the lead buttons from the insolubles are reserved. Standard sodium chloride solution is added to the nitric acid solutions in amount sufficient to precipitate all of the silver as chloride, but any considerable excess of the precipitant is to be avoided. The silver chloride is stirred briskly until it agglomerates and is then allowed to stand for an hour until it settles and the supernatant liquid becomes clear. If it remains cloudy, rapid stirring is repeated and it is again allowed to settle. The clear solutions are filtered through double filter papers and the silver chloride precipitates transferred to the filters by a water jet and there washed slightly with water. The beakers are washed well with a wash-bottle jet and any traces of silver chloride remaining in them are wiped off with small pieces of filter paper which are placed in the filters. Filters containing the silver chloride are transferred to scorifiers which have been glazed on the inside by melting litharge in them and pouring away the excess. The glazing is done to prevent the porous scorifiers from absorbing moisture from the damp paper, and as a further protection, a small disc of pure sheet lead is placed beneath the filter papers. The scorifiers are transferred to a closed oven heated to about 250° – 300° C., where they are dried and the paper is slowly charred until it is practically all consumed. This method of burning the filter papers is an essential step, since it avoids losses of silver chloride which are apt to occur if the burning is done rapidly in a muffle. Fine test lead is sprinkled over the burned silver chloride residues and the lead buttons resulting from the crucible fusions or scorifications of the corresponding insoluble residues are added. Scorification is then conducted at a low temperature so as to obtain 15-gram lead buttons. These are cupeled at a low temperature, care being taken, in the case of large silver beads, to avoid "spitting" at the end of cupellation.

The combination method is acceptable to the smelters since it does not include slag and cupel corrections. Inasmuch as all impurities likely to effect variations in the volatilization and slag losses are removed prior to the fire work, the results of assays made on different days and in different muffles, under different conditions, are more uniform than when the untreated ores are assayed directly.

Small amounts of bismuth occurring in the Cobalt silver ores are a source of irregularity in "all-fire" methods because bismuth is retained to some extent by silver after cupellation. In the combination method, bismuth is eliminated before any fire work is done.

THE ASSAY OF TELLURIDE ORES.

The determination of the precious metals in ores containing tellurium has always been considered more than ordinarily difficult. Results obtained by different assayers and even duplicate assays by the same man have often been widely divergent. The literature of telluride ore assaying is extensive and none too satisfactory; however, it is safe to say that most of the reported differences between duplicates and between different assayers have been due more to difficulties in sampling than to the chemical interference of the element tellurium. When it is considered that most of the telluride ores which are mined contain less than 0.1 per cent of telluride mineral, it is apparent that more than ordinary care must be taken to ensure obtaining a fair proportion of this in the final assay portion. The telluride mineral itself may contain as much as 40 per cent of gold, so that one 100-mesh particle more or less in the assay portion may make a difference of several hundredths ounces of gold to the ton. To obviate, as far as possible, this lack of homogeneity, all telluride ores should be pulverized to at least 150- and preferably 200-mesh and then very thoroughly mixed before the assay portions are weighed out.

Effect of Tellurium. — Tellurium is a close associate of both gold and silver and is difficult to separate from these metals either in the crucible, scorification or cupellation processes. It is not, however, often found in abundance, and even in high-grade ores tellurium itself is found in comparatively small amounts. For instance, in two high-grade ores used by Hillebrand and Allen* in their experiments on the assay of telluride ores, containing respectively 15 and 19 ounces of gold per ton, there was tellurium amounting to 0.074 and 0.092 per cent respectively. It seems unreasonable to expect such small quantities of any element to influence seriously the results of a fire-assay.

In order to study the effects of tellurium in the gold and silver assay it is necessary to experiment with ores or alloys containing much more tellurium than those above mentioned. The following facts regarding the behavior of tellurium in cupellation and fusion are mostly due to the work of Holloway,† Pease‡ and Smith,‡ whom we have to thank for coördinating and elucidating much information which was hitherto much scattered and of doubtful value.

Effect of Tellurium in Cupellation. — The presence of tellurium in a lead button causes a weakening of the surface tension of the molten metal. The result is that the metal tends to " wet " the

* Bull. 253, U. S. Geol. Survey.

† The assay of Telluride Ores, G. T. Holloway and L. E. B. Pease, Trans. I. M. M., **17**, p. 175.

‡ The Behavior of Tellurium in Assaying, Sydney W. Smith, Trans. I. M. M., **17**, p. 463.

surface of the cupel, and this allows some particles of alloy to pass into the cupel while others are left behind to cupel by themselves on its surface and form minute beads. In the case of a button containing 10 per cent or more of tellurium with an equal weight of gold or silver, complete absorption may take place. As the proportion of lead in the alloy is increased, the amount of absorption becomes less; when the lead amounts to eighty times the tellurium very little loss of precious metal occurs in a properly conducted cupellation.

Tellurium is removed comparatively slowly during cupellation, particularly in the early stages, as might be expected on comparing the heat of formation of its oxide with that of lead oxide. Rose* gives the following figures for the heat of combination of these metals with 16 grams of oxygen, —Pb to PbO 5030 calories, Te to TeO_2 3860 calories. To avoid danger of undue loss in cupellation of buttons from the assay of such ores, as much as possible of the tellurium should be removed before cupellation. It is also evident that the assayer should allow for large lead buttons in order that the ratio of lead to tellurium may be high.

Silver in the alloy protects gold from losses due to the presence of tellurium. It appears to act as a diluent for the gold and should always be added to every gold assay for this reason, if for no other.

In the case of imperfect cupellation, tellurium is retained by the bead and gives it a frosted appearance. In perfect cupellation the final condition of the tellurium is that of complete oxidation to TeO_2. Owing to its effect in reducing surface tension, as a result of which minute beads are often left behind, it would be well to use a cupel having a finer surface when cupeling buttons containing tellurium. Smith states that the loss due to subdivision and absorption in this case is much less when a "patent" (magnesia) cupel is used. Losses of gold and silver by volatilization, during properly conducted cupellation of lead buttons from ordinary telluride ores, is extremely small.

Effect of Tellurium in Fusions. — Tellurium was formerly believed to be oxidized to the dioxide during fusion and to go into the slag as a sodium or lead tellurate. Smith disagrees with this and argues that tellurates are decomposed at a red heat, and that lead tellurate is white, while he found the litharge slags ob-

* Trans. Inst. Min. Met., **14,** p. 384.

tained in the fusion of telluride compounds to be black. He believes that tellurium exists in the slag as the black monoxide, TeO.

The slag best suited to the oxidation and retention of tellurium in crucible assaying is a basic one containing a considerable excess of litharge. The temperature of fusion should be moderately low, as a high temperature prevents the satisfactory oxidation and slagging of the tellurium, owing probably to the formation of lead silicates before the litharge has had time to oxidize the tellurium. Smith gives the following reaction for the oxidation of tellurium:

$$2PbO + Te = Pb_2O + TeO.$$

In support of this he claims to have found the black suboxide of lead in the slag.

Practically all authorities agree that the scorification process is not reliable for telluride ores. When a button from a crucible assay contains too much tellurium for direct cupellation Smith recommends fusing or "soaking" the button under an ample amount of litharge at a moderate temperature *i.e.*, 700–900° C.

Hillebrand and Allen used the following charge for ores containing from 15 to 19 ounces of gold and 0.074 to 0.092 per cent of tellurium.

Ore	1. A. T.
Sodium carbonate	30 grams
Borax-glass	10 "
Litharge	180 "
Reducing agent	for 25-gram buttons
Silver	2½ to 3 times gold

They find slag losses no higher than with ordinary gold ores and no serious cupellation losses. With ores containing much more tellurium than the above, the quantity taken should be reduced and the rest of the charge maintained as before.

THE ASSAY OF ORES AND PRODUCTS HIGH IN COPPER.

Crucible methods for the assay of matte and ores high in copper have largely supplanted the older scorification method. This is due to the fact that a larger amount of pulp may be used for each individual assay, thus increasing the accuracy of the results. The copper is eliminated, as it is in the scorification assay, by the solution of its oxide in the basic lead oxide slag. The assay thus combines the advantages of the scorification with those of the crucible assay.

Perkins* has made a careful study of this process, and calls attention to the fact that the litharge used must be in proportion to the amount of copper and other impurities in the ore. The amounts he uses are very large, from 137 to 300 parts PbO to 1 part Cu, and make the method an expensive one. Others have reduced this amount considerably, and still manage to get buttons which will cupel.

The Slag. — The slag should be decidedly basic, for if the litharge is combined with large amounts of silica and borax, it will no longer retain its power of holding the copper in solution. A small amount of silica is necessary to prevent, to some extent, the action of the litharge upon the crucible. One part of silica to from 15 to 20 parts of litharge is generally allowed in the charge. Borax should be entirely omitted as it decreases the copper-holding capacity of the slag, and also causes boiling of the charge. Perkins states that the best results are obtained with a slag which exhibits, when cooled and broken, a somewhat glassy exterior gradually passing to litharge-like crystals towards the center. The amount of crystallization which takes place is, of course, a function of the rate of cooling and will depend among other things upon the size of the charge, the temperature of the charge when poured, and of the mold, so that too much weight should not be given to the above. The slag should, however, be crystalline and resemble litharge; a slag which is dull or glassy throughout indicates the presence of too much acid for a good elimination of copper.

Conduct of the Assay. — On account of the very corrosive action of the litharge slag it is especially necessary that the fusion be made rapidly. The muffle should be hot to start, 1000° to 1100° C., the hotter the better, and the fusion should be finished in from twenty to thirty minutes. This not only preserves the crucibles, but also, as a necessary sequel, prevents the slag from

* The Litharge Method of Assaying Copper-Bearing Ores and Products, and the Method of Calculating Charges, W. G. Perkins, Trans. A.I.M.E., **31**, p. 913.

becoming charged with silica and thus forcing the copper into the button. The slag melts at a low temperature and a very high finishing temperature is not necessary. With a quick fusion there is less chance for oxidation of lead with the consequent reduction of too small a lead button.

For the best work the hole in the back of the muffle should be closed and a reducing atmosphere maintained in the muffle. This may be accomplished by filling the mouth of the muffle with charcoal or coke, or by placing a few crucibles partly full of soft coal near the front of the muffle and using a tight-fitting door. If this precaution is not observed part of the silver will be oxidized and lost in the slag.

The following charges kindly furnished by the Boston and Montana Reduction Department of the Anaconda Copper Mining Company, Great Falls, Montana, are recommended for these ores.

TABLE XXV.

CHARGES FOR COPPER-BEARING MATERIAL.

Material		Approximate analysis	Charge for silver (In 20-gram crucible)		Charge for gold (In 30-gram crucible)	
Concentrates	Cu	9–15 per cent	Sample	½ A. T.	Sample	1 A. T.
	SiO_2	15–23 "	Soda	20 grams	Soda	30 grams
	FeO	33–40 "	Litharge	100 "	Litharge	150 "
	S	33–40 "	Silica	5 "	Silica	8 "
	Ag	3–5 ounces	Niter	15–25 "	Niter	40–60 "
	Au	0.015–0.025 ounces	Cover mixture		Cover mixture	
Matte	Cu	30–45 per cent	Sample	½ A. T.	Sample	½ A. T.
	Fe	40–30 "	Soda	18 grams	Soda	25 grams
	S	30–27 "	Litharge	100 "	Litharge	200 "
	Ag	10–18 ounces	Silica	7 "	Silica	12 "
	Au	0.07–0.11 ounces	Niter	6 "	Niter	18 "
			Cover mixture		Cover mixture	
Matte	Cu	45–60 per cent	Sample	½ A. T.	Sample	½ A. T.
	Fe	30–15 "	Soda	18 grams	Soda	25 grams
	S	27–24 "	Litharge	25 "	Litharge	240 "
	Ag	15–25 ounces	Silica	7 "	Silica	12 "
	Au	0.10–0.14 ounces	Niter	4 "	Niter	14 "
			Cover mixture		Cover mixture	

The cover consists of one-quarter inch of a mixture of 4 parts sodium carbonate, 2 parts borax and 1 part silica. Fusions in 20-gram crucibles require about thirty minutes, those in 30-gram crucibles about fifty minutes. It will be noticed that occasionally as much as 60 grams of niter is used in a single fusion. With the proper muffle temperature there is said to be no danger of a crucible boiling over even though the crucible be filled to within half an inch of the top.

ASSAY OF ZINC-BOX PRECIPITATE.

The gold and silver precipitated from cyanide solutions by means of zinc always contains more or less metallic zinc as well as more or less copper, lead and other readily reducible metals which may be present in the ore, or which may have been introduced during the process. Gold precipitate usually contains a good deal of metallic zinc and is generally given a preliminary acid treatment before being melted. Silver precipitate, on the other hand, is comparatively free from zinc and may be melted directly. Besides metals, the precipitate may also contain hydroxide, cyanide and ferro-cyanides of zinc, as well as iron oxide, silica, alumina, etc.

The materials as received by the assayer will usually have been passed through a 16- or 20-mesh screen for the purpose of removing the short zinc, and may or may not have been acid-treated. The peculiarities of this material are (a) the presence of more or less metallic zinc which has a reducing power of 3.17 and which boils at 930° C., (b) the presence of various compounds containing zinc oxide, which is difficultly soluble in litharge, (c) its richness and spotty character, which necessitate the most painstaking care to secure commercially satisfactory results.

On account of the amount of gold and silver contained, the sampling and grinding should be carried out in a special room, well separated from the regular assay office, to avoid danger of salting. A corner of the clean-up and melting room may be used if available, and there should be provided for this purpose a special bucking board, as well as special samplers, screens, brushes, etc.

The assay sample, weighing 2 or 3 pounds, should be thoroughly dried and ground to pass at least 80-mesh. A convenient quantity of the final pulp is 150 or 200 grams, and the 80-mesh sample may be cut down to this and then ground, preferably on the bucking board, to at least 150-mesh. This final sample should be thoroughly mixed and dried again, cooled in a desiccator and kept there until the final samples are weighed. This precaution is observed both to prevent the material from taking on moisture from the air and to prevent oxidation of the zinc, which in some cases would cause a measurable error due to change in weight of the sample.

The fine pulp may be assayed by crucible fusion and cupellation or by one of several wet or wet-and-fire methods. The crucible assay is always corrected by a reassay of the slag and corrections are also applied for cupel absorption.

The following crucible charge is recommended by Magenan,*

   Precipitate...... 0.1 assay-ton
   Sodium carbonate. 5 grams
   Borax-glass...... 2 "
   Litharge......... 70 "
   Flour............for 25–30-gram buttons
   Silica........... 5 grams

A thoroughly glazed crucible should be used for this purpose, to ensure against any of the precipitate adhering to the walls above the level of the fusion. A narrow-bladed spatula is convenient for sampling the precipitate. The weighing should be done on an analytical or exceptionally accurate pulp balance. It is customary to make at least six assays and to average the results. The fusions should be heated rather gradually to the full temperature of the muffle.

According to Layng,† a high temperature at the beginning is productive of low results. Apparently it is better to oxidize the metallic zinc with litharge than to allow it to volatilize.

For silver-bearing precipitate the Volhard or Gay-Lussac volumetric methods may be used, but the latter should be avoided in the presence of mercury, which interferes. There is no great advantage in the combination wet-and-fire methods unless the precipitate contains considerable copper or other metals which might contaminate the bead or cause extra losses in cupellation.

ASSAY OF ANTIMONIAL GOLD ORES.

The niter method is universally recognized as being the best method for the sulphide ores of antimony. Considerable litharge

---

* Min. and Sci. Press, **80**, p. 464.
† Mexican Mining Journal, Feb. 1913, p. 90.

is necessary to keep the antimony out of the lead button. The following charge is recommended by two English authorities:*

Ore	0.5 A. T.
Na_2CO_3	10–20 grams
Borax-glass	5–10 "
Litharge	100–120 grams
Niter	19 "
Silica	10 "

A preliminary assay to determine the reducing power is of course necessary. The above charge will be found to correspond almost exactly with our standard for sulphide ores, with litharge according to Lodge's rule.

George T. Holloway, in discussing this method, recommended the use of a much larger proportion of soda in the charge, *i.e.*, three times as much as stibnite, in order to aid in the retention of the antimony in the slag as a sodium antimonate.

ASSAY OF AURIFEROUS TINSTONE.

C. O. Bannister† finds a crucible assay with the following charge to be the most satisfactory method:

Ore	25 grams
Sodium carbonate	40 "
Borax	10 "
Red lead	60 "
Charcoal	1.5 "

In this method the tin is converted into a fusible sodium stannate. The author found no tin reduced during the fusion, as shown by the fact that the button cupeled without difficulty. In all ores carrying over 1 ounce of gold per ton, the slags were cleaned by a second fusion with 10 grams of soda, 30 grams of red lead and 1.5 grams of charcoal.

Various other methods of assay were tested but none were as satisfactory as this.

CORRECTED ASSAYS.

In the assay of high-grade ores and bullion it is often desirable to make a correction for the inevitable slag and cupel losses.

---

* William Kitto, Trans. Inst. Min. Met., **16**, p. 89.
  William Smith, Trans. Inst. Min. Met., **9**, p. 332.
† Trans. Inst. Min. Met. (London) **15**, p. 513.

This is done in one of two ways: either by the use of a "check" or synthetic assay, or by assaying the slags and cupels resulting from the original or commercial assays.

In correcting by a "check" assay, a preliminary assay is first made and then an amount of proof silver or gold, or both, approximately equivalent to the amount present in the sample, is weighed out and made up to approximately the composition of the sample by the addition of base metal, etc. The check thus made is assayed in the same furnace, parallel with the real assay. Whatever loss the known amounts of precious metal in the check sustain is added to the weight of metal obtained from the sample as a correction, the sum being supposed to represent the actual metal present in the sample. This method of correction is always used in the assay of gold and other precious metal bullions, and is sometimes used in the assay of high-grade ores. A more detailed description of the method will be found in the chapter on the assay of bullion. This method, when properly applied, is the better. and gives a very close approximation to the actual precious metal contents of a sample.

In the case of rich ores and furnace products other than bullion, a correction is usually made by assaying the slags and cupels resulting from the original assay. The weights of gold and silver thus recovered are added as corrections to the weights first obtained. This method, while approximating the actual contents of an ore, may occasionally give results a little too high, for although gold and silver lost by volatilization is not recovered and the corrections themselves must invariably suffer a second slag and cupel loss, yet on the other hand, the cupeled metal from both the first and second operations is not pure and may retain enough lead and occasionally other impurities from the ore and extra litharge used to more than offset the above small losses. The results of assays corrected by this method are evidently somewhat uncertain, but are nevertheless much nearer to the real silver content than are the results of the uncorrected or ordinary commercial assay.

Smelter contracts are almost invariably still written on the basis of the ordinary or uncorrected assay and when the corrected assay is made the basis of settlement, a deduction is made amounting to the average correction. This amounted to 1.1 per cent in the case of certain Cobalt ores.

Assay of Slags. — Assay slags are of such variable composition that no one method af analysis is universally applicable. Almost any plan of treatment whereby the slag is fused and a lead button reduced will result in the recovery of an additional amount of silver, but to make sure of obtaining practically all of the precious metals is quite another matter. Keller[*] states that to obtain a full recovery of the silver from slags it is necessary to reduce practically all of the lead from the charge and it is recommended that this procedure be followed.

In general, it is best to have the second slag differ materially from the original in order to ensure complete decomposition. It should be noted that the acid lead silicates are not decomposed by carbonaceous reducing agents, so that the slags resulting from Class 1 ores will have to be decomposed by means of metallic iron. Some additional borax may be required as a flux for the ferrous silicate resulting from the reaction of iron on lead silicate and if necessary an additional amount of sodium carbonate may be added.

In decomposing slags from niter assays by means of iron, it is advisable to carefully separate and reject the layer of fused sulphates which will be found on top of the cone of slag. If this is not done, the nails will be greatly corroded and even cut in two by the reaction with the fused sulphate; the formation of iron oxide and the production of an alkaline iron sulphide will result. The reaction is probably as follows:

$$Na_2SO_4 + 3Fe = Na_2S + Fe_3O_4.$$

If the lead button obtained is too large for cupellation, as will be the case in the decomposition of slags resulting from excess litharge fusions, it may be scorified to 20 or 25 grams.

Slags resulting from iron-nail assays should be fused with an excess of litharge, to ensure decomposing all of the sulphide with which the precious metals are combined. Borax and silica may be added, if necessary, to slag the resultant iron oxide as ferrous singulo-silicate. The slag resulting from an iron-nail assay of pure pyrite will probably contain about 3.5 grams of sulphide sulphur. This would reduce about 90 grams of lead from an excess of litharge. By limiting the amount of litharge it is possible to obtain a smaller lead button, which should, however, in this case, collect practically all of the gold and silver contained in the slag.

[*] Trans. A.I.M.E., **46**, p. 782.

ASSAY OF COMPLEX ORES AND SPECIAL METHODS

Assay of Cupels. — Cupel materials are all refractory, particularly magnesia, and for this reason all unsaturated cupel material should always be rejected before the cupel is pulverized. The student should also bear in mind that both Portland cement and magnesia are basic and require the addition of a considerable amount of acid reagents to make a slag of satisfactory character. When a corrected assay is to be made the original lead button should not weigh more than 28 grams, or too large an amount of cupel material will have to be handled. The fluxes have to be carefully proportioned; and in order to get complete recovery of the silver all of the absorbed litharge must be reduced. For this reason it is generally best not to use any litharge flux. In the charges which follow the proportions of reagents are all based on the weight of bone-ash, dry cement or magnesia in the material being assayed. This may be determined, closely enough for practical purposes, by calculating the weight of litharge corresponding to the lead button cupeled, and subtracting this calculated weight from the weight of saturated cupel material.

BONE-ASH. — To assay a bone-ash cupel, first remove and reject the unsaturated part of the cupel, in order to have as little of this refractory material as possible to deal with. Weigh the saturated part, which will be about 50 per cent bone-ash and 50 per cent litharge and grind to 80- or 100-mesh on a clean bucking-board.

Finally clean off what sticks to the board and muller by grinding a quantity of 20-mesh quartz equal to the silica requirements of the charge. For an ordinary assay this will be about 10 grams. This quartz is added to the charge and serves as a flux for some of the bases.

To flux bone-ash add one and a half times its weight of normal sodium carbonate, two-thirds of its weight of borax-glass, half its weight of fluorspar, and one-third its weight of silica. In assaying a cupel, an excess of flour is added to reduce all of the litharge. For example, the charge for a bone-ash cupel would work out as follows:

Cupel material (30 grams bone-ash, 30 grams litharge)	60 grams
Sodium carbonate	45 "
Borax-glass	20 "
Silica from cleaning the bucking-board	10 "
Fluorspar	15 "
Flour	4 "

Put into a 30-gram crucible, mix and place in a hot muffle so that it will fuse rapidly. Have the atmosphere neutral or slightly reducing and finally bring to a light yellow heat. Pour after half an hour at this temperature. The lead button obtained should weigh almost as much as the button first cupeled, i.e., the assay of a cupel in which a 30-gram lead button was cupeled should yield somewhat more than 28 grams of lead.

The slag will be an almost colorless, clear glass. The lead button is cupeled and the bead weighed and parted.

CEMENT. — To assay a Portland cement cupel, remove and reject the unsaturated part. Weigh the saturated part, which may contain as little as 40 per cent of cement, and grind it to 80- or 100-mesh. Clean the bucking-board and muller by grinding 15 grams of 20-mesh quartz, and add this to the charge, where it will serve as a flux for some of the bases. It must be included when considering the quantity of silica required for the charge.

To flux, add twice as much sodium carbonate as there is cement, an equal amount of borax-glass and twice as much silica. Add 4 or 5 grams of flour and fuse rapidly in a neutral or reducing atmosphere. The charge for a Portland cement cupel would work out as follows:

Cupel material (20 grams cement, 30 grams litharge)	50 grams
Sodium carbonate	40 "
Borax-glass	20 "
Flour	5 "
Silica	40 "

This yields a clear-green glassy slag and a lead button weighing about 90 per cent as much as the original button. The silver recovery is not as good as that obtained from bone-ash cupels, probably because the lead recovery is not so good.

MAGNESIA. — To assay a magnesia cupel proceed as for Portland cement. The patent magnesia cupels are the least porous and therefore the least of all suited for corrected assays, because so very much more flux will have to be provided for them. The saturated part of a magnesia cupel is almost 60 per cent magnesia. Therefore, the quantity of magnesia used in absorbing a given quantity of litharge is more than twice the quantity of Portland cement required to absorb the same quantity of litharge. Consequently twice as much of the reagents will have to be used to assay the magnesia.

CHAPTER X.

THE ASSAY OF BULLION.

Bullion, from an assayer's point of view, is an alloy containing enough of the precious metals to pay for parting.

The different bullions are usually named to correspond to their major components, for instance, copper bullion, an alloy of copper with small amounts of other impurities, as well as some gold and silver. In the same way we have lead, silver and gold bullions. Doré bullion is silver bullion containing gold as well as a small percentage of base metals. Doré bars differ in silver content from 600 to 990 parts per thousand; the base metals consist chiefly of copper, lead and antimony. The term base bullion is used in two different senses. According to the lead smelter's definition, base bullion is argentiferous lead, usually the product of the lead blast-furnace; according to the mintman's and refiner's definition it is bullion containing from 10 to 60 per cent of silver, usually some gold, and a large percentage of base metals, particularly copper, lead, zinc and antimony. Fine gold bars are those which are free from silver and sufficiently free from other impurities to make them fit for coinage and use in the arts, usually 990 to 999 fine.

The results of lead and copper bullion assays are reported in ounces per ton as in the case of ore assays, but in the assay of silver, gold and doré bullions the results are reported in "fineness," *i.e.*, so many parts of silver or gold in one thousand parts of bullion. Thus sterling silver is 925 parts fine, that is to say, it is 92.5 per cent silver.

Weights. — In assaying gold, silver and doré bullion, a special set of weights, called gold-assay weights, are used. This is termed the "millième" system; the unit, 1 millième, weighs 0.5 milligram, and therefore the 1000 millième weight equals 0.5 grams. Ordinary weights in the gram system may be used, but as 0.5 gram is the quantity of bullion commonly taken for assay the use of the millième system saves computation in obtaining the fineness.

SAMPLING BULLION.

Bullion may be sampled either in the molten or in the solid condition. When it may be melted and kept free from dross the dip or ladle sample is usually the more accurate method. As the weight, as well as the assay of the bullion must be known in order to value it, the sampling of large lots of bullion by the dip sample method often presents difficulties, owing to changes in weight or purity in the considerable length of time necessary for pouring. Again, it is not always convenient to melt a lot of bullion to obtain a sample, and other means must be found. Sampling solid bullion by punching, drilling, sawing or chipping, under certain conditions, may be made to yield good results. Lead bullion is usually sampled by punching one or more holes in each bar, and combining and melting the punchings. Copper bullion is now generally cast in the form of slabs or anodes, and these are drilled.

Sampling Molten Bullion. — The most satisfactory method of sampling bullion is to melt the whole in a suitable vessel, stir thoroughly with a graphite rod or iron bar to mix and then, immediately before pouring, ladle out a small amount and granulate it by pouring into a pail of water. If these operations are correctly performed there is no chance for segregation, and each particle of the granulated metal should be a true representative of the whole. If a granulated sample is not desired, a ladleful of the mixed molten metal may be poured into a thick-walled flat mold so that it chills almost instantly, and a drill or saw sample may be taken from this. When a ladle sample is taken, the ladle must be so hot as not to allow the forming of any solidified metal or "sculls," as this would interfere with the homogeneity of the sample. This method of sampling is most satisfactory for bullions which do not oxidize or form dross on melting, as this of course, adds a complication for which it is difficult to allow.

Sampling Solid Bullion. — The principal difficulty encountered in sampling bullion in the form of bars or ingots is due to the irregular distribution of the various constituents caused by segregation in cooling. If it were possible to cool a bar instantly, segregation could be prevented, and a chip or boring taken from any part would be representative. As instant cooling is impossible, the sampling of bars of the ordinary dimensions is usually a difficult problem. Occasionally a bar of bullion may be entirely homogeneous, but this is rare; and unfortunately there are no characteristics by which this homogeneity can be recognized. Heterogeneity is the rule, and the explanation for this common condition is found in the presence in almost every bullion of constituents having different freezing-points. In slow cooling, solidification begins first on the walls of the mold and the constituent having the highest freezing-point starts crystallizing here, forcing the part which is still liquid away from the walls.

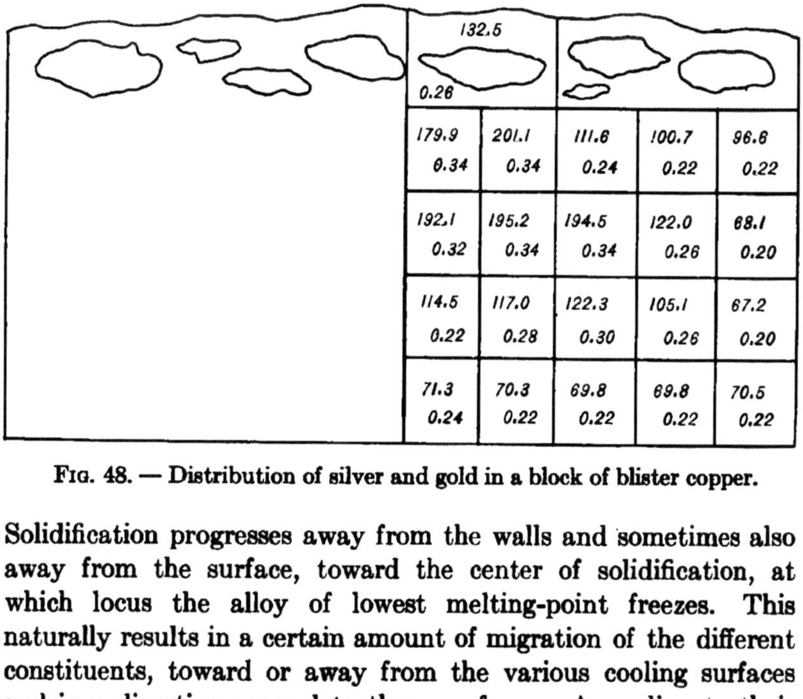

	132.5 0.26				
	179.9 0.34	201.1 0.34	111.6 0.24	100.7 0.22	96.6 0.22
	192.1 0.32	195.2 0.34	194.5 0.34	122.0 0.26	68.1 0.20
	114.5 0.22	117.0 0.28	122.3 0.30	105.1 0.26	67.2 0.20
	71.3 0.24	70.3 0.22	69.8 0.22	69.8 0.22	70.5 0.22

FIG. 48. — Distribution of silver and gold in a block of blister copper.

Solidification progresses away from the walls and sometimes also away from the surface, toward the center of solidification, at which locus the alloy of lowest melting-point freezes. This naturally results in a certain amount of migration of the different constituents, toward or away from the various cooling surfaces and in a direction normal to these surfaces. According to their amount, as well as upon the nature and amount of the other constituents of the alloy, the gold and silver may concentrate either toward or away from the center of solidification.

Figure 48 shows the distribution of silver and gold in a block of blister copper. To obtain these figures the block was cut in two, half of the section was laid off into squares as indicated and a sample was taken by drilling a hole in the center of each square. The upper figure in each case represents the silver assay in ounces per ton and the lower one gold in ounces per ton. In this case, the precious metals, particularly the silver, have concentrated toward the center of solidification, which is slightly above the geometrical center of the solid. It is obviously next to impossible to locate a drill-hole which would take a representative sample of such a block, and no chip taken from a corner could possibly give anything like the truth. A saw-section through the center would probably be satisfactory, provided the entire amount of sawings were assayed. Figure 49 shows another example of the distribution of the precious metals in copper

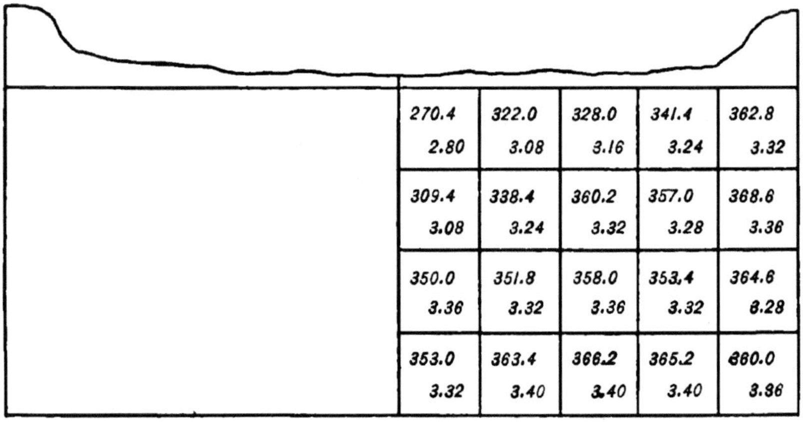

	270.4	322.0	328.0	341.4	362.8
	2.80	3.08	3.16	3.24	3.32
	309.4	338.4	360.2	357.0	368.6
	3.08	3.24	3.32	3.28	3.36
	350.0	351.8	358.0	353.4	364.6
	3.36	3.32	3.36	3.32	3.28
	353.0	363.4	366.2	365.2	360.0
	3.32	3.40	3.40	3.40	3.36

Fig. 49. — Distribution of silver and gold in a block of refined copper.

bullion; but in this case the concentration was in the opposite direction, *i.e.*, toward the part which solidified first. The same thing which is illustrated here for copper is true to a lesser extent for lead bullion and for impure precious metal bullions, and in these cases too the concentration may be either away from or toward the center of solidification.

The amount of this diffusion or segregation is dependent upon a number of factors, the most important of which are the composition of the alloy and the rate of cooling. The shape and thickness of the mold, as well as its initial temperature and the temperature of the alloy when poured, are also important factors in this problem.

It has been conclusively demonstrated that it is impossible to obtain samples of sufficient accuracy from copper bars or pigs of the usual dimensions, except by sawing, which is entirely too expensive a proceeding for everyday use.

To eliminate the difficulty of sampling from a bar, Keller[*] recommends casting the metal in a thin plate or slab, and this practice has now been almost universally adopted by the copper smelters. The slabs are usually made some 30 or 40 inches square and only 1 or 2 inches thick. Of course, some concentration takes place here, also, but as the plate solidifies so much faster than the same metal cast in a bar or ingot this factor has less weight.

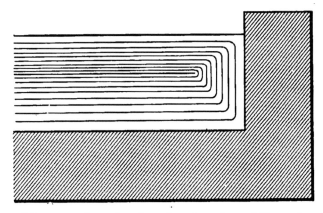

FIG. 50. — Diagrammatic section through a plate of metal illustrating direction of segregation towards or away from center of solidification.

Figure 50 is an ideal section through a part of such a slab. The concentric lines indicate the progressive cooling toward the center of cooling. It may be assumed that solidification progresses so as to form even layers from all the surface planes of the slab and that each successive layer differs in composition from its predecessor. On the right-hand side of the figure, just beyond the center of solidification, is shown a region, not wider than the thickness of the plate, where concentration has taken place both horizontally and vertically. All around the slab there will be a strip like this. Inside of this strip, the width of which is the same as the thickness of the slab, there can be movement only in a vertical plane. Therefore, the solid constituting this strip contains in its entirety a fair proportion of all the constitutents

[*] Trans. A.I.M.E., **27**, p. 106.

of the alloy, but it is impossible to sample this correctly. The solid inside of this strip also contains a fair proportion of all the constituents of the alloy, and as here there is concentration in the vertical direction only, a hole drilled through the plate anywhere should yield a correct sample of the whole. The method advocated by Keller has been demonstrated to yield satisfactory results and has now become standard in the copper industry.

Some typical methods of sampling lead and copper bullion follow.

Sampling Lead Bullion. — Lead bullion is sampled both in the liquid and in the solid state. In either case it is now customary to transfer the lead from the blast-furnace either into a reverberatory furnace or into large kettles holding 20 to 30 tons. Here the lead is purified by cooling to a little above the melting-point of pure lead. By doing this, a large part of the impurities which are held in solution by the superheated lead separate out as a dross which is carefully removed by skimming. The remaining lead, now in a better condition to sample, is drawn off and cast into bars of about 100 pounds.

In taking a dip sample, a small ladleful is taken at regular intervals from the stream coming from the drossing kettle. These individual samples are carefully remelted at a dark red heat in a graphite crucible, the melt is well stirred and cast in a heavy-walled shallow mold, making a cake about 10 inches long, 5 inches wide and $\frac{1}{2}$ inch thick. This cools so quickly that there is little or no chance for segregation. The final assay samples are taken from this cake by sawing and taking the sawdust, or by boring entirely through the slab in a number of places, and taking the borings, or by cutting out four or more 0.5 assay-ton pieces from different parts of the bar and using these directly.

Another and more modern method of sampling lead bullion, which does away with the remelting, is to take a number of dip samples in the shape of gum-drops. While the material in the kettle is being thoroughly stirred, the mold, which has six or eight conical depressions and is provided with a long handle, is inserted and heated to the same temperature as the molten metal. The "gum-drops" are dipped out and cooled in the mold, by dipping the bottom of the latter into water. These "gum-drops" which weigh from 15 to 25 grams, are weighed without clipping and cupeled, and the results are computed.

Bars of solid lead bullion are sampled by means of a heavy punch which takes a cylindrical sample about 2 inches long and $\frac{1}{8}$ inch in diameter. There are naturally a number of different systems, but the most common method is to place five bars side by side and face up, and punch a hole in each extending halfway through. Each bar is punched in a different place and in such a way that the holes make a diagonal across the five bars. The bars are then turned over and another sample is taken from each along the opposite diagonal. Usually a carload of about 20 or 30 tons is sampled as one lot. The punchings from such a lot, weighing from 8 to 15 pounds, are melted in a graphite crucible and cast into a flat bar, from which the final assay samples are taken by sawing, drilling or cutting.

Sampling Copper Bullion. — The sampling of copper bullion may be classified into smelter methods, and refinery methods. The bullion is quite universally cast in the form of anodes at the smelter, and shipped to the refinery in this form. This renders remelting at the refinery unnecessary, and the result is that the refiners sample the solid bullion by drilling. The smelters, having the bullion in the molten condition, generally sample it in this condition on account of the greater ease and less expense.

Probably the most satisfactory smelter method of sampling is the "splash-shot method," which consists in shotting into water a small portion of the molten stream of copper as it flows from the refining furnace, by "batting" the stream with a wet stick. This operation is repeated at uniform intervals during the pouring, the amount taken each time being kept about the same. The samples are dried and dirt and pieces of burned wood are removed. All material over 4-mesh and under 10-mesh is rejected, and the remainder taken as the sample. This method, when properly carried out, gives results which check within practical limits with the drill sample of the anodes taken at the refinery.

Another method which is used to some extent for sampling molten copper bullion is known as the "ladle-shot method." This consists in taking a ladleful from the furnace or from the stream of the casting machine and shotting it by pouring over a wooden paddle into water. In this method at least three ladlefuls are taken, one near the beginning, one at the middle, and one near the end of the pour. The shots are treated in the same manner as before. This method is not thought so well of as the previous one on account of segregation toward or from the " sculls " which are left in the ladles.

Instead of shotting and taking the shot for the final sample, W. H. Howard of Garfield, Utah, recommends ladling into a flat disc. This "pie sample" is sawed radially a number of imes, and the sawdust is used for the final sample.

The following description of the method of sampling anodes at Perth Amboy, N. J., is typical of refinery methods of sampling and is the method developed by Dr. Edward Keller. The copper is received in the form of anodes 36 inches long, 28 inches wide and 2 inches thick. These are carefully swept to remove foreign matter, and then drilled with a 0.5 inch drill completely through the anode, all of the drillings being carefully saved. A 99-hole template is used to locate the holes which are spaced $3\frac{1}{16}$ inches center to center, and the outside row is approximately $2\frac{1}{2}$ inches from the edge of the anode. The holes of the template are used in continuous order, one hole to the anode.

For very rich anodes some refiners use a template having as many as 240 holes, but it seems doubtful if this arrangement of spacing a single hole in each anode will yield any better sample.

With low-grade, uniform bullion every fourth anode only is drilled. A 30-ton lot of anodes in which each one is drilled will yield 6 or 8 pounds of drillings, which are ground in a drug-mill fitted with manganese steel plates and reduced by quartering to about 2 pounds. This sample is reground until it will all pass a 16-mesh screen, and is then divided into the sample packages.

Sampling Doré Bullion. — Doré bullion is sampled in the molten state by dip-sampling and in the solid state by drilling.

The doré bullion at one plant is cast into plates 18 inches by 7 inches by $\frac{3}{8}$ inch and sampled by drilling $\frac{3}{32}$ inch holes in it, on the checker-board plan. The drillings are ground to pass a 30-mesh screen. An electromagnet is used to remove from the sample all the iron from the drills and mill.

Sampling Gold Bullion (United States Mint Method). — Every lot of bullion or dust received at any United States Assay Office or Mint is immediately weighed and given a number. It is then melted in a graphite crucible with borax to make the deposit uniform, and cast into a bar whose horizontal dimensions are approximately $12\frac{1}{4}$ inches by $5\frac{1}{4}$ inches. Usually no attempt is made to refine it unless it is very impure. Occasionally, in the case of very impure bullions, a small dip sample is taken and granulated, but in general the whole melt is cast and sampled as noted below. The slag is poured with the bar and when solid is ground and panned, and the recovered prills are dried, weighed and allowed for in computing the value of the bar.

After the bar is cleaned of slag it is dried, weighed and numbered, and if it is thought to be homogeneous, two samples of 3 or 4 grams each are chipped from diagonally opposite corners. These are flattened with a heavy hammer, annealed and rolled into sheets thin enough to be easily cut with shears. The use of the shears can only be learned by practice, but assayers become very skilful after a time, and it is no unusual thing to see a bullion assayer weigh out five samples in almost as many minutes.

Cyanide bars, which do not give checks from chipped samples, are drilled halfway through on two opposite corners of the top at a point about 1 inch from each edge. These drillings are mixed and assayed as the top sample. The bottom sample is taken in the same manner, except that the drilling is done on the other two corners. The top and bottom samples are kept separate.

THE ASSAY OF LEAD BULLION.

A description of the cupellation assay of lead bullion has already been given in the chapter on cupellation. In smelter control work the assay is usually made in quadruplicate. If the bullion contains sufficient copper, arsenic, antimony, tin or other base metals to influence the results of the cupellation assay, three or four portions of 0.5 or 1.0 assay-ton are scorified with the addition of lead until the impurities are eliminated, when the resultant buttons are cupeled.

CORRECTION FOR CUPEL LOSS. — In some instances the slags and cupels are reassayed and the weight of the gold and silver found is added to that obtained from the first cupellation. There is no fixed custom as yet regarding the use of corrected assays. In most of the custom smelters, the uncorrected assay is used as the basis of settlement; but some of the large concerns who have their own refineries are using the corrected assay in their interplant business.

THE ASSAY OF COPPER BULLION.

Copper bullion may be assayed by the scorification method, by the crucible method or by a combination of wet-and-fire methods. In the combination method the bullion is treated with sulphuric or nitric acid which dissolves the copper and more or less of the silver but leaves the gold. The silver is precipitated by suitable reagents and filtered off together with the gold. The filter paper and contents are put into a scorifier or crucible with reagents and the assay finished by fire methods.

The Scorification Method. — The following method, commonly referred to as the "all-fire" method is a modification kindly supplied by Mr. H. D. Greenwood, Chief Chemist for the United States Metals Refining Co., Chrome, N. J.

Sample down the finely ground bullion on a split sampler in such a way as to obtain a sample of about 1 assay-ton which will include the proper proportion of the finer and the coarser parts of the borings. This sampling must be conducted carefully, as the precious metal content of the finer portion differs somewhat from that of the coarser portion of the sample. Portions "dipped" from the sample bottle or from the sample spread out on paper are likely to contain undue amounts of coarse or of fine.

Weigh out four portions of copper borings of 0.25 assay-ton each, mix with 50 grams test lead, put in 3-inch Bartlett scorifiers, cover with 40 grams test lead and add about 1 gram SiO_2. Scorify hot, heating at the end so that they will pour properly. Add test lead to make weight of buttons plus test lead equal to 70 grams, add 1 gram SiO_2 and scorify rather cool. Pour, make up to 60 grams with test lead, adding 1 gram SiO_2 and scorify again.

Combine the buttons two and two, and make up each lot to 85 grams with test lead, adding 1 gram SiO_2, and scorify very cool. Make up buttons to 70 grams by adding test lead, add 1 gram SiO_2 and scorify for the fifth time. The buttons should be free from slag and weigh 14 grams.

Cupel at a temperature to feather nicely, and raise the heat at the finish. Cupels should be made of 60-mesh bone-ash, and should be of medium hardness.

Weigh the beads and part as usual. Dry, anneal and weigh the gold. The two results should check within .02 ounce per ton, and the average figure is to be reported. If the silver contents of the bullion is low, add enough fine silver before the first scorification to make the total silver in the mixture equal to about eight times the amount of gold.

The scorification method was until recently accepted as standard for gold and most smelter contracts involving this material stated that "gold shall be determined by the all-fire method or its equivalent." The silver results obtained by the scorification method are not acceptable, owing to the considerable slag and cupellation losses which average perhaps as much as 5 or 10 per cent. Reassay of the slag and cupels will permit recovery of most of the silver and approximately 1 per cent additional gold. The scorification assay is expensive as regards both time and material, and is falling into disfavor.

The Crucible Method. — The crucible method for gold and silver in copper bullion was first described by Perkins* and as described by him showed no great advantage over the scorification method as to saving in time, cost of materials, or increased furnace capacity. The following modified procedure requires about one-third of the materials, time and furnace capacity necessary for that described by Perkins, and yet gives buttons sufficiently free from copper to be cupeled directly.

Sample down the finely ground bullion to about 0.25 assay-ton and adjust the weight of the sampled portion to exactly 0.25 assay-ton. Place in a 20-gram crucible and mix with it 1.2 grams of powdered sulphur. Cover this with a mixture of 15 grams of sodium carbonate, 240 grams of litharge, and 8 grams of silica; but do not mix with the sulphur and copper, which should be allowed to remain in the bottom of the crucible. Cover with salt or flux mixture and place in a hot muffle so that the charge will begin to melt in six or eight minutes. The fusions should be quiet and ready to pour in twenty-five or thirty minutes.

If a salt cover is used the lead buttons should weigh about 32 grams; if a flux cover is used they may be somewhat smaller. With a properly conducted assay the buttons are soft enough for direct cupellation; but the cupels are quite green. If the assayer prefers, the buttons may be made up to 50 or 60 grams with test lead and scorified in a 3-inch scorifier to further eliminate the copper. After cupellation the beads are weighed and

* An "All-Fire" Method for the Assay of Gold and Silver in Blister Copper, W. G. Perkins, Trans. A.I.M.E., **33**, p. 670.

parted as usual. It is well to make four fusions, and to combine the beads, two and two, for parting.

REMARKS. — As soon as the sulphur melts it combines with the copper to form a matte. This matte is later decomposed and most of its copper is oxidized and slagged by the litharge of the charge. The fusions melt down very quietly, almost without boiling, and with a short period of fusion the crucibles are not badly attacked. The final temperature need not be higher than a good bright red or full yellow. The slag is heavy but very fluid, and should not contain any lead shot.

The method gives results in gold equal to the scorification method; but, as in any method using high litharge, the silver is apt to be somewhat low.

Nitric Acid Combination Method.* — Sample down the finely ground bullion on a split sampler in such a way as to obtain a sample of about 1 assay-ton which will include the proper proportion of the finer and coarser parts of the borings. This sampling must be conducted carefully as the precious metal content of the finer portion differs somewhat from that of the coarser portion of the sample. Portions " dipped " from the sample bottle or from the sample spread out on paper are likely to contain undue amounts of coarse or of fine.

Weigh out two portions of copper borings of 1 assay-ton each, and carry the assay through, on each portion, as follows:

Place in a No. 5 beaker, add 100 c.c. of distilled water and 90 c.c. HNO_3, sp. gr. 1.42, the latter being added in portions of 30 c.c. each, at intervals of about one hour. When all is in solution, precipitate a small amount of silver chloride with salt solution in order to collect the gold, filter through double filter papers and wash the filter papers free from copper. To the filtrate add the calculated amount of salt solution to precipitate all the silver and a slight excess, measuring the solution with a burette and varying the amount added with the richness of the bullion. Allow to stand over night after stirring well. Filter the silver chloride through double papers, wash papers free from copper, then sprinkle 5 grams of test lead in the filter paper and fold into a $2\frac{1}{2}$-inch Bartlett-shape scorifier, the bottom of which is lined with sheet lead. To this add also the filter papers containing

---

* Procedure kindly supplied by Mr. D. H. Greenwood, Chief Chemist, for the United States Metals Refining Company, Chrome, N. J.

the gold. Dry and ignite the filter papers carefully, cover with 35 grams of test lead and a little borax-glass, and scorify at a low heat so that the resultant button will weigh about 12 grams. Cupels should be feathered nicely. Cupels should be made of 60-mesh bone-ash and should be of medium hardness. Weigh the bead and part. Anneal and weigh the gold. The two results on gold should check within 0.02 ounce per ton, and the silver within 1 per cent.

The nitric acid combination method has for a long time been the standard for the determination of silver in copper bullion. In laboratories where many such determinations are made, a number of most ingenious labor-saving devices have been developed. For a description of these the student is referred to two papers* by Edward Keller.

The nitric acid combination method is recognized as giving low results in gold. Van Liew† attributes this to the solution of the gold in the mixture of nitrous and nitric acids present. He found a loss of 33.7 per cent of gold, on treating gold leaf with a mixture of nitrous and nitric acids for two and a half hours. He gives a method of slow solution in cold dilute acid which reduces this loss to a minimum.

Various attempts to overcome this difficulty have been made but none have been completely successful.

The unconnected silver results obtained by this method are from 1.5 to 4 per cent low, according to the amount of silver contained, and unless this loss is taken into account, it is certain to cause a great deal of uncertainty in the statistics of the smelting industry.

Keller‡ recommends the following method for determining the slag and cupel loss. The slag and cupels are crushed, ground and thoroughly mixed. The whole or an aliquot part is fused in G crucibles with the following charge:

Slag and cupels..................200 grams
Sodium carbonate................. 70 "
Borax........................... 70 "
Flour........................... 10 "

* Labor-saving Devices in the Works Laboratory, Trans. A.I.M.E., **36**, p. 3 (1906); **41**, p. 786 (1910).

† Eng. and Min. Jour. **69**, p. 496 et seq.

‡ Recent American Progress in the Assay of Copper Bullion, Trans. A.I.M.E., **46**, p. 782.

The resulting lead buttons are scorified and cupeled. Keller states that it is necessary to reduce practically all of the lead in the slag and cupels in order to obtain full recovery of the silver and gold.

Mercury-Sulphur Acid Method. — The copper bullion sample, which has been ground to pass a 16-mesh screen, is first separated into two portions by means of a 40-mesh screen, and each portion is weighed. As the precious-metal content of the fine differs somewhat from that of the coarse portion, it is important to include a proper proportion of each in the sample taken for assay. Calling " C " the weight of the coarse and " F " the weight of the fine, weigh out $\dfrac{29.166}{\dfrac{F}{C} - 1}$ grams of coarse and make up the remainder of the assay-ton with fine. Transfer to an 800 c.c. beaker, add 30 c.c. of water and 10 c.c. of mercury nitrate solution (Hg 0.25g). Shake the beaker until the copper is thoroughly amalgamated, then add 100 c.c. of strong sulphuric acid, cover the beaker and place on the hot plate and heat until the copper is all dissolved. This will take from one to two hours according to the temperature and the state of division of the sample. The apparent boiling of the liquid during this time is only bubbling and is due to the evolution of sulphur dioxide gas. This completed, the supernatant liquid assumes a dark green color, finally changing to a light grayish-blue, which is the indication of the finishing point.

Remove the beaker and allow to cool. The contents will be a semi-liquid sludge. When this is cool, add about 100 c.c. of cold water and mix, then add 400 c.c. of boiling water and stir until the copper sulphate dissolves. Add sufficient salt solution to precipitate all of the mercury and silver present. With 100 milligrams of silver and 0.25 grams of mercury, 30 c.c. of a solution containing 19 grams of NaCl per liter is sufficient. Any material excess should be avoided.

Boil the solution to coagulate the silver chloride, remove from the hot-plate, dilute to 600 c.c. with cold water and allow to cool. Filter through double filter papers, wash the beaker and filter with hot water. Finally wipe the inside of the beaker with filter paper and add this to the material in the filter. Thorough washing of the filter is not necessary.

Transfer the wet filter and its contents to a 2½-inch scorifier which has been glazed on the inside by melting litharge in it and pouring away the excess.

Burn off the filter paper at a low temperature, preferably in a closed oven which may be heated to, say 175° C. This chars the paper slowly without danger of loss of silver.

When the paper is consumed, add 30 grams of test lead and scorify; pour so as to obtain a 12-gram button, cupel as usual to produce feather litharge, weigh the gold and silver bead and part with dilute nitric acid.

The mercury solution mentioned above is made by dissolving 32.5 grams of mercury nitrate in a liter of water. This makes a solution containing approximately 25 grams of mercury per liter. It should be noted that with comparatively pure copper the amount of mercury nitrate may be reduced, while with copper high in sulphur an increase in the amount of mercury nitrate will be required.

The object of adding mercury is to secure an easy solution of the copper in sulphuric acid. If the copper is treated directly without previous amalgamation, it is very difficult to dissolve it in sulphuric acid. In fact a considerable portion of it will remain insoluble, partly in the form of sulphide of copper. If, on the other hand, the copper be amalgamated, solution proceeds smoothly until practically all of the copper is dissolved. When the bullion is low in precious metals, say less than 50 ounces per ton, no silver dissolves in the sulphuric acid. No gold dissolves whatever the grade. If the bullion is very rich in silver a little of the latter may dissolve in the acid.

The assays should be made in duplicate or triplicate, and the average results reported. Differences in silver seldom exceed 0.2 ounce; the gold results are usually exactly the same. The sulphuric acid used should be chemically pure and full strength (1.84 sp. gr.).

The mercury-sulphuric acid combination method gives silver results equal to the nitric acid combination method and superior to the all-fire, or scorification method. When the scorification and cupellation losses of each method are taken into account the gold results obtained by the mercury-sulphuric acid and the scorification methods are substantially identical. The mercury-sulphuric acid combination method is now generally accepted as standard for gold and is fast coming to be considered standard for silver as well.

If the copper is not all dissolved, as is sometimes the case, particularly with very impure bullion, this method may give high silver results, due to the possibility of some copper being retained in the silver bead.

THE ASSAY OF DORÉ BULLION.

This method is the one generally adopted by assayers in this country, and may also be used for the assay of silver bullion. A better method for the accurate determination of silver in doré or silver bullion is probably the Gay-Lussac or salt titration, also known as the mint method. This later method requires considerable equipment and preparation, and for this reason the occasional assay is more easily performed by fire methods.

The Check. — In order to correct for the inevitable losses in cupeling as well as for any other errors in the assay, silver, doré, and gold bullions are always run with a check. This check or "proof center" is a synthetic sample made up of known weights of pure silver, gold and copper, to approximate as closely as possible the composition of the bullion to be assayed. It is cupeled at the same time and under the same conditions as the regular assays, and whatever gain or loss it suffers is added as a correction to the regular assay. To obtain data to make up the check a preliminary assay is made. This gives the approximate composition of the bullion.

Preliminary Assay. — A sample of 500 milligrams of bullion, or as nearly this amount as possible, is weighed out on the assay balance, and the exact weight recorded. This is compactly wrapped in 6 or 8 grams of lead foil and cupeled in a small cupel with feather crystals of litharge. The cupel should be pushed back in the muffle for the last two or three minutes, to ensure the removal of the last of the lead. After the play of colors has ceased it should be drawn toward the front of the muffle and then covered with a very hot cupel to prevent sprouting. It is then removed gradually from the muffle and when it is cool the bead is cleaned, weighed and parted in the ordinary manner. The gold will require more than the ordinary amount of washing, on account of the large quantity of silver present.

If the cupeling has been properly conducted it will be fair to assume a loss of 1 per cent of silver in determining the approximate silver. The weight of gold may be taken as approximately correct. The sum of the weights of approximate gold and silver is subtracted from the weight of bullion taken to obtain the amount of base metal. This will usually be copper, but the assayer should be able to determine what it is from the appearance of the bullion and the cupel.

Final Assay. — Three portions of approximately 500 milligrams are weighed accurately and wrapped in the proper amount of lead foil as shown by the following table in which the impurity is assumed to be copper.

TABLE XXVI.

LEAD RATIO IN CUPELLATION.

Fineness of Au. + Ag.	Wt. of lead	Fineness of Au. + Ag.	Wt. of lead
950	5 grams	750	11 grams
900	7 "	700	12 "
850	8 "	650	13 "
800	10 "	600	15 "

Two checks are made up with C. P. silver and proof gold, equal to the approximate silver and gold found by the preliminary assay, and the necessary amount of copper or other base metal. These are wrapped up in the same amount of sheet lead as was used for the bullion. The lead for these assays is best cut into equal-sized rectangles with proportions approximately $1\frac{1}{2}$ inches by $2\frac{1}{2}$ inches, and twisted into the shape of little cornucopias with the bottoms folded up. The bullion and metals going to make up the check are transferred to these directly from the scale-pans, and are then folded over and made into compact bundles.

The cupels are placed in a row across the muffle, and when they are hot, the buttons are dropped quickly into them with the checks in the second and fourth cupels. They should be cupeled at a low temperature so that plentiful crystals of litharge are obtained all around the buttons, but toward the end the temperature should be increased to make sure of driving off the last of the lead.

The beads are cleaned, weighed and parted, and the gold is weighed. The per cent loss of gold and silver is determined and a corresponding correction made to the weights of gold and silver found. From these figures the fineness in both gold and silver is determined. The gold should check within 0.1 part and the silver within 0.5 parts.

Notes: 1. When the doré contains antimony the samples are weighed into 2.5-inch scorifiers with 30 grams of test lead. Proofs are made up according to the preliminary assay. All are scorified in the same muffle at the same time. Should the weight of these lead buttons vary over a gram, they are made up to the same weight with lead foil before cupeling. The assay is carried on from this point as if no impurities had been present.

2. When the doré contains bismuth, selenium or tellurium, three one-half gram portions are weighed out into 2½-inch scorifiers with forty grams of test lead and scorified, and the lead buttons are flattened out into sheets about 3 inches square. These sheets of lead are dissolved in about 200 c.c., of dilute HNO_3 (1-3) and the solutions are boiled to expel all red fumes. They are then diluted to 400 c.c., filtered through triple-folded 15 cm. filters, and the precipitate is washed once. To the filtrate is added sufficient NaCl solution to precipitate all the silver. The solutions are heated to boiling and allowed to stand over night. The silver chloride is filtered off through 15 cm. filters and the precipitate is washed only once. The two filter papers are placed in a 2½-inch lead-lined scorifier, dried and burned in an oven, then covered with 30 grams of test lead and scorified. When the scorifiers have entirely closed over, the muffle door is closed and the heat raised. When hot, the fusions are poured and the lead buttons treated exactly as those from bullion containing antimony.

3. If the silver fineness of the doré is not three or more times greater than the gold fineness, another set of assays must be run with the addition of sufficient proof silver to allow for parting.

Instead of attempting to prevent sprouting by covering with a hot cupel, the student may try the following little-known method, first described by Aaron.* After brightening, the cupel is drawn to the front of the muffle and gently tapped on one side with the tongs. At the instant when the bead ceases to vibrate in response to the taps, by which is indicated the beginning of solidification, it is pushed back into the hottest part of the muffle and left for about a minute. After this it may be entirely withdrawn and will not sprout, being solid all through, as shown by a " dimple " in its surface, caused by contraction.

* Assaying Gold and Silver Ores, p. 67.

On being drawn to the front of the muffle, the cupel is cooled, and as the bead begins to solidify it is pushed back where the heat thrown down on it prevents the surface from solidifying, or melts it again. The partially cooled cupel, absorbing the heat, causes the bead to solidify from below and thus the gas is allowed to escape quietly.

UNITED STATES MINT ASSAY OF GOLD BULLION.

Preliminary Assay. Assay for Bases. — To determine the approximate composition of the bullion a preliminary assay is made. A sample of 1000 millièmes (500 mg.) is weighed out, wrapped in five grams of lead foil, and cupeled. The weight of the bullion taken, less the weight of the bead obtained, gives the base metals.

The bead now consists of gold and silver, the approximate relative proportions of which must be determined. This may be done by adding silver, cupeling and parting, or by touchstone. This latter method is used at the Government Assay Offices and Mints. The touchstone method consists in rubbing the sample on a piece of black jasper and comparing the mark with marks made by alloy slips, "needles," of known composition. The needles range from 500 to 1000 fine and are 20 points apart. This gives the fineness within 2 per cent, which is close enough to show how much silver to add in order to inquart the main assay and to make up the check or proof center.

Final Assay. — The final assay is usually made by two assayers, each working on one of the chip or drill samples. In the case of a small bar, each makes one assay, while in the case of a large bar each assayer makes two or more assays. The balance used for the assay is usually adjusted so that a deviation of the needle of 1 division on the ivory scale amounts to some simple fraction of the weights used. Thus, at one assay office a deviation of the swing of 1 division on the ivory scale amounts to 0.1 mg. = 0.2 millièmes. With this adjustment it is not necessary to make so many trials with the rider to get the final weight, nor is it necessary to weigh out exactly an even half gram of bullion for the assay. Instead we weigh out 1000 ± 3 divisions on the ivory scale, record the difference, and make a corresponding correction when the gold cornet is weighed.

As stated above the weight of bullion taken for each assay is 1000 millièmes. To this is added sufficient silver to make the ratio of silver to gold 2 to 1, and the whole is wrapped up in 5 or 6 grams of lead foil. The lead foil pieces are all cut to exact size, about 1½ inches by 2½ inches, and rolled up into the shape of a cornucopia with the bottom pinched in. The bullion is poured directly into these from the scale-pan. The silver is added in the form of discs made, for convenience, in four or five different sizes. These discs are punched out of sheets carefully rolled to gage, so that the punchings will weigh exactly even tens and hundreds in the gold weight system. If the bullion contains no copper it is advisable to add about 30 millièmes. This copper may be alloyed with the silver used for parting.

One or more proofs of pure gold weighing usually 900 millièmes (0.450 gram) are also weighed and made up to the 2 to 1 ratio, and copper is added to approximate that in the bullion. These are wrapped in the same quantity of lead foil as the bullion, and one or more are run in each row of cupels in the muffle. The lead packets are pressed into spherical shape with pliers specially designed for the purpose.

The lead packets are put in order as prepared in the numbered compartments of a wooden tray and taken to the furnace room where they are cupeled in a rather hot muffle. The cupels are surrounded by a row of extra cupels so that the temperature may be kept as uniform as possible for all the assays. The cupels are withdrawn while the beads are still fluid. With a 2 to 1 ratio of silver to gold, and with copper present, there is no danger of sprouting.

The beads are removed from the cupels by means of pliers and carefully cleaned from all adhering bone-ash. They are then placed on a special anvil and flattened by a middle blow and two end blows with a heavy polished hammer. They are then annealed at a dull red heat and passed twice through the rolls which are adjusted each time, so that after the second passage they are about 2½ inches long by ½ inch wide, and about as thick as an ordinary visiting card. It is important that the fillets be all of the same size and thickness and that they have smooth edges. They are then reannealed and each one is numbered on one end with small steel dies to correspond with the number of the assay, after which they are rolled up into "cornets" or spirals between the finger and thumb, with the number outside. It is important that an even space be left between all turns of the spiral, in order that the acid shall have easy access to all parts of the gold.

The cornets are parted in platinum thimbles, which are supported in a platinum basket, and the whole is placed in a platinum vessel containing boiling nitric acid of 32° B. (Sp. Gr. 1.28). They are boiled for ten minutes and then transferred to another vessel containing acid of the same strength and boiled ten min-

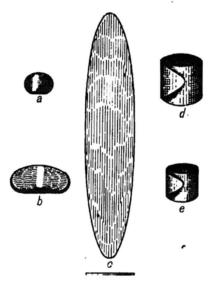

Fig. 51. — Stages in preparing bead for parting in gold bullion assay. (a) bead (b) after flattening (c) fillet (d) cornet before parting (e) cornet after parting and annealing.

utes longer. The basket, with its contents is then washed by dipping it, vertically in and out, in three changes of distilled water. It is now drained, dried, and annealed, usually in the muffle.

The various stages in the conversion of the bead to the parted cornet are shown in Fig. 51.

When cold, the cornets are ready to be weighed. The gold should be entirely in one piece, and the original numbers easily discernible on the parted cornets. The proofs are weighed first and the corrections applied to the weight of the other cornets. The proofs always show a slight gain in weight. The correction thus determined is termed the "surcharge," and is really the algebraic sum of all the gains and losses.

When more than fourteen cornets are parted at one time the lot is given a preliminary three minute treatment in an extra lot of acid, followed by the two regular ten minute boilings.

The purpose of the copper which is added to the assays is to render the button tough and permit of its being rolled out into a smooth-edged fillet. Without the copper, the fillet is apt to crack in rolling, or to come through with a ragged edge which might give rise to a loss in parting. The action of copper in this case is probably due to its effect in aiding in the removal of the last of the lead in cupeling.* The time required for cupellation is approximately twelve minutes.

* Rose. Trans. Inst. Min. Met., **14**, p. 545.

CHAPTER XI.

THE ASSAY OF SOLUTIONS.

A large variety of methods for the assay of gold- and silver-bearing solutions have been published in the technical press, and quite a number of these have been adopted by assayers. These methods may be classified as follows:

1. Methods involving evaporation in lead trays with subsequent cupellation, or scorification and cupellation, of the tray and contents.

2. Methods involving evaporation with litharge and other fluxes, followed by a crucible fusion and cupellation.

3. Methods in which the precious metals are precipitated and either cupeled directly, or first fused or scorified and then cupeled.

4. Electrolytic methods in which the precious metals are deposited directly on cathodes of lead foil, which are later wrapped up with the deposit and cupeled.

5. Colorimetric methods (for gold only) all of which depend upon obtaining the "purple of Cassius" color which may be compared with proper standards.

Evaporation in Lead Tray. — This method is a good one for rich, neutral solutions containing only salts of the precious metals. A tray of suitable size is made by turning up the edges of a piece of lead foil. If many of these assays are to be made it is well to have a wooden block as a form on which the trays may be shaped. A tray 2 by 2 inches and ¾ inch deep is about right to hold 1 assay-ton of solution.

Having made a tray which will not leak, the assayer adds the solution and carefully evaporates it to prevent spattering. The tray is then folded into a compact mass and dropped into a hot cupel.

Among the disadvantages of the method are the following: It does not permit of the use of a large quantity of solution, and therefore is suited only to rich solutions. If the solutions are acid they will corrode the tray, and if they contain salts other than those of gold and silver these will interfere with cupellation. As both AuCl₃ and KAu(CN)₂ are volatile at moderate temperatures, many assayers do not consider the method a reliable one for solutions of these salts on account of the possibility of loss of gold.

Evaporation with Litharge. — (First Method). A measured quantity of the solution is placed in a porcelain evaporating dish and from 30 to 60 grams of litharge is sprinkled over the surface. The mixture is allowed to evaporate at a gentle heat to prevent both spitting and baking of the residue. When dry the residue is scraped out, mixed with suitable fluxes, transferred to a crucible and fused in the ordinary manner. The last portions remaining on the dish may be removed by means of a small piece of slightly moistened filter paper which is afterwards added to the charge.

Some assayers add a little fine silica and charcoal with the litharge. The soluble constituents of a crucible charge, soda and borax, should not be added to the solution as they form a hard cake which is difficult to remove from the dish. The most important point in the process is the proper control of the temperature. If this is right, there will be no spattering and the dry residue will come away from the dish practically clean, after it has been pried up with the point of a spatula.

Evaporation with Litharge. — (Second Method). A measured amount of solution is evaporated to a small volume in a porcelain or enameled iron dish, without the addition of any reagents, and the concentrated solution is then transferred to a small dish of very thin glass, known as a Hoffmeister's dish. The solution is evaporated to dryness either with or without litharge, and the dish and contents broken up directly into a crucible containing the usual fluxes. The assay is finished in the usual manner. The advantage of this method lies in the fact that there is no chance of losing any of the residue by not properly cleaning the dish, as the dish and all are fused.

The evaporation method, while somewhat long, is the most reliable and accurate one known, and is the standard with which all other methods are compared. If arrangements are made for allowing the evaporation to run over night, the samples taken one night may be assayed and reported early next morning. The method is adapted to the treatment of solutions in any quantity and of almost any character. If the solution contains much sulphuric acid, the litharge may be converted into lead sulphate, which is not suited either to act as a flux or to provide lead for a collecting agent. A fusion made on such a substance with a carbonaceous reducing agent, will give either no button at all, or a button of matte. The reaction between lead sulphate and carbon is as follows:

$$PbSO_4 + 2C = PbS + 2CO_2.$$

If the solution is one of $AuCl_3$, a little charcoal should be added during the evaporation, to ensure the reduction and precipitation of the gold, as in this way we avoid the danger of loss of gold by volatilization as the chloride. The gold, being precipitated on the charcoal, is in the best possible position to be alloyed with the lead which will be reduced by the carbon.

Precipitation by Zinc and Lead Acetate. The Chiddey Method. — (For Cyanide Solutions). This method, which was first described by Alfred Chiddey[*] is suitable for both gold and silver and is used almost exclusively in this country for the assay of cyanide solutions. It works equally well on strong or weak, foul or pure solutions, and almost any quantity may be taken. Many changes of detail have been suggested and innumerable modifications of the original process have been described in the technical press. The following method has been found satisfactory:

Take from 1 to 20 assay-tons of solution in a beaker or evaporating dish, and heat. Add 10 or 20 c.c. of a 10 per cent solution of lead acetate containing 40 c.c. of acetic acid per liter. Then add 1 or 2 grams of fine zinc shavings rolled lightly into a ball. The gold, silver and lead will immediately commence to precipitate on the zinc. At first the solution may become cloudy but will soon clear as more of the lead is precipitated. Heat, but not to boiling, until the lead is well precipitated. This usually takes about twenty or twenty-five minutes. Then add slowly (about 5 c.c. at a time), 20 c.c. hydrochloric acid (1.12 sp. gr.), to dissolve the excess zinc. Continue heating until effervescence stops. It is often found that action ceases while there is still some undissolved zinc remaining. This is entirely covered and thus protected from the acid by the spongy lead. To be sure that all the zinc is dissolved, feel of the sponge with a stirring rod and drop a little hydrochloric acid from a pipette directly on it.

[*] Eng. and Min. Jour., 75, p. 473, (1903).

As soon as the zinc is dissolved decant off the solution and wash the sponge two or three times with tap water. Next, moisten the fingers and press the sponge, which should be all in one piece, into a compact mass. Dry by squeezing between pieces of soft filter paper or by placing on a piece of lead foil and rolling with a piece of large glass tubing. Finally roll into a ball with lead foil, puncture to allow for escape of steam, add silver for parting, and place in a hot cupel.

As soon as the zinc is dissolved the assay should be removed from the heat, and the sponge removed. If this is not done the lead will start to dissolve and the sponge will soon break up. Washing by decantation and manipulation with the fingers may appear crude, but after a little practice the operator becomes so proficient that there is practically no chance of losing any of the lead.

If any considerable amount of water is left the assay will spit in the cupel. To avoid this danger some assayers dry the assays on the steam table before cupeling. Any zinc left will also probably cause spitting. Chiddey recommends placing a piece of dry pine wood in the mouth of the muffle immediately after charging the cupels, probably with the idea that this aids in preventing spitting when some zinc has been left undissolved. When working with small quantities of solutions it is best to add water occasionally to maintain a volume of at least 100–150 c.c. The secret of keeping the lead from breaking up is not to allow the solution to come to a boil at any stage of the procedure.

Zinc dust is used by many chemists in place of zinc shavings, a small amount being added on the end of a spatula. Many chemists agree that half a gram is sufficient.

William H. Barton* suggests the addition of a small piece of aluminum foil dropped into the solution after the hydrochloric acid is added, to prevent the dissolving of the lead and the consequent breaking up of the sponge by the hydrochloric acid after the zinc is all dissolved.

T. P. Holt† recommends the substitution of a square of aluminum foil for the zinc. The lead sponge is removed from the aluminum with a rubber-tipped stirring rod. Care must be taken to use a sufficiently thick sheet of aluminum (1/16 inch does

---

* Western Chemist and Metallurgist, **4**, p. 67, (1908).

† Min. and Sci. Press, **100**, p. 863, (1910).

well), to prevent small pieces becoming detached. These would remain with the lead sponge and might cause the cupels to spit.

Precipitation as Sulphide.* — Acidify 5 or 10 assay-tons of solution with HCl and heat to boiling. While it is boiling add a solution containing 2 grams of lead acetate and pass in a current of hydrogen sulphide until all the lead is precipitated. Allow to cool somewhat, still passing in H_2S, then filter and dry. Collect the gold and silver with lead, either by a crucible fusion or a scorification assay. The method is said to be quick, accurate and economical.

Precipitation by Cement Copper.† — To 8 assay-tons of the solution add a few cubic centimeters of sulphuric acid, and 1 gram of finely divided cement copper. Heat to boiling and boil ten minutes. Filter through a strong 7-inch paper and place on the drained filter one-third of a crucible charge of mixed flux. Place the filter in a crucible containing another third of a charge of flux, and cover with the final third. Fuse and cupel as usual. The filter itself furnishes the reducing agent for the assay. If cement copper is not available, a solution of copper sulphate may be added, together with a small piece of aluminum foil. Boil until all the copper is precipitated and add the remaining aluminum foil to the fusion. This modification takes more time than the first.

Precipitation by Silver Nitrate.‡ — (For Gold in Cyanide Solutions). Add an excess of silver nitrate solution which will cause the gold and silver to precipitate as an auric-argentic-cyanide. Allow the precipitate to settle, filter through a thin paper, and wash several times. Dry the filter and either scorify with test lead or fuse in a crucible with litharge and the regular fluxes. The method gives fairly good results with solutions not too low in gold. With solutions very low in gold the precipitation of the gold is not perfect.

Precipitation by a Copper Salt.§ — (For Cyanide Solutions Only). Add to 1 liter of solution in a 2-liter flask 25 c.c. of a 10 per cent solution of copper sulphate, then add 5 to 7 c.c. of concentrated

---

* Henry Watson, Eng. and Min. Jour., **66**, p. 753, (1898).

† Albert Arents, Trans. A.I.M.E., **34**, p. 184.

‡ Andrew F. Cross, Jour. Chem. Met. and Min. Soc. of South Africa, **1**, p. 28, and **3**, p. 1.

§ A. Whitby, Jour. Chem. Met. and Min. Soc. of South Africa, **3**, p. 6.

hydrochloric acid and lastly 10 to 20 c.c. of a 10 per cent solution of sodium sulphite. Shake vigorously for at least two minutes, then filter, dry, and fuse the filter and precipitate in the usual way. With weak solutions it is best to bring up the strength by the addition of cyanide before adding the copper salt. The gold and silver are carried down by the precipitate of cuprous cyanide formed. Assays may be completed in three hours, and the results are said to be good on both low- and high-grade solutions.

The Electrolytic Assay of Cyanide Solutions. — The following method is abstracted from the Journal of the Chemical, Metallurgical and Mining Society of South Africa* in which is described the method and installation used at the Kleinfontein Group Central Administration Assay Offices.

Ten-assay-ton samples of the solution to be assayed are placed in No. 3 beakers, which are held in a frame, and electrolyzed with a current of 0.1 ampere. The anodes used consist of ordinary $\frac{5}{16}$-inch arc lamp carbons which are held in position in the center of each beaker by suitable clamps. They are arranged so that they may be lifted out of the solution when no current is passing. The cathodes are made from strips of ordinary assay lead foil $2\frac{1}{2}$ by 9 inches, with the lower edge coarsely serrated to allow for circulation of the solution. To connect with the battery a $\frac{1}{4}$-inch strip is almost severed from one end of the foil, and turned upward to make a terminal. The two ends of the lead are brought together and connected by folding the edges, making a cylinder about 3 inches in diameter.

The time required for the complete deposition of the gold is four hours, after which the carbons are removed, the lead cathodes disconnected and dried on a hot-plate. When dry, they are folded into a compact mass and cupeled.

With weak solutions a small quantity of cyanide should be added in order to decrease the resistance and thus accelerate the deposition of the precious metals. The author reports no difficulty in obtaining a complete and adherent deposit of the gold, which separates as a bright yellow deposit.

This, of course, was the only metal worked for on the Rand, but there seems to be no reason why silver as well as gold cannot be determined by this method.

* Vol. **12**, p. 90, C. Crichton.

The principal advantage of the method lies in the small amount of actual personal attention required. The method works as well for a 20 assay-ton sample as for one of 10 assay-tons. The time required for the deposition of the gold is somewhat longer than for some of the precipitation methods and this appears to be the principal disadvantage of the process.

Colorimetric Methods. — (For Gold only). Several attempts have been made to adapt the "Purple of Cassius" test to the estimation of gold in chloride and cyanide solutions. So far as the author is aware, none of the methods have beeen adopted as practical assay laboratory methods in this country. They were used for a time in one or two South African plants, but have never come into great favor. The two most promising methods were described by Henry R. Cassel (Eng. and Min. Jour. 76 p. 661) and James Moir (Proc. Chem. Met. and Min. Soc. of South Africa, 4, p. 298), and to those original articles the interested reader is referred.

CHAPTER XII.

THE LEAD ASSAY.

The fire assay for lead consists of a reducing fusion with iron, fluxes, and some carbonaceous reducing agent, and is conducted much as is the iron-nail assay for gold and silver ores, except, of course, that no litharge or other lead-bearing flux is added. The object of the fusion is to reduce and collect all of the lead in a button free from other elements.

Lead Ores. — Lead ores are classified by metallurgists as oxidized or sulphide ores, also as pure or impure ores. The oxidized ores contain the lead principally in the form of carbonate, occasionally as sulphate and rarely as oxide or in combination with phosphorous, molybdenum, vanadium, chromium, etc. The corresponding lead minerals are cerussite, $PbCO_3$ (77.6 per cent Pb), anglesite $PbSO_4$ (68.3 per cent Pb), minium Pb_3O_4 (90.6 per cent Pb), pyromorphite $Pb_5Cl(PO_4)_3$ (75.6 per cent Pb), vanadinite $3Pb_3(VO_4)_2 PbCl_2$ (72.4 per cent Pb) and wulfenite $PbMoO_4$ (56.5 per cent Pb). The most important sulphide lead minerals are galena PbS (86.6 per cent Pb) jamesonite $Pb_2Sb_2S_5$ (50.8 per cent Pb) and bournonite $PbCuSbS_3$ (42.5 per cent Pb). The principal associated minerals are argentite, pyrite, chalcopyrite, sphalerite, stibnite, quartz, calcite and dolomite, as well as the oxidation compounds of the above sulphides. Impure ores, from the assayer's point of view, are those containing more or less arsenic, antimony, bismuth, copper, zinc, and other rarer metals which interfere with the lead assay.

Besides ores, the assayer may have brought to him various furnace products such as litharge, slag, matte, flue dust and cupel bottom.

The fire assay for lead is not as accurate as a carefully made wet determination, but it is so simple, inexpensive and rapid that for a long time it served to govern the purchase and sale of all lead ores. Today it is still largely used by the smelters and others for the assay of pure ores, although for ores containing such base metal impurities as antimony, copper, zinc, etc., the wet method is usually preferred. The results of the fire-assay may be either lower or higher than the actual lead content, depending on the nature and quantity of the other minerals present in the ore.

Pure ores give low results owing to losses of lead by volatilization and slagging. Both the sulphide and the oxide of lead are volatile at moderate temperatures and for this reason great care must be taken to maintain the lowest temperature consistent with a proper decomposition of these minerals, during the early part of the assay. Lead oxide begins to volatilize at about 800° C., and the loss due to this cause is rapid at 1000°. Lead sulphide is more easily volatilized than the oxide. In a neutral or reducing atmosphere Doeltz* found that at 860° C., it lost 18 per cent in an hour, while at 950° it vaporized at the rate of 45 per cent per hour. Lead compounds, particularly the oxide, also tend to pass into the slag and this tendency is increased by the presence of zinc, and to some extent by arsenic and antimony.

Impure ores containing arsenic, antimony, bismuth and copper usually give high results, as these metals are partly or wholly reduced and pass into the lead button.

Quantity of Ore and Reagents Used. — The amount of ore used is generally 10 grams, occasionally 5 grams. With low-grade ores 20, 25, or more grams may be used. The reagents used are the alkali carbonates, borax-glass, some reducing agent, usually argols or flour, and occasionally sulphur. Iron in some form is always used. It may be in the form of nails or spikes, or coiled wire, or the crucible itself may be of iron, and in this case will be used over and over again until worn out. A very satisfactory way of introducing iron is to use a rail- or boat-spike $2\frac{1}{2}$ or 3 inches long, and about $\frac{1}{2}$ inch through. In this assay it is customary to use a mixture of sodium and potassium carbonates, as the mixture fuses at a lower temperature than either one alone. The alkali carbonates act as fluxes for the silica, and serve to give a basic slag which is necessary in this assay. Usually two or three times as much alkaline carbonate as ore is taken. Borax-glass acts as a flux for the metallic oxides, for limestone and the other alkaline earths. From one-half to twice as much borax-glass as ore is used. An excess of reducing

* Métallurgie, **3**, p. 441.

agent is always used to maintain the highly reducing character of the slag which is required. Sulphur is used when an oxidized ore containing copper is being assayed.

In the lead assay it is customary to use a mixed flux called a "lead flux." This may be bought already prepared or may be made up in the laboratory. Many different formulas are given, including the following:

	1	2	3
Sodium carbonate	12 parts	4 parts	6.5 parts
Potassium carbonate	15 "	4 "	5.0 "
Borax-glass	7 "	–	2.5 "
Borax powdered	–	2 "	–
Flour	2 "	1 "	2.5 "

Nos. 1 and 2 are found in use in the Coeur d' Alene lead district where the fire assay for lead has been brought to the highest degree of perfection. No. 1 is better for ores having a basic gangue, No. 2 for siliceous ores. No. 3 is perhaps the best of all for general use.

About 30 grams of flux are intimately mixed with 10 grams of ore, one spike or four or five 10-penny nails are inserted and a cover of 8 or 10 grams more of flux is added. Very few assayers use a cover of salt in the lead assay, on account of the danger of the loss of lead as chloride.

The fusion should always be made in a muffle furnace owing to the better control of temperature available. In fact, the secret of the successful fire-assay for lead is largely in the proper manipulation and control of the temperature throughout the process.

At first the muffle should be just visibly red and the crucibles should be allowed to remain at this temperature for about twenty minutes. Then the heat should be gradually raised until fusion begins, and kept at this temperature for some time.

This is necessary owing to the fact that in the early part of the assay the charge is in active motion and particles of the various lead compounds are continually being brought to the surface, where, if the temperature were high, they would suffer an appreciable loss by volatilization. When the charge has finished boiling and most of the lead is reduced and collected in the bottom of the crucible there is less danger of loss by volatilization, first, because lead itself is not so readily volatile as are some of its compounds, and second, because it is difficult for the molecules to migrate through the heavy layer of reducing slag which covers the lead.

After the boiling has entirely ceased the temperature is raised to the highest heat of the muffle to decompose the lead compounds which still remain in the slag. These are principally the silicate and the double sulphide of lead and sodium or potassium, and require a bright-yellow heat for their complete decomposition. The fusion period is finished when the nails can be removed free from shots of lead. Sulphide ores require a much longer fusion than oxides, owing to the fact that their decomposition is effected principally by iron, and therefore time must be allowed for every particle of the charge to come into contact with the iron. Oxide ores, on the other hand, are decomposed by the carbon of the charge and as this is uniformly distributed a much shorter time will suffice. Sulphide ores will require from an hour to an hour and a half of fusion, oxide ores from three-quarters of an hour to an hour.

Influence of Other Metals on Lead Assay. SILVER. — Practically all of the silver in an ore is reduced and passes into the lead button. If it is present in sufficiently large quantities a correction for it may be made, *i.e.*, 291.66 ounces per ton equals 1 per cent.

GOLD. — This metal is also reduced and passes into the lead button, but it is usually present in such small quantities that it may be disregarded.

ARSENIC. — Arsenic is occasionally found in lead ores, usually in the form of arsenical iron pyrite. During the assay, part of the arsenic is volatilized as metal or as arsenic sulphide but the larger part remains in the crucible. Here it usually enters into combination with the iron, forming speiss. After the contents of the crucible has been poured, the arsenic will be found as a hard white button on top of the lead, from which it may be removed by hammering. Little if any arsenic enters the lead button. Under certain conditions, *i.e.*, a long fusion at a low temperature with high soda excess, the formation of speiss may be prevented.

ANTIMONY. — This metal is frequently found associated with lead, usually, however, only in small amounts. In the assay with iron, antimony is reduced and passes into the lead button. Buttons containing antimony are harder and whiter than those from pure lead ores and when they contain much antimony are brittle, breaking with a bright crystalline fracture.

If much antimony is present (over half as much as the lead) an antimony speiss will be found lying on top of the button.

BISMUTH. — This metal is rarely found associated with lead ores, but if present will be reduced and pass into the lead buttons.

COPPER. — Copper is often found in lead ores in the form of chalcopyrite, chalcocite, and oxidized copper compounds. If the ore is fully oxidized and a high temperature is employed most of the copper will pass into the lead button. If the ore contains much pyrite, or sulphur in other forms most of the copper will remain as a sulphide and be dissolved in the alkaline slag. A button containing copper will be hard and tough and may show a reddish tinge.

IRON. — This metal is often present in lead ores, usually in the form of iron pyrite. It goes into the slag, forming either a silicate or a double sulphide of iron with sodium or potassium. The lead button is practically free from iron.

ZINC. — Zinc is often found associated with lead in ores, usually in the form of the sulphide. During the assay, part of the zinc is volatilized and part remains in the slag. Zinc sulphide is only decomposed by iron at a very high temperature, so that only a very small amount of zinc passes into the lead button. Zinc sulphide is practically infusible; it makes the slag thick and pasty, and thus, if present in too great proportion, interferes with the separation of the lead.

Procedure. — Assay ores in duplicate, using 10 grams of ore and 40 grams of prepared lead flux. Use a 12- or 15-gram muffle crucible. Weigh out first 30 grams of lead flux, place the ore on top of this and mix thoroughly with the spatula. Insert a spike or nails, point downward, and finally cover with 10 grams more of lead flux. Have the muffle just visibly red and bring up the heat very gradually so that after the charges are put in it will take at least forty-five minutes to boil them down. Close the door of the muffle as soon as the crucibles are in, and after the charges are melted place two crucibles partly full of soft coal in the mouth of the muffle just inside of the door, which should be kept as tightly closed as possible. Raise the temperature gradually to a bright yellow and continue at this temperature until the nails can be removed free from lead.

Finally take the crucibles from the muffle, using a pair of muffle-crucible tongs, and without setting them down quickly remove the nails with a large pair of steel forceps, tapping against the side of the crucible and washing the nails in the slag to remove all adhering lead globules. Then pour into a deep, pointed mold. Work as fast as possible to prevent too great chilling of the slag in the crucible before pouring.

When cool separate the lead from the slag and hammer clean. Weigh to centigrams and report the results in percentage. Duplicates should check within 0.2 per cent.

The slag should be black and glassy. If it is dull, more borax-glass should be added. It should pour well from the crucible and immediately after it is poured, the crucible should be examined for shots of lead. If these are found it is usually an indication of too low a temperature at pouring.

Notes: 1. If the ore is an oxide and contains copper add a gram or two of finely pulverized sulphur to the charge to prevent the copper from entering the button.

2. The soft coal is added to ensure reducing conditions in the muffle and it may be renewed if necessary. When a muffle is used solely for fusion purposes the hole in the back is stopped up, preventing the entrance of so much air.

3. The removal of nails and the pouring must be done without a moment's delay as the charges are small and cool rapidly.

4. If the ore contains much silver the button should be cupeled and the weight of silver found deducted.

5. The lead should be soft and malleable and a fresh cut surface should have the bluish-gray color of pure lead. The button should be capable of being hammered out into a thin sheet without breaking or cracking. A button that is bright, brittle and brilliantly white in the fracture indicates the presence of antimony.

6. The lead button should be carefully examined for speiss before it is hammered. With a little care this may be pounded off without seriously affecting the weight of lead.

7. If there is doubt regarding the purity of the lead button it may be tested by cupellation. The only metals, except lead, likely to be present are gold, silver, antimony, copper and possibly bismuth; each of these gives characteristic indications in cupeling.

8. Crucibles may be used a number of times as they are but little corroded, but those used previously for gold and silver assays must not be used for this assay as the slag left in them contains lead. It is well to use a special size of crucible for the lead assay in order to prevent errors due to mixing crucibles.

9. If the fusion has been properly conducted the nails will show but little corrosion. If they are much corroded the results are bound to be decidedly low.

Assay of Slags, Furnace Products and Low-grade Ores or Tailings. — In the assay of low-grade materials, such as slags and tailings, a larger quantity of ore and a different mixture of fluxes should be used. The slag should be between a singulo- and a sub-silicate and part of the iron may be added in the form of filings. On account of the size of the charge it is well to add a number of nails, as this will lessen the time necessary for complete reduction.

The following charges have been found satisfactory:

Limestone ($\frac{1}{2}$–2 per cent Pb)	Slag	Slag
Ore 25 grams	Slag 25 grams	Slag 100 grams
Na_2CO_3 25 "	Na_2CO_3 25 "	Na_2CO_3 50 "
K_2CO_3 20 "	K_2CO_3 20 "	K_2CO_3 — "
Borax-glass 20 "	Borax-glass 10 "	Borax-glass 10 "
Flour 10 "	Flour 10 "	Flour 10 "
Nails 5 "	Nails 5 "	Nails 5 "
(20-penny)	(20-penny)	(20-penny)
20-gram crucible	20-gram crucible	30-gram crucible

Allow some time at a high temperature, so that all of the slag may have a chance to come in contact with the iron.

Corrected Lead Assay. — To recover any lead which may have been left in the slag the following procedure is recommended: Save all the slag and remelt in the original crucible with the spikes or nails formerly used. If the first slag was quite glassy and viscous in pouring, add from 5 to 15 grams more of sodium carbonate. Heat to redness and drop into each crucible a lump of about 5 grams of potassium cyanide. Close the door of the muffle, heat to a bright yellow and pour as soon as quiet. Add the weight of any small button found to the lead from the original fusion.

Chemical Reactions of the Lead Assay. — With an ore containing $PbCO_3$, $PbSO_4$, PbS, SiO_2 and $CaCO_3$ the following reactions may occur:

$PbCO_3 = PbO + CO_2$,   (Begins at 200° C.)
$2PbO + C = 2Pb + CO_2$,   (Begins at 550° C.)
$PbO + SiO_2 = PbSiO_3$,   (Begins at 625° C.)
$PbSO_4 + 2C = PbS + 2CO_2$,   (Begins at a dark red heat.)
$7PbS + 4K_2CO_3 = 4Pb + 3(K_2PbS_2) + K_2SO_4 + 4CO_2$.
                                  (Begins at a red heat.)

THE LEAD ASSAY

If carbon were not present some oxide and sulphate would probably remain to react as follows:

$PbS + 2PbO = 3Pb + SO_2$, (Begins at 720° C.)
$PbS + PbSO_4 = 2Pb + 2SO_2$, (Begins at 670° C.)
$2PbSO_4 + SiO_2 = Pb_2SiO_4 + 2SO_2 + O_2$. (High heat.)

Toward the end, as the heat is raised to a bright red and above, the reactions with iron become important, particularly the following:

$PbS + Fe = Pb + FeS$,
$PbSiO_3 + Fe = Pb + FeSiO_3$, (Requires a bright yellow heat for completion.)
$K_2PbS_2 + Fe = Pb + K_2FeS_2$. (Requires a bright yellow heat for completion.)

INDEX

Active flux, definition, 171.
Alumina, fluxing of, 168–170.
Annealing, 120.
  reasons for, 120.
Annealing cups, clay dish to hold, 38.
Antimony, assay of ores high in, 205, 206.
  behavior in cupellation, 110.
  behavior in iron nail assay, 189, 190.
  behavior in scorification, 128, 137.
  effect in lead assay, 243.
Argols, 11.
Arsenic, behavior in cupellation, 111.
  behavior in iron nail assay, 189.
  behavior in scorification, 128, 137.
  effect in lead assay, 244.
Assay-ton weights, 84, 86.

Balance, alignment of knife edges, testing, 84.
  assay, 73–75
  arms, equality, testing, 84.
  construction of, 73, 74.
  directions for use of, 77, 78.
  equilibrium, testing, 82.
  flux, 71, 72.
  multiple rider attachment for, 85, 86.
  pulp, 72, 73.
  resistance, testing, 82, 83.
  sensitivity, 73, 83, 84.
  stability, 73, 82.
  testing, 81–84.
  theory of, 75, 77.
  time of oscillation, 73, 82.
Basic ores, assay of, 164–170.

Basic ores, calculation of charge for, 166.
  slags for, 164, 165.
Bismuth, behavior in cupellation, 111, 115.
  behavior in scorification, 128.
  effect in lead assay, 244.
  in ores from Cobalt, 198.
Bone-ash, 89–90.
  best size for cupels, 90.
  fluxing of, 209.
  specifications for, 90.
  temperature of burning, influence of, 89.
  to preserve muffles, 28.
Bone-ash cupel, assay of, 209.
Borates, classification of, 4, 5.
Borax, 3–6.
  action in slags, 148–150, 152.
  cover, 152, 172.
  effect on elimination of copper, 202.
  quantity required, 164, 165, 172, 185.
Borax glass, 4–6.
Bullion, 211.
  copper, assay of, 220–226.
  doré, assay of, 226–229.
  gold, assay of, 229–232.
  lead, assay of, 99, 219.
  sampling of, 212–219.
  segregation of metals in, 212–216.
  silver, assay of, 226.

Capsules, parting, 38, 119.
Character of sample, determination of, 145, 146.
Charcoal, 11.

INDEX

Chiddey, method for assay of cyanide solutions, 235, 236.
Class 1 ores, assay procedure for, 170–173.
    slags for, 162–165.
Class 2 ores, assay procedure for, 186–188, 192–194.
    various methods of assaying, 173–174.
Class 3 ores, assay procedure for, 195.
Clay, fluxing of, 168–170.
Coal furnaces, 18–23.
    firing of, 23.
Cobalt, assay of ores containing, 196–198.
    behavior in scorification, 128.
Coke furnaces, 23, 24.
Colorimetric assay of solutions, 239.
Combination method of assay, 174, 194.
    for copper bullion, 222–226.
    for ores containing nickel and cobalt, 197, 198.
    for zinc-box precipitate, 205.
Copper, assay of ores high in, 201–204.
    behavior in cupellation, 111, 115.
    behavior in scorification, 128.
    color of crucible slags containing, 147.
    color of scorifier slags containing, 137.
    effect in cupellation, 98, 105–107, 232.
    effect in iron nail assay, 189–192.
    effect in lead assay, 244.
    matte, assay of, 139, 201–204.
Copper bullion, assay of, 220–226.
    sampling of, 217–218.
    segregation of metals in, 213, 214.
Corrected assays, 107–109, 115, 125, 140, 205, 206–210, 219, 246.
Cover, the, 152, 153.
Cream of tartar, 11.
Crucible assay, theory of, 143, 178–180, 182–184, 187.

Crucibles, 31–33.
    capacity of different sizes, 33.
    desirable properties of, 31, 32.
    sizes for various charges, 203.
    testing of, 32.
Cryolite, 14, 170.
Cupels, 89–93, 100.
    assay of, 209, 210.
    cracking of, 90, 111.
    effect of shape of, 92, 93.
    instructions for making, 91, 92.
    machines for making, 91, 92.
    magnesia, 116, 117
    Portland cement, 115, 116.
    size of, 93.
    specifications for, 92.
    testing, 109.
Cupel tray, 37, 38.
Cupellation, 89
    assay of lead bullion, 99, 219.
    correct temperature for, 94–97.
    description of process, 93–97.
    flashing of beads from, 95.
    freezing of assay during, 94, 95.
    indications of metals present, 96, 99, 109–114.
    instructions for, 97–99.
    loss of gold in, 102–105.
    loss of silver in, 90, 100–102, 116.
    regulation of temperature during, 94, 95, 97, 98.
    retention of base metals in beads from, 96, 98, 114, 115.
    spitting during, 92, 326.
    sprouting of beads from, 96, 98, 226, 228.
Cupellation losses, 90, 99–109.
    influence of copper on, 105–107.
    influence of impurities on, 105–107.
    influence of quantity of lead on, 101, 102.
    influence of tellurium on, 199, 200.
    influence of temperature on, 100, 102.
    effect of silver on gold, 103–105.
    progressive, 101.

INDEX

Cupellation losses, rule governing, 107–109.
   Sharwood's rule for determining, 107–109.

Desulphurizing agent, 2.
Doré bullion, assay of, 226–229.
   sampling of, 218.

Electrolytic assay of cyanide solutions, 238.

Ferric oxide, fluxing of, 168
   oxidizing effect of, 157.
Fire-brick, directions for laying, 29.
Fire-brick lining vs. tile lining, 18.
Flour, 11.
Fluorspar, 13, 170, 209.
Fluxes and reagents, 1–14.
Fluxing, 3, 5, 7, 9.
   principles of, 2.
Fuel, 17, 18.
Fuel-oil furnaces, 26–28.
Furnace repairs, 28–30.
Furnaces, 16–28.
   directions for firing soft coal, 23.
Fusion products, 14, 15.

Gas furnaces, 26.
Gasoline furnaces, 24–26.
Glass, 3.
Gold, weighing of, 78, 81, 120.
Gold bullion, assay of, 229–232.
   sampling of, 218, 219.
Gold ores containing coarse particles, assay of, 66–70.
Granulated lead, assay of, 138.
Grinder for assay samples, 63–65.

Inquartation, 121.
Iridium, behavior during cupellation, 113, 114.
   indications of in appearance of bead, 113.
   indications of in parted gold, 124.
Iron, 11, 12, 188.
   behavior in cupellation, 110.
   behavior in scorification, 128.

Iron, color of crucible slag, containing, 147.
   color of scorifier slags, containing, 137.
   effect in lead assay, 244.
   reducing action of, 11, 12, 189.
Iron nail assay, 173, 188–193.
   chemical reactions during, 189–191.
   limitations of, 191, 192.
   procedure for, 192, 193.
   slag for, 192.

Lead, 11.
   fire assay of ores, 240–247.
   granulated, assay of, 138.
   granulated to make, 11.
   ores, classification of, 240.
Lead assay, accuracy of, 240.
   assay of slags from, 246.
   chemical reactions during, 246, 247.
   conduct of fusion, 242.
   corrected, 246.
   influence of other metals on, 241, 243, 244.
   losses in, 241, 242.
   procedure for, 244, 245.
   slag for, 241, 242, 245.
Lead bullion, assay of, 99, 219.
   sampling of, 216, 217.
Lead button, 14, 151, 152.
   testing purity of, from lead assay, 245.
Limestone, fluxing of, 166–168.
Litharge, 9–11.
   assay of, 159–161.
   corrosive action of, 28, 133.
   disadvantages of excess, 176.
   quantity required to slag copper, 202.
   solubility of metallic oxides in, 127, 128.
   use in scorification assay, 133.

Magnesium carbonate, fluxing of, 167.
Magnesium oxide, fluxing of, 210.

Manganese, dioxide, oxidizing effect of, 157.
Manganese oxide, fluxing of, 168.
Matte, 15, 173.
  crucible assay of, 201–204.
  obtained in crucible assay, 173, 177, 180, 187, 193.
  scorification assay of, 139–141.
Metallic assay, 66–70.
Metallic oxides, heat of formation of, 128.
  solubility in litharge, 127, 128.
Metallic sulphides, heat of formation of, 190.
  ignition temperature, of, 128, 129.
Minerals, oxidizing power of, 157.
  reducing power of, 156.
Moisture sample, 60, 61.
Mold, crucible, 37.
  scorifier, 38.
Muffles, 31.
  care of, 28.
  directions for replacing, 29, 30.
  methods of supporting, 22.
Multiple rider attachment for balances, 85, 86.

Nickel, assay of ores containing, 196–198.
  behavior in cupellation, 110.
  behavior in scorification, 128, 130, 137.
  effect in iron nail assay, 192.
Niter assay, 173–188.
  calculation of charge, 182–186.
  chemical reactions during, 159, 178–180, 182–184, 187.
  conduct of fusion, 176–178.
  disadvantages of excess litharge in, 176.
  preliminary fusion, procedure, 180–181.
  regular fusion, procedure, 186–188.
  slags for impure ores, 175, 176.
  slags for pure ores, 175.
Niter, determining oxidizing power of, 182.

Niter, oxidizing power of, 158, 159.
  quantity required, 184.
  see also potassium nitrate.
Nitric acid, testing for impurities, 125, 126.

Oil furnaces, 26–28.
Ore, classification of, 1, 144, 240.
  determining oxidizing power of, 195.
  determining reducing power of, 180, 181.
  estimating reducing power of, 181, 182.
  in general, 1.
  reducing power of minerals, 156.
Osmium, behavior during cupellation, 113, 114.
  behavior during parting, 124.
Oxides metallic, heat of formation of, 128.
  solubility in litharge, 127.
Oxidizing agent, 2.
Oxidizing power, definition of, 153.
  of minerals, 157.
  of niter, 158, 159.
  of ores, determination of, 195.
  of red lead, 159.
Oxidizing reactions, 156–159, 178–180.

Palladium, behavior during parting, 124.
  indications of in appearance of bead, 113.
  indications of in parting, 124.
Parting, 118.
  acids for, 118, 119.
  in assay of gold bullion, 231.
  in porcelain capsules, 119–121.
  errors resulting from, 123, 124, 125.
  in flasks, 122, 123.
  disintegration of gold during, 123, 124, 125.
  indications of rare metals in, 124.
  influence of base metals on, 123, 124.

INDEX

Parting, preparing beads for, 116, 122.
  procedure, 119–121.
  recovery of gold lost in, 125.
  ratio of silver to gold necessary, 121.
  testing for completeness of, 120, 121.
Platinum, behavior during cupellation, 112, 114.
  behavior during parting, 124.
  indications of in appearance of bead, 112.
  indications of in parted gold, 124.
Portland cement, flux for, 210.
Potassium carbonate, 8, 9.
Potassium cyanide, 13.
Potassium nitrate, 12.
Pulverizer disc, 63–65.

Reagents, 1–14.
  testing of, 159–161.
Red lead, oxidizing power of, 159.
Reducing agent, 2.
Reducing power, definition of, 153.
  of minerals, 144, 155, 156.
  of ores, determination of, 180, 181.
  of ores, estimation of, 181, 182.
  of reagents, 154, 161.
  of reagents, determination of, 160.
Reducing reactions, 153–156.
Rhodium, behavior during cupellation, 113, 114.
  indications of in appearance of bead, 112.
Riders, 84, 85.
  multiple attachment for, 85, 86.
  testing, 88.
  Thompson, 85.
Riffle sampler, 51–54.
Roasting, 193, 194.
  period in scorification assay, 131.
  reactions in scorification, 135.
Roasting method of assay, 174, 193, 194.
Ruthenium, behavior during cupellation, 114.

Ruthenium, indications of in appearance of bead, 113.

Salt, 13.
  cover, 152, 153.
Sample, definition, 39.
  finishing the, 62–66.
  grab, 60.
  moisture, 60, 61.
Sampler, Brunton, 52, 53, 55–57, 59.
  Jones, 53.
  Snyder, 57, 58.
  Vezan, 56–58.
Sampling, Brunton's formula for, 44–46.
  bullion, 212–216.
  copper bullion, 217, 218.
  doré bullion, 218.
  duplicate, 62.
  gold bullion, 218, 219.
  grab, 60.
  hand, 48–54.
  lead bullion, 216, 217.
  machine, 54–59.
  methods, 40, 41.
  mill, complete, 59.
  moisture, 60, 61.
  object of, 39.
  ore, 39–70.
  ores containing malleable minerals, 66–70.
  practice, 47–62.
  principles, 42–47.
  Richard's rule for, 43.
  tables showing weights to be taken, 43, 46.
Scorification, 129.
  chemical reactions during, 134–136.
  effect of various constituents of ore on, 133.
  indications of metals present, 131, 136, 137.
  losses in, 139–141.
  ores suited, 133, 134.
  reagents used, 127.
  spitting during, 137, 138, 139.

Scorification assay, 127.
  charges for different ores, 142.
  for gold, 138, 220, 221.
  fractional elimination of metals in, 128, 129.
  of copper bullion, 220, 221.
  of copper matte, 139.
  procedure for, 130–133.
  use of large ore charges in, 141.
Scorifiers, 33, 34.
  sizes, 33, 127.
Screening assay samples, 65.
Segregation of metals in cooling, influence of on sampling, 212–216.
Silica, 2, 3.
Silicates, classification of, 147, 148.
  mixed, 151.
Siliceous ores, calculation of charge for, 162–164.
Silver foil, testing for gold, 126.
Slags, 14, 146.
  acid and basic distinguished, 151.
  action of borax in, 143, 148–150.
  assay of, 208, 246.
  color of crucible, 147.
  color of scorifier, 136, 137.
  for class 1 basic ores, 164–168.
  for class 1 siliceous ores, 162–164.
  for class 2, iron assay, 192.
  for class 2, niter assay, 175, 176.
  for crucible assay of ores containing copper, 202.
  fluidity of, 150.
  formation temperature of, 148.
  properties of good, 146, 147.
Slag factors, bisilicate, 163, 165.
  mono-silicate, 188.
Sodium bicarbonate, 6.
Sodium carbonate, 6–8.
Solutions, assay of, 233–239.
Speiss, 15.
  in crucible assay, 189.
  in lead assay, 243.
Split shovel, 51–53.
Splitter, sample, 51–54.
Sprouting, to prevent, 228.
Stack, height of, 22.

Stack, support of, 22.
Sulphides, heats of formation of metallic, 190.
  ignition temperatures of, 128, 129.
  reactions with iron, 189–191.
  reactions with niter, 169, 183.
  reactions with oxides, 136.
  reactions with oxygen, 135.
  reducing powers of, 155, 156.

Telluride ores, assay of, 198–201.
Tellurium, behavior in cupellation, 111, 199, 200.
  behavior in crucible fusions, 200, 201.
  behavior in scorification, 128.
  indications of, in beads, 99, 111.
Temperature, eye estimation of, 117.
Tin, assay of ores high in, 206.
  behavior in cupellation, 110.
Tools, furnace, 34–37.

Vanning, operation of, 145, 146.

Weighing, accumulative, 81.
  assay pulp, directions for, 132.
  by equal swings, 78, 79.
  by methods of swings, 79, 80.
  by "no deflection," 80.
  by substitution, 80, 81.
  check, 81.
  double, 77.
  general directions for, 77, 78.
  gold, 78, 120.
  silver, 78, 99.
Weights, 84–86.
  assay-ton, 84, 86.
  calibration of, 86–88.
  milligram, 84.
  millième, 211.
  recording, 78.
Wood furnaces, 23.

Zinc, behavior in cupellation, 110.
  effect in iron nail assay, 190.
  effect in lead assay, 244.
Zinc-box precipitate, assay of, 204, 205.